ON

DEMOCRACY.

BY

J. ARTHUR PARTRIDGE,

AUTHOR OF

"COALITIONS AND FRONTIERS IN 1860-1," "THE FALSE NATION AND ITS BASES; OR WHY THE SOUTH CAN'T STAND;" "THE MAKING OF THE AMERICAN NATION; OR THE RISE AND DECLINE OF OLIGARCHY IN THE WEST," &c., &c.

PHILADELPHIA:

J. B. LIPPINCOTT AND CO.

1866.

This work arose out of considerations suggested by another work, published concurrently herewith, and entitled "The Making of the American Nation, or the Rise and Decline of Oligarchy in the West."

The one is a study on the great, and indeed, only precedent of Democracy; its origin, history, qualities, conflicts, and reconstruction. The other work, the present one, is a consideration of the general theory of Democracy, with special reference to the traditions and future of England.

ON DEMOCRACY.

"If the popular party exceed more in quantity than they are excelled in quality, Democracy must prevail."—*Aristotle.*

"Every Government is composed of two distinct elements, its nature (or organisation) and its principle (or motive power). Laws ought to be no less relative to the principle than to the nature."—*Montesquieu.*

"European Society is in a state of transition from Feudal to Federal principles. This I conceive to be the sole cause of all the convulsions that have occurred and that are to occur." —*Disraeli.*

"Unity will once more be restored, but not through the *canon* and *feudal* law, for the new Catholic element was the People."—*Bancroft.*

"It is the third huge Gate of Barbarism, the monarchical Gate, which is closing at this moment. The nineteenth century hears it rolling on its hinges."—*Hugo.*

"*The History of the world is nothing but the development of the idea of Freedom.* Philosophy concerns itself only with *the glory of the idea* mirroring itself in History and the process of its development. That History is this process of *Development and realisation of spirit,* is the justification of God in History.

"Freedom of a low and limited order is mere caprice. Freedom does not exist as original and natural. Rather must it be first sought out and won; and that *by an incalculable medial discipline* of the intellectual and moral powers. Freedom is spirit in its completeness. *Society and the State are the very conditions in which Freedom is realised.* Reason is the comprehension of the divine work. The strength of a nation lies in the Reason incorporated in it. The conception of God constitutes the general basis of a People's character."—*Hegel,* "Philosophy of History," p. 38, 40-2-3, &c., Trans.

"The only possible purpose of nature, *to manifest and maintain Reason.*"—*Fichte,* Vocation of Man, p. 197.

"It is a work good and prudent to be able to guide one man; of larger extended virtue to order well one house; but to govern a nation piously and justly, which only is to say happily, is for a spirit of the greatest size and divinest mettle. And certainly of no less a mind, nor of less excellence in another way, were they who by writing laid the solid and true foundations of this science, which being of greatest importance to the life of man, yet there is no art that hath been more cankered in her principles, more soiled and slubbered with aphorisming pedantry, than the art of policy; and that most, where a man would think should least be, in Christian commonwealths. They teach not that to govern well, is to train up a nation in true wisdom and virtue, and that which springs from thence,—magnanimity (take heed of that); and that which is our beginning, regeneration, and happiest end,—likeness to God, which, in one word, we call godliness; and that this is the true flourishing of a land, other things follow as the shadow does the substance: to teach thus were mere pulpitry to them."—*Milton.*

PREFACE.

"The question as to what constitutes the State is one of advanced science, and not of popular decision. . . The great point is that Freedom has not subjective Will for its principle: the process by which *Freedom* is realised, is the *free Development of the successive stages of the Universal* (*God's*) *Will.* History is the Development of Spirit in time."—*Hegel*, on the Philosophy of History, pp. 28, 48, 45.

"De sorte que toute la suite des hommes pendant le cours de tant de siècles doit être considérée comme un même homme qui subsiste toujours et apprend continuellement."—*Pascal*, Pensées.

"The organisation and establishment of Democracy in Christendom is the great political problem of the time."—*De Tocqueville.*

"And though no one now living may be permitted to enter into this land of promise (a perfect system of legislation), yet he who shall contemplate it in its VASTNESS and BEAUTY, may rejoice, as did Moses when on the verge of the desert from the mountain top he saw the length and breadth of that good land, into which he was not permitted to enter and take possession."—*Jeremy Bentham*, on Influence of Time and Place.

"I need not ramble over earth and sky to discover a wondrous object woven of contrasts of greatness and littleness infinite, of intense gloom and of amazing brightness,—capable at once of exciting pity, admiration, terror and contempt. *I find that object is myself.* MAN springs out of nothing, crosses time, and disappears for ever in the bosom of God. He is seen but for a moment,—staggering on the verge of the two abysses; and then he is lost!"—*De Tocqueville.*

The organisation of the national thought concerning Democracy, is a necessary prelude to the peaceful organisation of Democracy itself, and whilst it is necessary to know the genius, nature, and average preparedness of our national manhood, it is necessary, above all things, *to believe* in manhood.

Whilst many political writers have pointed out the means whereby manhood will get the victory over privilege, and whilst some have clearly anticipated that result, it is strange that only one (De Tocqueville) has directly asserted that there is in every community a single preponderating power of which the only final and universal issue is Democracy ; and, as far as I know, only four, De Tocqueville, Bentham, Coleridge,* and Goldwin Smith, who have ventured to deride that God of English idolatry, "a mixed Government." "Preponderance" was bad, because it was the preponderance of sections, but arguments against preponderance are confidently and incessantly repeated as against Democracies,—as though the preponderance of the all could be anything else than equality, or as though the material, intellectual, and spiritual progress of nations could result in anything less.

As on the morrow of the new Reform Bill, England will be, not an Aristocratic, but a Democratic Republic, the subject is piquant.

This question of preponderance is indeed a paradox, which has taken in and done for many notable politicians. The whole recent Reform Debate on the Opposition side, was conducted on the assumption that it is possible to prevent the preponderance of Democracy.

* *See* "The Friend," v. ii, p. 57. Ed. 1844.

A preponderance, to do harm, must be either a preponderance of interest over right, or of ignorance over knowledge; in other words, a preponderance of a class, or of the uninstructed.

As long as power is in the hands of the one, the few, or the many,—autocrat, oligarch, or middle class, it is a partial and sectional, and, therefore, a sinister power. Such interest not only is, but must be, against right. And doubtless, if power could be shared equally by the uneducated all the result would be that disastrous contradiction,—"the servant ruling."

But as power gets out into the universal, and as the all become educated (without which their power were mere anarchy and confusion) the sectional disappears in the process, quality is added to quantity, the mass of individual units, is, as argued fully in the sequel, balanced by individual multiples, or men with material, moral, or intellectual accumulations of power, or by individual varieties, and local or party combinations. Capital and knowledge become multiples of labor, and make a property stake and interest universal, and the universal interest and right, not only are, but must be identical.

I say, then, that though a knowledge of history, tradition, and national genius is necessary to the conservatism of progress, a belief in manhood is essential to both. The tendencies of the whole race are to health and life, whilst those of the parts may be to disease and death, if not corrected by the universal.

Development, Organisation, Unity, are the gradations of the teaching of the past, and although civilisation may be, as Guizot says, in its infancy, we know that nothing contrary to these can continue.

Judæa gave us Law and Love and Immortality. Greece, liberty of thought,—"reason, her own starting point and guide." Rome, unity,—the organisation of municipality, church, and empire. Primitive Germany, the spirit of liberty and of voluntary association. France, feudality, or, "the fusion of property and sovereignty." Scandinavia, the organisation of monarchy as a confederation, of which the organic germ or unit was the hœrad or hundred. Anglo-Saxondom, the folk-mote, court-leet, shire-gemot, and witenagemot,—the local courts and the council of peers.

What element is there of all these that is not now in our Institutions, and that has not done its part in helping us on even towards the goal of politics,—Equality ?

Peers and Ecclesiastics united with Peasants until English liberties were safe. The local courts administered justice and kept freedom alive when centralisation must have meant tyranny. The hundred and the witenagemot organised our nation till money drew the sovereign into a limited partnership with it. Feudality was a modified sovereignty which organised downwards and defied upwards, when the relations between the individual and the nation were immature. Municipalities, have they not been reorganised by the Corporation Act? The spirit of liberty and the liberty of thought, our heirlooms from Germany and Greece, have worked, the one within, organising intellect, the other without, organising facts, till thoughts and deeds together, helped on by supernal inducements, and guided by the higher law, have combined in systems which are the net result of all the past.

Thus the great facts of the world conspire with the teaching of its greatest men. Unity and life depend upon organisation, and organisation depends upon the preparedness and education of the Units.

The substance of the boast of the "New York Times" is widely feared in this country. That paper lately said: "This is the beginning of an Americanising process in England. The new Democratic ideas are gradually to find embodiment. The separation of Church and State, a complete secularisation of politics, a removal of the Irish Church, the destruction of entail, and the greater freedom given to the transfer of land, the duty of a popular system of education apart from all associations with creed or Church."

However this may be, it is undoubtedly true that one of the primary institutions of Democracy is in the way to be adopted amongst ourselves. The "Caucus," or the submission of great questions beforehand to the People's initiative and will, and the discipline of parties and instruction of members accordingly, is becoming established here.

If the forms of the past and the power of the present point to the opinion of the majority as our future master, there is only the greater reason for educating "the royal infant, the People," while we may.

To be a politician, it is necessary to believe and to know.

To believe what? The Ideal and the Infinite, towards which the People always advance.

To know what? The People. Men and things. The practicable. The circumstantial. The actual. Human nature, which always advances towards the Infinite, which it will never reach.

The man who believes not is scarcely a man,—certainly not a Statesman.

He who cannot adjust belief to knowledge, the ideal to the actual, may be a poet or a lunatic, a madman or a demagogue, but he knows not Politics. "The perfect lawgiver," says Macaulay, "is a just temper between the mere man of theory who can see nothing but general principles, and the mere man of business who can see nothing but particular circumstances."

The science of Politics is *a science of adjustment*—the People and the System. "How much Reason is there in this nation, and in what classes and proportions does it exist?" is the question upon which all reform bills must be based. Or, to pass from Hegel to Mill, the equal objects in legislation are not only to take the "next step" rightly, but to prepare the way for "all future steps."

For "Constitutions," says Macaulay, "are in Politics what paper money is in commerce. They afford great facilities and convenience. They are not power, but symbols of power." And the power is in the quantity and quality of national manhood.

Thus a Statesman knows the People. What they want. Wherein they fail. What they have. How they will rise, and by what steps. And that as a whole they *will* rise,—if not in this country, in that.

Thus a man may be a Bonapartist in France, an Imperialist in Russia, a Constitutionalist in England, a Republican in America, and a Revolutionist in some places,—not for want of, but by reason of political intelligence and consistency.

The term "Radical," used as a party epithet, means a man who cannot adjust the ideal to the actual. His theories are too fine for facts.

The term "Tory" means a man who cannot adjust the actual to the ideal.

The first believes in the catholic and the absolute (comprehends, as some would put it, the "subjective" only), but knows not the People: the last knows only and certainly, what the People are *not*.

The first may be light, but he is not base. He believes in the angel, though his theories will not fit the ape. The last imputes his own nature to the People, and naturally refuses to believe in them.

The People! capable of all, realising what? The People, demoniac and angelic,—their Ignorance and Light, Brutality and Intellect, their nature, condition, rights, wrongs, wants, wishes, demands, and preparedness,—the Statesman must know all this, their present, and believe in all that, their future,—must rise to all their Heights, and measure all their Depths,—must at once believe and disbelieve in the People.

And this thoroughness and clearness of vision will especially avoid and condemn a trait which has become almost characteristic of English politics.

"There is in the English mind a highly salutary shrinking from all extremes. But as this shrinking is rather an instinct of caution than a result of insight, it is too ready to satisfy itself with any medium, merely because it is a medium, and *to acquiesce in a union of the disadvantages of both extremes* instead of their advantages. . . . The celebrated theory of the three powers was got up, which made the excellence of our constitution consist in doing less harm than would be done by any other form of Government."—*Mill's* "Dissertations," v. i, pp. 430-3.

Statesmanship is always catholic in conception, but conservative in action.

It is necessary ever to bear in mind the twin Principles of Politics,—that Human nature always advances, and that if any succeed in withholding the rudiments of Development from a given nation, they cannot obstruct Human nature, but may destroy the material, mental, and moral greatness of that particular country.

Some forms of freedom may, it is argued, be dangerous without the others. Government education, for instance, may be objected to where the State could instil servile ideas by means of it, or where freedom so little prevails, that a fixity or sameness of type might be communicated to the national mind by school forms. And this last was Baron W. von Humboldt's objection.

In reference to the present state of preparedness of England for political equality, I see in our Institutes of Feudality, and in corporate anti-popular interests both in Church and State, abundant elements wherewith to "temper" the advance of Democracy, and to neutralise for ages any possible or impossible "class preponderance" of an equal voting Demos. But no possible obstructions can resist its ultimate triumph.

Bearing in mind, therefore, the educational preparedness of England, nor forgetting how our Democracy is handicapped, and the strength and onesidedness of our upper class rule and system, I conclude that *the equal voting representative power of all adult males having a fixed and registered residence, and not being paupers, lunatics, or criminals, is the goal towards which the advanced guard of liberalism may safely press.*

This is not "Manchester meat for roughs," on the one hand, nor do I suppose, that according to Mr. Lowe's exquisite illustration, Democracies, when educated, require to be "held together like a piece of coal by a pair of tongs." This is a requirement, not of Democracy, but of vast size.

There is with us the Sovereign, the symbol and centre of unity.

There is the true aristocracy of all ranks; an aristocracy of culture, intellect, genius, leisure, earnestness, or power. This class leads the van of the nation's manhood, organises its opinion, and always, sooner or later, commands its Will.

This is the "class" that with us always "preponderates."

Of it England breeds more than all other nations besides,—but it is, I say, handicapped.

For there is amongst us another class, also recruited from all ranks, except the lowest. They are sometimes called the great middle-class, but differ far from the middle-class of former years.

They are not, as of old, the advanced guard of the People, with energies trained by conflict with necessity. Nor on the other hand have they the qualities of a ruling race, or of individual achievement. They have the conservative instincts of plutocracy, and divide instead of uniting the extremes of Society. The instincts of many of them are debauched, and their reason is not disciplined. They are often educated out of sympathy but not up to faith. They are refined enough to sneer, but not strong enough in head or heart, in fortitude, in enthusiasm, in leisure, in generalisation, or in ideas, to believe.

And why insist on this? Because this "great middling party" misleads the lower class, and mistakes the upper. Because the vis inertiæ of their ignorant conservatism obstructs progress. Because I fear that a new Reform Bill may bring in more of the dregs of this class, and shut out the true People.

And what is the remedy?

The union of sympathy which exists between the crown, the true aristocracy, and the People.

The developing, guiding, and moderating, of those true revolutionary, but practical and constructive energies, which always characterise the common People, educated, and in contact with reality.

Let us note well the advice of Bacon, "in the declining age of a State, mechanical arts and merchandise do flourish." Solon said well to Crœsus, "Sir, if another come that hath better *iron* than you, he will be master of all this gold." Of Demosthenes, "And you abandoned and despised; sumptuous indeed in your markets; but as to any real provision for your security, ridiculously deficient." Of Cyrus, "I am not afraid of a set of men who have a place marked out in the middle of their city, where they take oaths and deceive one another; to whom, not the misfortunes of others will be matter of consideration, but their own." Of Hannibal to the weeping merchants, "You are touched with public calamities only as they affect your private fortunes, you may quickly find that these tears have been shed for the least of your misfortunes." Of Montesquieu, "The mischief is when wealth destroys the spirit of wealth" (industry.) Of Burke, "Nation is a moral essence."

There is little hope for a country where *wealth and materialism* overshadow manhood, and this danger grows upon us. There is reason enough in the fears of the Hon. R. Lowe about Millionaires and Demagogues.

Nevertheless, every year will also lessen the objections to a residential manhood enfranchisement, take from the arguments of its opponents, and baffle and confound the politicians who fear manhood rule as the antidote of class rule, and who will neither trust manhood as it is, nor help to prepare it for the future, by free and full development.

The "rights" of the parts against the whole, whether those parts be Feudality or Priestcraft, will not now be maintained in theory by any who possess a reputation or are likely to require one.

An "established" Church is no longer required as the champion of arts against arms, of the serf against the seigneur, peace against war, or spiritual principles and powers against animal force.

As to feudality and its stronghold, the land, even there it is assailed, and assailed from the heights of conservative philosophy, witness the following dissertation of Mill on Coleridge.

> "The land, the gift of nature, the source of subsistence to all, and the foundation of everything that influences our physical well-being, cannot be considered a subject of property, in the same absolute sense as that in which no one has any interest but themselves. As Coleridge points out, such a notion is altogether of modern growth. The State fails in one of its highest obligations unless it takes means of providing that the manner in which land is held, the mode and degree of its division, and every other peculiarity which influences the mode of its cultivation, shall be the most favorable possible for making the best use of the land, for drawing the greatest benefit from its productive resources, for securing the happiest existence to those employed on it, and for setting the greatest number of hands free to employ their labor for the benefit of the community in other ways. We believe that these opinions will become in no very long period, universal throughout Europe." —*Mill's* "Dissertations," v. i, pp. 455-7.

The case of the sectional oligarchic slave South,

against the American nation, is the great leading case in the series, and it will be followed.

Priests and Oligarchs, as in Volney's famous vision, have now to exclaim in reality, "it is over with us, the multitude are enlightened!"

When such men as Fichte, Hegel, Humboldt, De Tocqueville, Macaulay, Hallam, Mill, Guizot, Goldwin Smith, and not least though last, Draper, concur that religious freedom ought to prevail, it is evident that the principle of inequality, whether in State or in Church, has no hold on England, but on its yet unextirpated class interests, ignorance and superstition.

And politically speaking, "the factors and conditions" of Democratic progress are becoming so well understood, that soon few will doubt De Tocqueville, that the organisation of Democracy is the great problem of our time, and that to obstruct it is to obstruct the will of God.

And here Mill considers "that the great difficulty in politics for a long time, will be how to govern by means of the specially instructed few, who shall be responsible to the People." He maintains that respecting any nation that possesses a fair share of the very ordinary wisdom to select such representatives as the general voice of the instructed points out as the most instructed, the argument for universal suffrage is irresistible; for the experience of ages, especially of all great national emergencies, bears out the assertion, that whenever the multitude are really alive to the necessity of superior intellect, they rarely fail to distinguish those who possess it. The points are that the people shall be able to discover such men who shall be responsible to the People, with the least possible direct interference from the People; but representatives must not be delegates. But the multitude will never believe the truths of political economy until tendered upon authority in which they have unlimited confidence, although he is satisfied this will be given as soon as knowledge shall have made sufficient progress among the instructed classes themselves, as to produce something like a general agreement in their opinions on moral and political doctrine.—"Dissertations," vol. i, pp. 469-70, 473-4.

As to competent leaders in extraordinary crises, we have therefore the opinion of this illustrious thinker, that the multitude discern and promote their true leaders. This also applies to heads of important departments in ordinary times.

As to matters of general local administration, the People themselves are equal to it, and the advantage claimed by Mill for a trained bureaucracy, must be balanced against the advantage claimed by De Tocqueville in the security for freedom by the transaction of the People's business by the People; bearing in mind that neither the change of office bearers with the President, as in America, nor the newness of that country, are chargeable on Democracy.

But throughout, we must remember, that in a true and instructed Democracy, the will of the nation, is, in its force, intuition, and instantaneous action, more the result of a *living organism*, than of what we are accustomed to call a "constitution," a "balance," or a "mixture." The national will expresses itself constantly, and is omnipotent.

Further, I would contend that the truths of political economy, and the principles of good Government are *not*, after all, of so recondite a character. That a tolerably instructed People penetrates and comprehends them, and that it is not the inherent difficulty or abstruseness of truth, but the operation of perverse and partial interests and influences, that under Governments of the one, the few, or the many, confound enquiry and perplex thought.

There is one peculiarity of this book, which perhaps needs no apology, as it is warranted, if not demanded, by the nature and traditions of the subject. The really valuable thinkers on political science are so few, and they present such a striking coincidence and concentration of authority on most important points, that I have thought it best to present their appropriate dicta together as mottoes at the commencement of each chapter, that their *combined* weight may be fully appreciated.

On the whole, I cannot better conclude this prologue than with the words of two Titans of a Titanic epoch. One of them talks grandly of the future; the other first put into shape that test-principle of trust of the People, of which we have lately heard so much, and experienced so little.

"Government is founded, not on force, as was the theory of Hobbs, nor on compact, as was the theory of Locke and the Revolution of 1668; nor on property, as had been asserted by Harrington. It springs from the necessities of our nature, and has an everlasting foundation in the unchangeable will of God. Man came into the world and into society at the same instant. There must exist in every earthly society a supreme sovereign, from whose final decision there can be no appeal, but directly to heaven. *This supreme power is originally and ultimately in the People*, and the People never did in fact freely, nor can rightfully make an unlimited renunciation of this divine right. Kingcraft and priestcraft are a trick to gull the vulgar. The happiness of mankind demands that this grand and ancient alliance should be broken off for ever.

"The omniscient and omnipotent Monarch of the universe has, by the great charter given to the human race, placed the end of Government in the good of the whole. The form of Government is left to the individuals of each society; and its whole superstructure and administration should be conformed to the *law of universal reason. There can be no prescription old enough to supersede the law of nature, and the grant of God Almighty*, who has given all men a right to be free.

"The first principle and great end of Government being to provide for the best good of all the People, this can be done only by a supreme legislative and executive ultimately in the People or whole community, where God has placed it; but the difficulties attending a universal congress gave rise to a right of representation. The grand political problem is to invent the best combination of the powers of legislation and execution; they must exist in the State, just as in the revolution of planets, one power would fix them to a centre, and another carry them off indefinitely; but the first and simple principle is EQUALITY and THE POWER OF THE WHOLE."

"Nor do the political and civil rights of the British colonists rest on a charter from the Crown. *Old Magna Charta was not the beginning of all things*, nor did it rise on the borders of chaos out of the unformed mass. A time may come when Parliament shall declare every American charter void; but the natural, inherent, and inseparable rights of the colonists, as men and as citizens, would remain, and, whatever became of charters, can never be abolished till the general conflagration."

"*Acts of Parliament against the fundamental principles of the British Constitution are void.*"

"The world is at the eve of the highest scene of earthly power and grandeur that has ever yet been displayed to the view of mankind.

"Who will win the prize is with God. But *human nature must and will be rescued from the general slavery that has so long triumphed over the species.*"—*Otis*, "On the American Crisis, 1764."

To this add the words of Jefferson:—

"Men by their constitutions," said Jefferson, "are naturally divided into two parties: 1. *Those who fear and distrust the People*, and wish to draw all powers from them into the hands of the higher classes; 2. *Those who identify themselves with the People*, have confidence in them, cherish and consider them as the *most honest and safe*, although not the most wise, depository of the public interests. In every country these two parties exist, and in every one where they are free to think, speak, and write, they will declare themselves."

But it must never be forgotten, that whilst the excellence of Statesmanship is that it understands the People and the system, and adjusting the one to the other, prepares to raise them both, yet the ultimate vindication and warrant of all political action consists only in this,—that it prepares fair conditions and a clear stage for the development of the *spiritual manhood of nations.* Thus, throughout, are politics related to the final, the universal, and the infinite.

Reform Club,
May, 1866.

ON DEMOCRACY.

CONTENTS.

Book I.

Book II.

DEMOCRACY:

ITS FACTORS AND CONDITIONS.

"Two elements enter into our enquiry. The first the idea of spirit; the second, the complex of human passions; the one the warp, the other the woof of the vast arras web of universal history. The concrete mean and union of the two is liberty under the conditions of morality in a State."—*Hegel.*

"A Commonwealth ought to be as one huge Christian personage, one mighty growth and stature of an honest man, as big and compact in virtue as in body; for look what the grounds and causes are of single happiness to one man, the same shall ye find them to a whole State, as Aristotle, both in his ethics and politics, from the principles of reason, lays down."—*Milton.*

"*Freedom can exist only where Individuality is recognised as having its positive and real existence in the divine Being. Secular existence*, as merely temporal—occupied with particular interests—*is only relative and unauthorised*, and receives its validity only in as far as the universal soul that pervades it—its principle—receives absolute validity, which it cannot have unless it is recognised as the definite manifestation, the phenomenal existence of the divine essence. *On this account it is that the State rests on Religion.*"—*Hegel's* Philosophy of History, pp. 348, 396, 53, trans.

"With regard to the limits of its activity, the State should endeavour to bring the actual condition of things as near to the true theory as possible. Now the possibility consists in this, that men are sufficiently ripe to receive the freedom which theory always approves. The other consideration, that of opposing necessity reduces itself to this, *that freedom if granted is not calculated to frustrate those results without which all further progress is endangered.* In both cases the Statesman's judgment must be formed from a careful comparison between the present condition of things and the contemplated change, and between their respective consequences."—*Baron W. von Humboldt,* "Sphere and Duties of Government (The Statesman)," pp. 201–2.

"What is the first part of policy? Education. The second? Education. And the third? Education. Fewer laws, but strengthen the principle of laws by education. Before the State found the commune, *before the commune found the man*. Only the education given in the commune ought to emanate from the State."—*Michelet.*

"The Peoples of Christendom present in our day a frightful spectacle. The movement that bears them on is already too strong to be arrested, but not to be guided. Instruct Democracy. An entirely new world demands a new political science."—*De Tocqueville.*

"The State's activity should always be determined by necessity, the principle towards which as to their ultimate centre all the ideas advanced in this essay immediately converge.

"In theory the limits of this necessity are determined solely by consideration of man's nature as a human being; but in application we have to regard in addition, *the individuality of man as he actually exists.* This principle of necessity should prescribe the grand fundamental rule to which every effort to act on human beings, and their manifold relations, should be invariably conformed.

"The necessary chiefly requires negative measures, since owing to the vigorous and elastic strength of man's original power, necessity does not often require anything save the removal of oppressive bonds.

"There is no other principle so perfectly accordant with reverence to individuality and solicitude for freedom. Finally the only infallible means of securing power and authority to laws, is to see that they originate in this principle alone."—*Baron W. von Humboldt,* "Sphere and Duties of Government (The Statesman)," pp. 201-2.

'There is a general principle in every nation which is the invariable basis of power, and when once this principle is too much loaded, it infallibly shrinks into smaller dimensions."—*Montesquieu,* v. 3, p. 172. Edition 1777.

CHAPTER I.

DEMOCRACY:

ITS FACTORS AND CONDITIONS.

"To build on a rock means to establish a Government on Democratic Principles."—*Napoleon III.*

"The first and simple principle is Equality and the power of the whole."—*Otis.*, 1764.

"Let no one quote the old proverb against me, that *whosoever builds upon the People, builds upon sand.* When a Prince puts his confidence in the people, who is a man of courage himself, and knows how to command others, nor deficient in other necessary preparations, he will never be deserted by them."—*Machiavel*, "The Prince."

"Men are governed by several kinds of laws, *and the sublimity of human reason consists in perfectly knowing to which of these orders the things that are to be determined ought to have a principal relation*, and not to throw into confusion those principles which should govern mankind."—*Montesquieu.*

"On this ground, then, a man engaged in a design like that which is the object of this work, might lay claim to the attributes of UNIVERSALITY AND ETERNITY for the rectitude of his doctrines,—with as little arrogance as he could claim for them the most confined and temporary expediency—*provided that* in the execution of his plan he has boldness and strength of mind enough to set apart all along *whatsoever is peculiar to certain times and places*, and to raise his contemplation to that elevated point of view from which the whole map of Human interests and situations lies expanded to his view."—*Jeremy Bentham*, "On Influence of Time and Space."

Government consists of two things,—the first is called the Spirit, or passion, or motive power; the second is the organisation.

In all Governments but Democracy, the two are separate, and, to an extent, hostile.

The motive power of all Government is manhood. The excellence of Government consists in the amount of manhood it can represent and "organise." Often the question of questions is, Is there more of this manhood *in* the Government, or out of it?

And the essential value and power of Democracy consists in this,—that it combines, as far as possible, power and organisation; THE SPIRIT, MANHOOD, *is at one with* THE BODY, ORGANISATION.

Only the parallel cannot be complete, because as systems must be worked by men, in all systems but that in which the aggregate manhood *entirely preponderates,* there is a permanent and dangerous official corporate life and interest.

"There is," says Montesquieu, "in every nation a general spirit upon which power itself is founded. When power clashes against this spirit it clashes against itself, and is necessarily stopped." The question is, whether Education can develop and organise the general universal spirit of Humanity, so that manhood, which has always ruled by Individuals or Sections, may rule universally.

Democracy is Government by the People. It is a national Royalty.

"The People" is the whole (approximate) manhood of a nation. The necessary exceptions are Paupers, Lunatics, and Criminals.

"Government" involves Power, Organisation, and Unity.

"Government by a whole People" must of course be by representation, and by freedom and equality of representation,—Freedom as between Individuals and the State; Equality, the only Freedom as between Individuals, and its only guarantee as against the State.

Democracy, therefore, becomes possible when the whole national manhood can organise itself on a basis of Equality: and the two-fold question is whether Government can *so* be organised, and how?

The first and general question, "Can Democracy organise itself?" is one of principle. If there be no radical, essential, and unalterable difference between the political capacity of races, bloods, castes, and classes, then Democracy is possible;—if not, not. If there be such a difference, oligarchy has its warrant in Principle, and will be eternal.

But assuming, as here we must, that there is no such difference, then education will of necessity organise the national intellect on a common platform of political truth.

Education, therefore, is the factor of Democracy, and *cannot but be so*, for when quality is added to quantity, "Democracy must prevail."

But the second question, "whether Democracy can organise itself upon a basis of freedom *and* equality?" is not, upon the surface of it, so easy.

For if it be true that to give Freedom and Equality to numbers is to erect a class preponderance, then to give an equal voting power to the masses is *not to abolish Despotism, but to establish it*, and so Freedom and Equality involve a contradiction in express terms and in essential principles.

This supposition, however, is as puerile as it is specious. The answer is five-fold. First; if true it is unavoidable, for the causes that have brought on Democracy to its present shape will now act with accelerated force, and we are already doomed to this "Despotism of numbers!" Second; the People, if uneducated, *cannot organise*. Third; if educated, they will be trained to the discovery of *truth*. Fourth; representation is not Government, and the people's representatives have always been men of a higher class. Fifth, the People are naturally as divided in opinion as any other class; and, as to class interest, Despotism and outlawry alone now cause them to unite.

The present, however, is not the place for this discussion.

The third question, "*how* Democracy can be organised," is one of detail and circumstance, and of principle.

The principle, we say, is that of Development or EDUCATION of the national *Intellect* and *Character*. This must be *of a certain quality and quantity* to become the means of Democratic organisation.

Education means, therefore, *universal Free common Schools.* "Free," because some cannot pay. "Common," because no more should be done than is necessary.

Free Press, which, however, to be free, must be cheap, otherwise its proprietary and constituents will both belong to the exclusive classes.

Free assembly is equally necessary for education of the national manhood, and for the declaration of its will.

Free Church, also, must educate the character, and will always and only mean a Church paid for by those who want it and use it. A Church paid by the State always and only means a Church that *obeys* the State, and that is based on physical force and social servility.

As a question of detail and circumstance, this four-fold freedom has, as in America, to be introduced at once and wholesale by the immigration of a prepared people, or it has, as in old countries, to be prayed, thought, and fought for.

But it is an inevitable *à priori* conclusion, and demonstrated also in the only country where it has been tried, that this four-fold freedom not only capacitates men for *Association,* but compels them to it. It is the necessary habit of men with ideas in common, and it is the notorious custom of free countries.

Thus education begets association, and the association of educated men is already political power. Education begets association; association begets Equality. That is the genesis of Democracy. These are the epochs and the principles by which the world ascends.

And a national unity based on opinion is of *a higher order* and more enduring texture than one based on force.

And a national unity compacted of the infinite ramifications and varieties of free intelligence is *stronger* than any other.

If anything can solve the problem of the political eternity of nations, it is this principle of Equality, which gives a fair chance and a free career to the best of every man, which incorporates every man with the State, and arouses everything that belongs to the Soul.

Therefore Democracy tends to make the loftiest, strongest, most lasting, and most united *nation*, and Equality is the goal of national political progress.

Amongst Democratic nations, the quality and the quantity of Development mark the grade.

"NATION" is a LIVING ORGANISM, but it is only as a nation is also a Democracy, that it can complete its material Bases, its organic Functions, and its Individuality or character,—it is only as it organises the power, and the life, and the will of *the all*, that it organises *the whole*.

And nations thus prepared can alone enter as units into those vaster *Federal* combinations towards which the most advanced nation points.

Thus, to ascend to the *universal* we must complete in Freedom and Equality, the *Individual*:

getting Freedom and Equality, we get variety and complexity of relationship and interests: getting this we get "Power, Organisation, and Unity" of the loftiest and most lasting character, and of hitherto unconceived proportions.

WE MAKE DEMOCRATIC FEDERAL EMPIRES POSSIBLE.

§

Thus the question of the organisation of Democracy is two-fold,—of the institutions, and of the nation;—of principle and preparation.

As Government consists of *Power and Organisation*, so at every step in national progress, the administration partakes of the knowledge and the ignorance, the advantages and the defects, of the actual ruling class.

And organisation either expresses the national Intellect and Will, or is used to suppress it. In the first case there is harmony, whatever the status of the nation. In the second, there is revolution and reaction, or death.

The organisation of Democracy is of necessity the problem of every advancing age or People, and the one deadly unpardonable sin of nations is the failing to revolt against bad Government.

Wherever the best governing qualities govern, —wherever the actual administration is adjusted to the real power, there is good Government.

With the *Power* of the one, the few, the many, and the all, let there be also *administration* of the one, the few, the many, or the all. It is a question of Adjustment. If those who have the franchise are more numerous than those who deserve it, there is anarchy,—if less, Despotism.

Adjustment is the law of Politics : non-adjustment, its license. For Politics means Power, and any fancies or fictions about that lead straight to Chaos, Despotism, or national Death.

But whereunto are systems to be adjusted ?

To the actual political competency, at any given epoch, of the ever advancing People. Until this tide is at the full, "no everlasting mansions" can be built upon its verge. But there will be always building there asylums for Idiots or Lunatics, who would confine the Power of the few to the function of the one, the Power of the many to the function of the few, the Power of the all to the function of the many,—and who would call *that* "Statesmanship!"

But to reasonable men we would say,—"either affirm the necessary and eternal subordination of the masses, and to support *that*, affirm further an essential and absolute difference of races and bloods,—do this, we say, as "the South" has done, and be honestly destroyed, you and your theories together in open fight, or acknowledge your foregone defeat, and that at last the Crown and the Purple of Empire must descend upon the People."

The *Theory* has been always with us. Now, yonder, in America, is *the fact*. All that obstructives can do is to suppress and aggravate the danger, and make Revolution of that which might have been order. The time is past for the good old Tory drivel that repression and safety are one, and the true alternative is pondered well, that the People must be let in, or education kept out.

The equal voting power of so much of the country's manhood as is at any given time educated or developed,—that is the right governing power of the country, whether it be power of autocrat, oligarch, middle class, or Demos.

The equal voting power of the (approximate) whole educated manhood of a country is Democracy, for there is no power without organisation, no organisation without education, and no Democracy without the People.

§

Of any *system of Government*, except a Democracy, it may be safely said that it is only a transition system, for the system must advance or the nation recede. If the nation advance, the system must advance with it or be cast off; if without advancing, it retains its hold on the nation, it must destroy it.

Every *nation* is in its youth and immaturity, in its manhood, or in its Dotage. If in its minority, and without the equal voting power of its universal manhood, all intelligent patriots will seek to hasten on its manhood: if in its manhood, they must look well to preserve the bases of Democracy. If it be in its Dotage, and incapable of any advance, gradual or violent, towards Democracy, then the sooner it gets itself out of the way of the world the better.

The question therefore respecting any nation is, "Is it prepared for democracy or national self-Government, or must it still be governed from above or from without? And if the latter, has it such a measure of preparation as to allow of middle class rule, or is it only fit for that of the few, or of the one?" The rule of the all being possible, national unpreparedness is the only warrant for the rule of the one, the few, or the many.

And respecting Democracy, or the Manhood of a People, the only question is that of time and adjustment. There is no *question* of Principle. He who would inaugurate Democracy too soon or too late may truly be no Statesman. But he who denies the ultimate universality of Democracy is only too plainly a fool.

The whole world gravitates towards Democracy, and those parts of it that do not obviously partake of this movement, and that yet have before them a future, do in fact tend to Despotism or to anarchy first, that they may be prepared for Democracy afterwards.

It is the Policy of *Conservatives* to graduate Reform in order to forestall Revolution. It is the Policy of *Liberals* to consider how large a portion of privilege can be destroyed, and how soon. *Statesmanship* has to do in this view with two situations. In the one, where nations have not the elements of self-Government, to supply them, for all Government that is not self-Government is but an expedient and an interregnum.

In the other, where national self-Government is

a *fact*, to reconcile, as gradually and peacefully as may be, forms with fact.

The first is all that can yet be done in England. Educate and prepare. And whosoever helps to educate the English, prepares them for Democracy (and what perhaps he might call Revolution), whatever else he *thinks* he does. Whosoever obstructs education, obstructs Democracy,—but he does two other things also. He prepares for anarchy and Revolution, as well as for the relative degradation of his country.

Who then, we ask, are the Statesmen,—they who advance to Democracy through education, or they who would advance to it through anarchy?

Theoretical question of Democracy there is none, but the double question always remains of Institution and People,—are they fitted for one another. If the nation is not fitted for Democracy, why is it not fit, and how shall it be made fit. If the Institutions are not fitted for the People, how are those institutions soonest to be modified or destroyed?

There is, first, the question of Development of the country's manhood; second, the question of its *assertion* of its right to rule.

Respecting Europe, although it is certain that every advance leads it towards Democracy, it is probable that it can never reach it by a peaceful road.

Notwithstanding all the culture of former ages, the natural fruits of Development and association were never reaped within the reach of the associated tyrannies of Europe, till the British Channel and the sword of Cromwell defied their interventions.

The lesson taught by European history in this connection is, that notwithstanding the mutual exhaustion of hostile Despotisms, and the many separate efforts of *Freedom*, it was never able to consolidate and secure itself in the face of associated tyrannies, alliances, and coalitions, until it was partially isolated from them in England.

And even in England, Freedom could never blossom into *Equality*, because of the many hostile associations against it. Freedom was gradually overcome and forced back by centralisation in Church and in State, and had, after its one glorious success, to yield to the Stuarts and to the families, and to their one hundred and seventy years of reaction, and to seek in America a still completer isolation, before the principle of Equality could live.

The world owes it to three thousand miles of ocean that the first nation is now constituted on a basis of Equality.

It is evident to all who have considered this question in any connected or reasonable way, that all questions of "Government," being questions of the distribution and organisation of Power, will practically be decided by the strongest, and that *strength is a question of Development and of numbers.* That the People will not obtain power till they can conquer it, and that (non-intervention being a fact) they will conquer when they deserve it. That when they can conquer it others will cease to govern them, for there are involved interests too deep and universal, passions too strong and absorbing, to allow any but the strongest to govern. That the possession of political Power depends therefore upon the acquisition of governing qualities. That these are acquired by education in the widest sense of the term, and that as education opens to all, so governing qualities and consequent power become at once universal, impartial, and safe.

Further, that the craft of the sections cannot long postpone the recognition of the manhood of a nation that has really come of age, and that whilst to emancipate too soon or too late is equally dangerous, to deny emancipation altogether is the *last* extreme of folly.

True it may be a question, and sometimes a very fine one, how large a majority in numbers must become possessed of these governing qualities, or what proportion the educated must bear to the whole, before the whole can be enfranchised, but that in all living nations a greater and ever greater proportion must and will vote, till at last "the all" will be admitted,—of this there can be no doubt possible. The only question is whether the nation is to continue to live and to maintain its relative position in the world.

Political questions have to do with nations and systems of three kinds ;—

1st. With dying nations, destroyed by the suppression of the national manhood,—killed by conflicts with Democracy, or by victory over it.

2nd. With living and progressive nations that are advancing loyally towards the Democratic era, or that have entered upon it.

3rd. With nations that have reached some sort of completeness as to the elements of national life, and that have become Democracies.

Of the last, America is as yet the only complete example. England follows, and is nearer to her than is supposed, because our forms of Feudality have not been adjusted to the power of the People.

Every Government tends to some preponderating power or to anarchy. All so called mixed Governments are at best prolonged constitutional conflicts between different and hostile principles of Government, and whatever the local partial or temporary impulses, the one universal tendency is towards Democracy, or the power of the all,—towards a more equal diffusion of the elements of knowledge, of material advantages, and of the means of organisation.

As therefore every progressive state tends to one preponderating power, which will ultimately represent national unity, and become the equal rule of the all, it is but safety, economy and common sense to admit and prepare for our future rulers.

And since Democracy involves Conservatism,

and is the *postulate of a new and unknown progress, —the organiser of civilisations more complete, and national unities, whose life need never decay, and whose proportions are vaster than have yet been conceived of,—since it is also perhaps the germ of an universal Federation,* it presents a problem of vast interest, and of world-involving issues,—a problem for which all past ages and peoples have prepared the present.

In this chapter we propose merely to state certain rudimentary propositions :—

1st. What is meant by that *manhood,* the equal universal rule of which is Democracy.

2nd. The right *test* of manhood.

3rd. The *bases and stages* of its Development.

4th. How it combines results sought in vain through other systems.

And firstly, we consider the root of the matter ;—

WHAT IS MANHOOD?

Manhood is of the *Body, Mind, and Character*, and implies (1) Physical maturity, (2) Mental Development or Education, and (3) Character.

This definition of course excludes Minors, Paupers, Imbeciles, Lunatics, and Criminals. It does *not* exclude civil servants, and the army and navy.

But the vexed and crucial question about this manhood doubtless is,—What is to be

THE TEST?

And the answer is, that broadly speaking, *all*

tests of manhood are, to those who deny and to the manhood that seeks enfranchisement, arbitrary, useless, or superfluous.*

This is a self-evident proposition, as appears in considering what the real question at issue is.

There are three parties concerned in every question of enfranchisement.

1st. The obstructives, the privileged, the careless, the trimmers, the doubters, and haters of the People, the doctrinaires, and the go-betweens,—an exceedingly great army.

2nd. A small band of the philosophical and thoughtful, whom truth influences in questions of other men's interests.

3rd. The indignant alienated mass of the unenfranchised thundering at the Gates of the constitution.

The real question is, not what the second class can or will do. *That* but smooths the way and levels the ground between the hostile ranks. The real and only question is, what power can the last bring to bear against the first?

The question of the promotion of a disenfranchised class is not mere "*fitness*," nor ever has been.

It is a question of their power and organisation. It is a question of Battle,—constitutional battle, if there be a constitution,—if not, not.

Between the class that is privileged, and the classes that are not, are the conditions, *not* of dis-

* Physical manhood is of course not a question, being a mere matter of formal certificate.

cussion and of right, but of war. Of course the weapons are those of the People and of the age.

And the question on which side is the prevailing power and organisation, is again a question of manhood.

For organisation, two things are necessary,—a common platform of thought, and mutual confidence, permanently possible only to "*character and education.*" For Power, add to these qualities, *numbers.* How can the problem be otherwise expressed, when once the phrase has been heard, than in the everlasting words of Aristotle,—"when the popular party shall exceed more in quantity than it is excelled in quality, Democracy must prevail."

Tests may be and are useful to keep a victorious Democracy pure and competent,—they are but forms, farces, delusions, pretences, mockeries, and snares, as applied to a Democracy struggling against prerogative or privilege for place and power. To be weak is to be disfranchised. Men are not kept out because they are not fit, but because being unfit, they are not strong.

A test is a form of capitulation, or a cartel of defiance. Privilege capitulates to those whom it is obliged to recognise: it defies those whom it can exclude. If the three, five, six, or ten-pound renters can be kept out, they will be, and the "test" is the badge of their subjection. If they cannot be kept out, the test admits them for the same reason that battered walls admit besieging armies.

§

To the anticipated objection that the manhood may be too low or too little for political copartnership, we answer that at least it cannot be lower or less than the average of that through which by constitutional means, it has just forced an entrance. And further, it *cannot* be too low where education is universal.

Education of the rudimentary sort should be made and kept universal by an immutable law, and this not so much that the People should be thereby fitted for the franchise before they attain it, but that having attained it, the ruling reason of the nation should never be debased or lowered to an undisciplined, uneducated, or undeveloped condition.

It should be the policy of every nation to make education universal, in order that (not the political only, but) *all the requisite results* of manhood be developed. The "man" is prior to, and includes the "citizen," and the State can still less afford that any of its citizens should not be "men," than that being men, they should fail to do a certain act (to vote) of citizenship once in three or seven years.

All men should be educated, and mental Development is as much an element of manhood, as bodily maturity, or legal majority. Universal free common schools, not only can and must, but will be established in all free countries, and no manhood can exist or be recognised, that on the average, is not educated.

We have here, therefore, nothing to do with the average quality of the manhood of any given country. If it be not high enough it will not become a Democracy. If it be a Democracy, and should fall from it by reason of failing in these qualities, it would fall from them as soon, and no doubt a great deal sooner, under any other form of Government.

According to the English census of 1860, there were 3,739,505 houses at an average rental of £15 5s. Of these by far the largest number, 1,277,956, was at from £6 to £10, and there were only about half that, or 659,724, at from £3 to £5, which equals 1s. 2d. to 2s. weekly.

This proves two things :—

1st. That there is very little *numerical* difference between residential Manhood and a £5 rental, for there are twice as many rentals from £6 to £10 as from £3 to £5. For the latter, it is *a question of principle*, and with an universal system of education, few average men of health, ability, and character, could rent under £5.

2nd. That if they rented ever so low, the proportion of rentals under £5 would, unless our country is greatly to degenerate, be as 660,000 to 3,740,000, or less than one-fifth of that part of the constituency whose average is £15 5s.

§

What, then, is the difference between manhood, and an educational, rating, or rental suffrage ?

1st. Manhood suffrage is based upon a statesmanlike appreciation of the *necessity* of qualifying all the country's manhood for the country's Government,—of the deficiencies which all other systems must labour under. It recognises that *all* Government is *by, for, and through* manhood.

2nd. Rental or rating suffrage adopts a false principle, that of measuring manhood by money, and it sanctions a low and materialistic habit of thought.

3rd. Manhood suffrage declares that the all, or the vast majority, *can*, and *must*, and *shall* be educated into citizenship and self-support. Money suffrage either denies or ignores this great national fact and duty, and is content with its million or so of paupers vibrating on the edge of anarchy, vitiating the morals of the People, and weakening the resources of the country.

4th. Manhood suffrage recognises all partial suffrages as expedients and instalments, or compromises, and thus rightly forms the public mind on political questions, and prepares it for political advance.

5th. The only value of money suffrage is, that it is a bad measure or test of manhood.

6th. Manhood suffrage affirms at once the final principle of Government. It says clearly and boldly, "Suffrage follows manhood." If the all are not fit to govern they *cannot* govern, not because they lack money, but because they lack manhood. The all must become fit to rule, and then they shall rule; for *the proportion of men without manhood*, is the measure of national anarchy, disease, retrogression, or death.

7th. Because an educational suffrage smacks of

the pedagogue and the forcing system. Manhood is wanted, not a reading machine. School education, which is but one of the means of manhood Development, can never become its measure or substitute.

And there is this further inevitable result of these principles. The fact of the political minority of a nation is an impeachment of the whole political past of that nation, or of those sections or parties in it that have obstructed either its political, religious, or material progress. *Anything* of monopoly or privileges, in Church or in State, *anything* that restricts knowledge or weighs upon material progress ; *all interests and men that obstruct the means of material, political, or religious freedom and equality, obstruct manhood*, and, as such, have already the sentence of political death working against them.

The third inquiry respects—

MANHOOD DEVELOPMENT ; its BASES and STAGES.

We have seen that there are four things which have been the making of the only Democracy that has ever endured.

The first is free universal common schools.

The second is free public assembly for political purposes.

The third is a free and *cheap* Press.

The fourth is free worship, or the absence of political inducement, penalty, or control, in religion.

At first sight these four forms of freedom may appear contradictory, inasmuch as the first demands State intervention, and the others repudiate it. The first says, let the State enable men to acquire the elements of citizenship. The others say, seek not to come between the citizen and his fellow on the forum, or between the citizen and his God in the Church.

There are, however, innumerable arguments and precedents, not to be repeated here, why the State *should* put within reach of every man the elements of citizenship, and why it should not follow up that interference with patriarchal or priestly domination.

Free schools are the basis of Democracy. Without them, there has as yet been no complete national manhood Development. As political life compels men to associate, so education enables them to associate rightly.

Free assembly involves the principle of complete and equal representation, for *its essence is the rule of the majority, all voting who are present.*

Free Church can acknowledge no irreversible State-imposed formularies ; no political master, no legal or money bond to the State, for *its essence is ideal and absolute Freedom.*

These cannot fail to complete a threefold Freedom, material, political, and religious. They also impress on the nation an intense *Individuality* and Ideal, which constitute the very spirit of a nation, whilst the *power* and the *culture* of the all give the utmost wisdom and impartiality to the national councils, and the utmost strength, concentration, and stability to the national Executive.

The four provide the elements of national manhood and of political and religious Unity. The educated national *Intellect* is the best diviner of what is *True*, and acts directly on the Legislature and Executive. The Churches, on the other hand, have no direct bearing on politics, except as they elevate and purify the national manhood, but they constitute a number of independent and incorruptible republics within the State, appealing through the *conscience* to the *Right*, and upholding the real national Unity, inasmuch as the Right and the True are one. They teach a grander ideal, a sterner resolve, and stronger passions, than mere patriotism, while they render patriotism itself imperishable.

The Development and Organisation of Manhood has been the great work of the world, and it ends in Democracy or failure.

Not Development alone, or Organisation alone; not the Development and Organisation of a fraction of the man, nor of a section of men, *but the Development and Organisation of the bodily, mental, and spiritual manhood of nations.*

According as you develop and organise the One, the Few, the Many, or the All, *as to numbers,* you have Barbarism, Oligarchy, Middle-class Government, or Democracy. As society advances from Barbarism to Civilisation, it advances always and inevitably from the Royalty of the One to the Royalty of the All.

According as you develop and organise man partially, *as to qualities,* you get physical, mental, or moral paralytics ; a Society that is rotten, a nation that is doomed. Democracy is the manhood of nations. It ends the conflict between Conservatism and Progress, for its Progress is conservative, its Conservatism is progressive.

Development of the *Intellect* enables man to find and to accept a common platform of Truth. *Conscience* disposes him to yield to others their rights. The *Spiritual* gives the irrevocable impulse and the higher Law. Thus, Development, *if it be sufficiently complete in character, and sufficiently general in numbers,* prepares for association. Thus, the Revolution and the Reformation always advance together, for Christianity is the mother of Democracy.

The first great step in the world's advancement was the advent of the one perfect man. This epoch was prepared for during more than two thousand years.

It took sixteen centuries more before *a nation* was sufficiently developed to associate. The interim was filled up with the trial of various separate, sinister, or partial systems of Development,—with Developments that destroyed each other, or that were incompatible with equality, the right and the interest of the all.

But the Puritan or true Republican stock, born of and living upon these elements, Press, School, Church, and Assembly, can never be beaten down, and will leaven the lump of the world, unless human nature be changed, and the order of Providence reversed. It gets its inducements from Heaven and from Hell. The prizes of Eternity glitter before its believers. Hell frowns in their rear. Paradise blooms in their front, and beckons their advance.

"Religions," false or fettered, are against it, and will be destroyed or set free. Nations that cannot associate for public acts are either immature, or doting and debased. Where childhood is not educated, manhood cannot exist.

This universal four-fold free system is self-dependent, self-contained, and of necessity and nature tends to an universal Equality.

The root of them all is in Christianity. Without that knowledge would be taught, but not wisdom or Charity, and civilisations would blossom only to wither away! Our right of political assembly may indeed have *begun* in German woods, as the page of Tacitus relates, but German manhood after fifteen hundred years is still Austrianised and Prussianised. It had to cross the channel to Puritan England before it conquered Freedom. It has now to cross the Atlantic, and has waited ever since Tacitus wrote, ere the next step in this world-logic could be secured, and Germans also advance from their primitive right of association or "assembly," to Equality.

In the beginning, Government may even create a nation. In its Infancy it must protect and guide it; in its manhood it must represent and obey it.

Government is but a function of the national manhood, and the proportion the *manhood* of a nation bears to its population as *men*, decides the character of the Government. It is against nature for that which is weaker or worse than another to govern it.

Hence, Government by the all is a necessary and inevitable incident of the political maturity of nations.

Autocracy may secure power and unity, but they depend on a life. Oligarchy may secure wisdom and a high tone, but it is selfish and immoveable. Middle-class rule is materialistic and wanting in initiative. Democracy is not possible except in an advanced social and political state, but every partial distribution of power is obviously provisional and precarious.

4thly.—We consider the

RESULTS OF MANHOOD-DEVELOPMENT.

All systems are to be tested by their result on *Individuals, Institutions,* and *Nations.*

The right and Development of the INDIVIDUAL are the very postulates of Democracy. It is, in fact, the amount of these in a nation that necessitates more or less advanced Institutions. They are the basis of all combinations that are either stable or complete.

There are three standpoints from which SYSTEMS of Government are judged.

First. Concerning the constituent; *Individual right to representation.*

Second. Concerning the first branch, the Legislature; or the best means of securing *good representatives.*

Third. Concerning the second branch, the Executive: How much of Individual action is compatible with freedom, and what system of Representation will secure *the best administration?*

Of these in due course.

But the all-involving test is that of NATIONALITY.

A complete nation is one that has complete and sound its *Material Bases*, its *Individuality and Unity*, and its *Organic Functions.*

By the first it exists; by the second it exists as a nation; and by the third it thinks, administrates, and acts.

The *Material Bases* of a nation consist of its *Territory, Labour, and Population.*

Its *Individuality or Unity* consist of a oneness of circumstance, ideas, and interests, and this results from a oneness of *Institution, Race, Boundary, Language, and Religion.*

Its *Organic Functions* are its *Legislature* and *Executive.*

And leaving out the mechanical items of Territory and Boundary, it is manifest, as to "*Material Bases,*" that Democracy develops Labour and Population. As to "*National Individuality,*" that Democracy tends to oneness of Institution, Race, and Language,—for all are equally interested in the first; there are no castes to separate the second; and all study the third, while Religion, being free, secures the essential condition of its own life. Also as regards "*Organic Functions*," the collective universal educated reason is undoubtedly the best means of choosing the best Legislature, and procuring the best Executive.

§

If Democracy be the best system, it must combine the "right," the "means," and the "end." It must satisfy Individual Right, select the best representatives, and secure the best system of Government; or, at the least, it must do these things, on the whole, better than other systems.

First, then, this book contends throughout that Democracy satisfies *Individual Right* in the only possible way,—by preparing men to exercise it satisfactorily. The only Democracy in the world has established universal free common schools. All other systems deny Individual Right as a Principle, and defy it as a power, and confide it either to the one, the few, or the many in trust for the all. Democracy says the franchise right is as much, *and no more*, a trust than any other right.

In the second place, Democracy, thus understood, secures on the whole the *best representation*,—of material interests, political truth, and moral right. Material interests, for every man can judge of his own. Political truth, for the Collective Reason is its highest exponent. Moral Right, for the interest of all is the right of each.

As to the *best Executive,* the system that can organise the will and the *Power* of the all must be the strongest, as the system that develops the *Intellect* of the all must be the wisest. To combine intensest Unity with completest Freedom, is the perfection of Executive, for it supplies the greatest amount of power, and the best organisation of it. It will, in fine, be seen that Democracy alone can meet the requirements of advanced civilisation. With interchange instant and constant, of ideas, men, and things, systems that do not or cannot *represent, express, and enact the universal,* will soon become mere Governments of revolt, and administrations of chaos or obstruction.

The completer the freedom, the more intricate and involved the relationships, the more centralised will be the administration, and the greater the nation : for "right," "representation," "Government," and "nationality," all support and complement each other.

The objects of the scheme of Hare, namely, representation of minorities, and representation by the eclectic intellect of the country, are better attained by the principles of Democracy, which "represent minorities" in the only practicable way, by preparing the People to comprehend all just ideas entertained by the few. To enable voters to remove their names from the local registry and enter them on the national one, with a view to the certain election of the foremost intellects, would be a good substitute for Democracy if that system did not exist. And as to minorities, they would probably obstruct equality, and fail to elect the best men.

Democracy, as an organised system, maintains the maximum of the three essentials of Government, *Security,*—for the all consent; *Power,*—for the all think, and act, and govern; *Honesty,*—for they will govern for themselves. It makes a truer nation than can otherwise be made. *It makes a nation of men, instead of a nation of classes and corporations.*

The fact is that *as Manhood, the essence, culminates, Diplomacies and forms recede.* With the majority of souls in a nation incapable of self-control and restraint, you must have your Blondins of Statecraft with their long poles of elaborated Institutions to balance withal. With the majority educated and free, the People will stand as men, not only not by means of, but in spite of all Statecraft to the contrary. Systems which seek to govern for and by the Few, are forced to balance one mistake by another,—mobs by Primogeniture, Ignorance by standing armies. Democracy leaves Truth and Principle to balance themselves.

There are many American regiments that, give them but materials, can, amongst themselves, build boats, bridges, pontoons; construct railways, engines, carriages; conduct newspapers or magazines; preach, pray, and build chapels; make garments, books, or constitutions. Such being the citizens, what sort of Statesmen would it take to enslave them?

The nation that does not adopt Democracy is either in a *rudimentary* or a *falling* state,—it is slowly labouring up to the true ideas of right, representation, good Government, and nationality, or it is going slow or fast, but surely, to destruction.

Democracy, or Government of, by, and for the whole People, is that system which begins in a free and therefore a varied *Development* of the qualities of citizenship, which sees all the complex forces and functions of its manhood thus matured and prepared for *Association*, and by association for self-Government or political *Equality ;* which having thus created a national manhood, finds it *a living organism of intense vitality and unmatched power*, perfect in the completion of its Individual forces, compact in a loyalty to itself, strong in an all-pervading habit of Association, immutable in an equality which makes every man royal, with an Executive as intense as the will and the arm of one man can make it, with an administration based on the universal will and upheld by the universal voice, yet everywhere and always free as the living soul called public opinion, which lightens through and leavens the mass.

Behold at last the making of a complete nation and of a settled Government. That is Democracy. Add to it the principle of Federation now settled upon a due adjustment of local and general interests and jurisdictions, and of local and imperial Sovereignties, and you have a principle which may encircle the world with Federations, whilst it gives to the Individual his freedom, to local Governments their minor life centres, and to the nation Power, Balance, and Unity.

You cannot get deeper than Individual Freedom and Development, you cannot build safer than by allowing no bastard sub-sovereignties of Church or of "State Right" to mock at individual freedom, or to out-balance, hamper, or defy the aggregate Sovereignty. You cannot invent a completer Executive Unit than a President, you cannot have a broader foundation than the universal suffrage of the universally educated, nor a safer society or more stable Government than is formed by an universal habit of association, which forecasts the national policy and forms opinions abreast of facts.

It is a Unity reposing on nature, and on a basis of truths, interests, and forces, universally shared and understood.

Writing from a country which in thirty years has made such great advances towards Democracy, —and of a country which shows us the only Democracy in the world, it is necessary here shortly to notice their relative positions.

England progresses in Freedom, but will probably never reach Equality.

Our Diplomacy is more open, our taxation more direct, our suffrage will soon be extended, and toleration is more complete. But six Englishmen in seven are still unrepresented; we have no House of "Commons," religion is still endowed by unbelievers, and established by the State.*

Europe stops half way between Development and Association. We have secured partial Freedom, and our neighbours an equality tempered with Despotism. Development has prepared for Association, but the hierarchical principle everywhere interposes minor Associations of corporate bodies, to negative those of the People.

It is in vain to speculate as to whether remote ages will or will not find England still an aristocracy. All her Independencies are becoming democratic, and this at least is certain respecting herself,—she will become comparatively depopulated or comparatively Democratic. But in England and Europe the Revolution and the Reformation have been arrested.

Men of confused thought, and of too much or too little education, or taught to admire institutions and constitutions of a narrow and restricted tendency, separate the means, Democracy, and the end, good Government, and actually consider them hostile the one to the other.

They are accustomed to say that "your conclusions depend on your point of view, and that the points of view are, *either* the necessity of giving

* "The History of the Reformation does not close where many European authors have imagined. It made another enormous stride when at the American Revolution the State and the Church were solemnly and openly dissevered from one another . . . That (*toleration*) is perhaps as far as the movement has at this time advanced in Europe."—*Draper's* "Intellectual Development of Europe," v. ii, p. 220.

to individuals their civil rights, *or* to Society, good Government."

This is the pitfall for those who hiccup about the British Constitution, without knowing that that Constitution reasonably adapted to the present times, is the very last thing which they, as the opponents of Democracy, would wish for.

When will statesmen learn that it is impossible to permanently secure good results by bad agents? The only way to secure "good Government" is to develop by education the minds and the manhood of those for whom you would claim "civil rights." Until the majority are fit for self-Government, Democracy is impossible, and until Democracy be possible, good Government is not possible, for *Government by, is always and everywhere Government for.*

§

In a Democratic nation there are two forces which naturally balance or neutralize each other's evil action, and which cannot otherwise be balanced.

The first may be called the vis inertiæ and of flunkeydom. The tendency of all persons in comfortable circumstances and position to avoid all extremes, all great efforts ; to renounce and abjure the ideal and the absolute ; to look to the lead of those above, not to the wants of those below ; and to consider the convenient rather than the right.

The second principle comes up against this in the shape of the almost *revolutionary energies* of men in contact with the soil and with reality, and who are protected by no realised property from the immediate personal pressure of evil institutions and of want.

Where the all have the vote-power, this principle becomes loyalty and a true conservatism. Where they have it not, their work can only be done by agitation or revolution, and after perhaps, as in England, thirty years of the former.

As the all obtain power the oscillations become less vehement. We approach a balance of one excess by the other, and we recede from war.

Moreover in all countries where the all do not govern, there exists the immutable basis of an alliance between certain alternate governing factions, against the People. There is the fact of the People's exclusion, and the wish to perpetuate it.

In England the Whigs and Tories, the "Inns" and the "Outs," thus combine against the unenfranchised. In America, Slaveholders and Democrats, against the Negro. In all cases where the People do not govern, the combination exists. The holders of power may contend amongst themselves, but they will always unite against the People.

Taking the position and relations between Whigs and Tories to be to Englishmen the most intelligible application of this general principle, it is evident that representing between them the party and the cause of *property,* they can usually command the powers of the press, the purse, and the screw.

The Whig or more advanced section, is of the two decidedly the more dangerous to progress, for they obstruct progress in the name of progress, and divide liberalism against itself. They can always reckon on the Tories to plump or split with them against the Radical, and often on the Radical to split with them against the Tory, whilst they can effectually use against the Radical, force, intimidation, and corruption.

In such countries the powers of retrogression are always strong. There are but three parties;—the Few who happen to be in; the Few who happen to be out; and the People, who are always out.

The first two know that with them it is only a question of *interchange* of position, and they know that if once they let the People in, the position will not be changed but *destroyed.*

There is therefore the hopelessly retrograde party that gets in between the accesses of the People's indignation and the epochs of their advances. There is also the party that from time to time uses the People to recover power. It is only by a determined and skilful use of their needs or of their terrors, that the third party, the People, can prevail; and in the order of providence, *the millionaire,* the owner of so many English boroughs, the furthest removed from sympathy with manhood, and the most determined unbeliever in it, is ever haunted with its approach, and shakes with fear at its apparition.

Yet till the power of the veritable People preponderates, it is evident that faction and not country will be the best and the easiest paymaster, and that representatives of ordinary abilities will fear to commit themselves against such a combination.

In the House, Whigs and Tories coalesce against the People. Out of the House, *in almost every constituency* that is not Tory, *a Committee or Association rules, and consists of men above and without the People.*

The remedy is, in the House *a determined phalanx of men around an honest and capable leader;* out of the House, *numbers*, and organisation, to work and balance the constitution against those who destroy its action by farming the constituencies.

Thus, we say, until "the party of the People" is formed, powerful enough to swamp the sections or any combination of them, the power, the falsehood, the corruption, and the hypocrisy of the great Whig party will always exist and prevail, and Government will still consist, not of acts done or abstained from on considerations of Statesmanship, but, as at present, to a great extent, of a series of spasms and jerks of agitation, met by sheer obstruction. There can be no complete Statesmanship without the People, but the theory and practice of Whigs and Tories alike is, that conservatism shall not claim their counsels nor progress their energies, that they shall not, according to the English Constitution, be included in "The State," and that their exclusion, which causes inertia within, shall only be remedied by periodical storms of discontent, in which they enforce their will from without.

This question involves for England that same two-fold question of Good Government and of abstract right, of which we have discussed the position in America,—for neither practical nor abstract rights are ever conceded as long as the Few can combine to exclude the all.

Allowing for the difference of circumstances, there are, in both countries (as in all others), the same parties and the same objects. The Tories are as much slaveholders as they can be in England. The Whigs resemble the "Democrats," and by turns, use the Tories against the People and the People against the Tories. They are neither of, from, nor for the People. Out of office, they have been intriguers and liars, in office, they may become liars and intriguers. In the bright exceptions, nature overcomes party. The Radicals, pure, determined, logical, consistent, and honest, are few and far between, until a crisis swells their ranks into a host, and they move with and as the People. Republicans in America, Radicals in England, their natural enemies are Tories, Whigs, and Slaveholders.

The Tories think, and say, and stick to it, that for the People to be represented, would be dangerous to Church, King, State, and Constitution. The Whigs know better but do worse. They act as though they believed it, and talk as though they did not. Practically, the creed of the two is one, and it is this, to take office and place, turn and turn about, one in, the other out, one out, the other in,—a large party, keeping it all in the family.

They consider the Constitution saved as long as the people are kept from restoring its balances and from interpreting it by the ancient spirit and by present facts, and they admit as much talent as is necessary to make themselves respectable.

It may be said that every party when admitted is always apt to become Whiggish and conservative, that is, to look after its own interests as opposed to those of outsiders. This is true, and it is the great argument for Democracy. Admit sufficient numbers,—all the qualified of the People, and you have all interests looked after, you combine conservatism with progress, *for the interest of all is the right of each.*

As to England, let us remember that the chief duty of all her citizens everywhere, is *to recognise that Democracy* MUST *prevail, and that Education* SHALL *prepare the People for it; and to see to it that no traitorous or foolish schemes for plural or fractional voting* (the reversal of which would be one of the first results of an universal education) are meanwhile foisted on them to create distrust, weakness, and revolution hereafter.

Nature cannot be forced. In political life, the foundation is the Individual; and the completion of his physical, mental, and moral nature, by which completion alone he can be free, is indeed the beginning of all national Unity. Freedom is variety and Development, and other foundation for Unity can no man lay, how stupendous soever may be the national or Federal combinations that hereafter shall organise and harmonise the world.

From a *chaos* where all is confounded together, to a *Development* where all appears to separate, to a *Unity* wherein all is organised,—that is the formulum of all progress, whether in worlds or in systems. As Guizot says: "All things at their origin are nearly confounded in one and the same physiognomy; it is only in their after-growth that their *variety* shows itself. Then begins a new *Development* which urges forward societies toward that *free and lofty unity*, the glorious object of the efforts and wishes of mankind."

There can be no absolutely sound political combinations that do not rest upon men prepared for political Equality. From that comes an intense and varied *Individuality*, but the secret is that *that very increase of complexity increases also the organised dependence of men upon one another.* That is Unity. When it has spread far enough it is Nationality. And the completion of the first nation upon the basis of individual political equality is the completion of the first great step of the series along which Humanity has to advance.

Such a national Unity is America, for itself a living Organism peerless in organisation and power, —for the world a moral propagandism which nought but the conversion of all nations to its principles can stay.

By Equality we mean of course political Equality.

The whole educated manhood of a nation

equally voting, is God's natural progress, conservatism, and balance, and only in proportion as it is realised, can these be secured.

To sum up, the object of this book is to show that an educated Democracy is the only final Conservatism ;—that the war in the West has indeed been the making of the first precedent for Democracy ;—that there can be no complete nation that is not also a complete Democracy ;—that the only safe bond of Unity is the preparation of the units, and that the vaster the conglomerate of Empire the more perfect must be the component atoms ;—that minorities should be treated as minorities, unless and until they can by the natural use of argument and discussion, convert themselves into majorities ;—that, in fine, the thoughts and will of the whole People are the true governing and progressive power, and that Statesmanship is of little value save as it prepares the Royalty and Universal Manhood of Peoples ; while *they* are but quacks and doctrinaires who, with infinite pains and trickery, seek out many inventions for Conservatism and balances without and against the People, and neglect, abuse, and refuse that true Democracy which is the end and aim of all political science.

It is by thoroughness of preparation, and through complexity of relationship, that national Unity obtains its completest form and highest expression.

Some politicians may object to Equality or Individual Development, and think to leave them out of the series, but both are in the order of Destiny. The law which makes Unity is an universal one, and "we must consent to go with the movements of the Universe, and to march to the step of Destiny," or be crushed under the resistless tread of advancing Principles and Peoples.

"Nation" is the mightiest unity yet. But there is a mightier to come, in which nations may be as Federated States. That Unity is HUMANITY. "It is," says Humboldt, "the idea of Humanity which History exhibits as evermore developing itself into greater distinctness, *setting aside the distinctions of Religion, Country, and Colour.*" "It is," says Fichte, "the vocation of our race to unite itself into one single body. This is the first great point. Then shall Humanity move onward."

DEMOCRACY:

WHAT IT IS.

"The universal Commonwealth."—*Fichte.*

"The state is here a living universal spirit, but which is at the same time the self-conscious spirit of the Individuals composing the community."—*Hegel.*

"In a despotic State a real division is perpetually kindled, and if at any time a union happens to be introduced, citizens are not then united, but dead bodies are laid together in the grave."—*Montesquieu.*

Freedom is the completeness of Spirit.
Democracy is the completeness of nations.

"Democracy does not confer the most skilful kind of Government upon the People, but it produces that which the most skilful Governments are often unable to awaken, namely an all pervading and restless activity, a superabundant force, and an energy which is inseparable from it, and which may under favourable circumstances beget the most amazing benefits. These are the true advantages of Democracy."—*De Tocqueville*, 140, v. 2.

Chapter II.

DEMOCRACY:

WHAT IT IS.

"The judgment of a whole people, if unbiassed by faction, undeluded by the tricks of designing men is infallible."—*Franklin.*

"Many maintain that nations are never their own masters. Such principles are false and cowardly, and can never produce aught but feeble men and pusillanimous nations."—*De Tocqueville.*

"Every man who is supposed a free agent ought to be his own governor, but it is fit the people should transact by their representatives what they cannot transact by themselves."—*Montesquieu.*

"A majority held in restraint by constitutional checks and limitations, and always changing easily with deliberate changes of popular opinion and sentiments, is the only true sovereignty of a free people."—*Lincoln.*

"The Statesman must allow all restrictions of freedom to remain which are once rooted in the present, so long as men do not show by unmistakeable signs that they regard them as enthralling bonds, that they feel their oppressive influence, *that they are ripe for an increase of freedom*, but when this is shown he must immediately remove them. Finally, *he must make men thus ripe for enlarged freedom by every possible means.* The last duty is unquestionably the most important, for by nothing is this ripeness and capacity for freedom so much promoted as by freedom itself."—*Baron W. von Humboldt*, "Sphere and Duties of Government," pp. 197, 201-2.

Development.—By free School, Press, Church, and Assembly.

Association.

These two produce Equality, and that is Democracy, or Government of, by, and for the People.

Development endows Individuals with Power, and when of a certain quality and universality, produces association for public purposes. In other words, it causes a common platform of material, Political, and Moral Truth, to be accepted and acted on by a competent number.

Thus, DEVELOPED AND ASSOCIATED MANHOOD, produces material, political, and moral power. In other words, it is strength and unity,—Power and Organisation.

POWER produces Equality or Revolution.

Take, in addition to these facts, the axiom in material as in political science, that *the smaller the molecules the stronger the unity.*

And that other maxim vouched by authorities and common sense, that a mixed Government is an unnatural or provisional state of things, and *that one power will necessarily preponderate in every living nation.*

And also the fact of the substantial oneness of the race.

Take also History.

The result is, that mankind has, has had, and can have before it, throughout all its nationalities and epochs, but three alternatives :—

To educate and develop, or to remain barbarous.

To develop and associate, or to be ruled from above or from without.

To associate for Equality, and to rule itself.

The nation that is a Democracy is also *the strongest nation.*

The nation that is a Democracy is *the only nation that while it moves can rest.* It has reached the highest political *form,*—that towards which or towards ruin, all Peoples for ever gravitate.

There the Government and the People are one. There power is rightly distributed, and completely administered.

"The organisation of Democracy" is therefore the problem, not only of Individuals, but of nations, not only of "the age," but (politically) of Souls and of Creation.

And the problem solving in Politics always is how power shall be developed, or how the policy and the politicians shall be destroyed.

The Development is an Imperial question; Providence secures it for the whole.

The Destruction is a Provincial question, each country may settle it for itself.

Order is the first law of earth,—freedom the next, or perhaps, in its perfect sense, the last. The Savage obeys the strongest individual. Society the strongest organisation. As Society advances, Equality advances, and "Individualities" (save as servants and helpers), and administrations recede. The Law of organised existence is, "as much freedom as is compatible with order, and no more; first unity, then the perfection of the units."

But order is useless, save as it leads to freedom, and when (as now at last in America) greater freedom for the Individual becomes possible, and there is enough organisation to work it, then comes Revolution, and out of that, again a more complete order, and more perfect unity.

Order and Freedom are, in the mind of the Supreme, the symbols of a mighty equation, but *whilst*, in the history of man, they work imperfectly towards that equation, they are in ceaseless and essential antagonism. Man, at each stage more complete, offers himself for a more complete organisation; the organisation wears out its system of law, and is again modified or destroyed by the man, again progressed, and further completed.

Perfect unity, or organisation, cannot be reached without perfection of the units, because their advancing perfection will destroy all other organisation, than the last or perfect one.

"How to Destroy?" becomes then, at certain stages, the question of questions. To graduate wrong into right, and if it may be, to abolish Revolution by enacting progress, or, if it must be, to summon, in the last resort, Revolution itself from the abyss.

When this question comes to be asked, it is the supreme one, and they who do not agree in the answering, or who will not abide by the answer, contend neither for Freedom or Revolution, Progress or order, but for anarchy—the negation of both.

Happy the People that has learnt to destroy by replacing!

Rights arise out of relationships. Political Relationships are between man and man, between the Individual and the State, and between States.

The requirements of man in communities are, protection of Property, Person and Life, conduct of affairs between States, and the payment of the expenses of these things.

In other words the Judicial, the Political, and the Economic departments of Government.

It is usual to say that the "rights" of man are relative or absolute, original or acquired. That his original rights are absolute, and that his acquired rights depend on his fulfilment of his duties. We, on the contrary, prefer to put it, that *all "rights" are absolute.*

But the *getting* of right depends usually on the getting of self-Government, and by the same reason, of *equal* self-Government.

The question is not whether rights are absolute,—that is a truism.

The question is, "*what are the rights?*"

Rights to protection of Property, Person, and Life, are called absolute, because they are absolutely clear, obvious, and simple, until forfeited.

Complex rights also are absolute in the ideal, but have got to be absolutely proved to be rights before they are known and accepted as such.

Political rights are complex. *They are rights to the best mode of obtaining rights.* They are absolute in the ideal, because truth is absolute; they are only absolute in practice as far as opinion coincides with Truth, *i.e.* as far as "the best mode of obtaining rights" is discovered, agreed upon, and enacted by Law.

"Man has Rights." True. "Manhood," also, has rights. True, also. And the whole circle of political error is caused by the confounding of "*Man*" with "*Manhood*."

The Rights of man depend upon what the man is, and he is everything from the angel to the ape, and from the ape to the Demon.

To say, then, that man has rights is to utter a bêtise, a truism, or a lie,—according to what is understood by "man."

Man has a right to the best possible mode of securing and obtaining his rights, *i.e.* to the best possible Government; but "Government" presupposes Unity, and strength and wisdom are the qualities whereby Unity is acquired.

Man will never get his rights (such is the blinding effect of self-interest) until he gets equal self-Government, and he cannot get equal self-Government until he has got the *Governing qualities,*—strength and wisdom.

It has been shown that Development (or Education) and association can alone supply these.

The question, therefore, "What *are* the rights?" depends upon the fact, "What is the manhood?"

The question, how any nation is *to get* the rights of manhood, depends upon getting the national manhood, by which alone equal national self-Government is possible.

The science of Politics, therefore, seems to exhaust itself in two problems.

First: What is the average educated or developed manhood of a country, and, therefore, its appropriate Government?

Second: What is the best mode of raising that average, and of moulding the Government to it?

For a low or one-sided Development, tyranny is the best Government, rising, with the Development, from the rule of the one to that of the few and the many, and at last attaining to that of the all.

The ideal best Government is of course national self-Government, and Conservatism joins with progress in seeking the consummation. Self-Government is safest, for it is the broadest base. It is the object of all progress, for it unites interest and right.

All theories of thinghood or Property, as opposed to manhood,—of three per cent., or bricks and mortar, if meant as aught but a rough test of the qualities of manhood,—are dismissed with the contempt they deserve. "Let them blare off into the inane without further note or comment." They are false, abject, anarchical, material, and retrograde, —fit only for millionaires or monkeys. All Property that derogates from Manhood is Robbery.

To raise the average national manhood is the work of Conservatism and the work of Democracy. You must either sink manhood to perpetuate the rule of the Few, or raise manhood to hasten on the rule of the All.

The rule of the all is the only finality. That must be a very low degree of *development* that does not see this, a very low degree of morality that will not seek to attain it, and an infinite measure of stupidity that thinks to withstand it.

§

The *basis* of the relationship of the unit with Unity,—the Principle of the reconciliation of Individual Freedom with Nationality, with Order, with Government, or any other real Unity,—is the fact that each Individual bears the same relationship to the Universal, and is therefore capable of Harmony with the natural laws, and with other Individuals. Things that are like the same thing may be like one another, and all are capable of advancing *together* towards the Infinite.

Progress consists in *an ever truer obedience, by an ever increasing number*, to the eternal laws, and as this progress but *develops* the natural relationship of man to his fellow and to the Supreme, so "Manhood Development" is the right name for the process.

And as nationality is the most comprehensive political Unity at present within the sphere of our knowledge, so, inevitably, as the next great step, the collective reason of a nation must become (if the nation is not to be destroyed) the best expression of the national mind. If any minds are excluded as incompetent, they degrade the national character, or, at least, weaken the national average, and any *fractional* reason must be, by comparison with the true collective national reason, weak, imperfect, arbitrary, and uncertain.

Every man, perfectly free, must, in a measure, have experienced in his own soul every stage and struggle for completeness that the world itself has passed through.

Every nation, truly democratic, must in like manner have conquered its right to Democracy.

The Individual wins freedom by a symmetrical manhood Development. Communities win freedom by those Powers of Association which are the natural and necessary result of Development. The two together give Unity and Strength, and can never fail to win Equality. The Individual contends with Individuals, and advances as an Individual. But when he contends for *political* rights he contends against Factions and Parties, and can only succeed by association.

Freedom is the completeness of Spirit.

Democracy is the completeness of nations.

As this question is often put—

"That is good Government which secures Order, Freedom, and Progress; and that is the best possible Government which secures the greatest possible amount of them."

"Is Democratic Government good Government? Can it,—*Does* it secure Order, Freedom, and Progress; or the greatest practicable amount of them?"

The "Can it" must be answered by Theory and Fact.

That it secures Order is admitted. Where "the all" govern, all obey.

And Democracy not only secures Freedom. It *is* Freedom.

As to Progress, progress is Development, and the great recommendation of Democracy is that it depends upon Development.

All these things are admitted as theory, and are established in the life of the American nation.

What, then, is the difficulty? What is the impeachment of Democracy?

Two-fold.

First: "The equal voting all would give an inevitable class majority to Labour. Democracy, therefore, after all, impugns *Freedom.* It would destroy Equality by Equality."

Second: "High culture, wealth, leisure, and high *Caste,* give to aristocracies grand and chivalrous exaltation of soul, breeding therein a love of glory and of beauty, to which dead level Democracies aspire in vain." But Equality is of the essence of Democracy, and if this accusation be true, Democracies do *not* promote the highest degree of *Progress.*

In other words, though Democracy secures Order, and also a mediocre average Development, it does not secure the greatest possible amount of Freedom and Progress.

The first theory is Mill's. The second, Aristotle's. The first is born of fears that can never be realised. The second, of assumptions which mechanical, industrial, and social science, and a completely altered state of Society, have for ever destroyed. We shortly proceed to examine both by the light of their own admissions,—by that of other great authorities,—and by that only true Democracy, and only complete nation, of the making of which we have written.

Fact, theory, and authority will perhaps show us that Development is the synonym of Order, Freedom, and Progress. That the faculty of Association (remarkable in Democracies) intensifies, multiplies, and accelerates progress by competition on an equal basis,—that it secures freedom by making public opinion irresistible, and enthrones Order in an intense executive Unity. That Development means intelligence of common interests, and Association, an instant, intense, and constant expression of the national will.

Behold at last the ditch wherein Conservatism, falsely so called, has got to die.

With Development universal,—national manhood Development or Education, vanishes the basis of Aristotle's objections to. Democracy, for Development is wealth, dignity, and glory, and the true national Unity which Association secures, secures also defence of national rights, and defence of Human rights. Where Families rule, but do not pay, their selfishness leads the nation to fight for privilege,—their subserviency leads it to fight for Prerogative. Where nations rule, as well as pay, there will be no ignoble wars; they will not fight for families or legitimacy, but they will fight for national existence or popular rights. As nations, they will fight for nations: as "The All," for Democracy.

Development being attained, and Association with it, there remains, therefore, the question of Equality, pure and simple, which *must* result therefrom, and that is the whole question; for if that is not right, then not Development, but *restraint*, is the true Gospel, and there is a hitch somewhere, not only in Democracy, *but in Creation.* Democracy means Development,—but *universal* Development. It means also Association,—but association of the All to promote the "rights of minorities," or the supremacy of the Few, is not only not Democracy,—it is nonsense.

The question of Democracy has to be developed in its entirety, but the only questions worthy of discussion amongst advanced thinkers, are those of Individual greatness, genius, and glory, and whether or not the whole equal voting (educated) Developed Manhood of a nation constitutes its natural Governing power, possessing the three attributes of all that is rightly Imperial, namely :—

1st. The conservative element, or the power to decide what at each stage is the right instalment of progress.

2nd. The progressive national force.

3rd. The central power, the national will, which combines these two and balances them, making progress conservative, and conservatism progressive, developing the thought, passion, and character of the nation for permanent national uses.

Whether the true, perfect, and complete *national*

Individuality resides in its *equal* voting developed manhood, or in some *unequal* artificially balanced *quasi* national manhood.

The latter position is that taken by Mr. Mill. He says that this equal voting all would *throw the nation off its balance* on questions which naturally affect the majority as a class.

That Equality, if it descend to the all, means class tyranny, and not freedom. In other words, that national Equality can never exist. And the same writer's theories about *special rights for minorities* are only another denial of the Principle of Equality. They deny it none the less that the scheme may not be pressed for present adoption.

Thought and fact have irrevocably settled every question of Polity in favour of Democracy, except this one of Equality.

Democracy says that this is a question of Education or Development. That an educated national manhood contains within itself a complete natural balance of forces and interests. Mill says that it does not.

The errors of the Human mind seem to reproduce themselves eternally.

Here again are the Hebrew old clothes of political judaism. Mill has got into the petticoats of the Hierarchy. The pharisees of civilisation would make broad their phylacteries over the manhood of the People. They would hide the nakedness and readjust the fulcrum of Creation. The "Balance of Power," recognised at last as a policy of idiotcy amongst *nations*, takes up its last refuge between *classes*. It is declared that a true People can never be, and that Genius, wealth, learning, and organisation, which must always belong to the comparatively few, will never be recognised and deferred to by the all, even when education shall have rendered their advantages, and the capacity to appreciate them, universal.

The latest and the least unfavorable form of this opinion is in Mr. Mill's letter of the 17th April, 1865:—

"I would not vote for giving the suffrages in such a manner that any class, even though it be *the most numerous*, could swamp all other classes taken together."

§

But there exist already, in fact, two complete and "balanced" Individualities, and their existence guarantees, to our thinking, the others.

God,—the All-One. The One-All.

Man,—(certain Individual men) politically complete and self-balanced.

Nation,—to be thus complete when its men are thus complete.

World,—to be thus complete when the constituent nations are thus complete.

We must reason through human nature on to order and God, or back to Chaos and the absolute void inane.

To affirm that the *world* cannot be thus complete, is to affirm that its constituent nations cannot be complete.

To affirm that a *nation* cannot be thus complete, is to affirm that its constituent men cannot be complete, that manhood tends to confusion, and that God is the author of it.

To affirm that *man* cannot be thus complete, is to deny God. It is to affirm that Individual completeness clashes with Political Unity. That the State and an universal political manhood are hostile interests. That Equality, the completion of Freedom, contends with Unity, the result of Freedom and order completed. And it proves nothing but that the Individual so affirming, is himself "unbalanced," by reason of excess of the critical and speculative faculty, or of deficiency in insight and faith.

Freedom is good because it conduces to Development. But when it has leavened the all, and made them fit members of the State, then, forsooth, the State meets development and its claims of Equality with a higher law, and says, "we must balance *interests or men.* If men are equal, Interests will be unbalanced. We prefer Interests.

True Conservatism criticises each instalment of progress to see that it is real.

True Democracy sees in God, the *One-All,* a guarantee that *Development must justify creation,* —that every Individual Development is not only not incompatible with, but essential to, a higher or wider Unity,—that the truths of Freedom and Unity can never clash,—that free will and Destiny are one. It therefore advances with confidence to the future.

False conservatism dreads each advance as approaching the final anarchy,—just as false Democracy patches up false immature unities. The one is ignorant of the true process; the other disbelieves in the final result.

Let us who believe in man—nation—world, because we believe in God, accept only such political theories as allow conservatism and progress, —manhood Development and national Development, to unite in hope and action for each and all.

Let us who believe that ONE NATION is *already Royal*, and owes its Royalty to Equality, denounce with every power of our soul and every effort of our understanding, the fears that would obstruct the road along which other nations follow. Let us hail the approach of every planet as it sweeps towards its predestined place in the political Heavens,—hail the fact and hail the theory, not only as right but inevitable,—unless we have the will and the power to banish from man, nation, and world, truth, nature, Destiny, Progress,—and God!

"The People will be able to sit down whenever the sovereignty of a king shall be exactly of the same dimensions as the liberty of a man."

The men of the Future must now say to those great ones of the Past, who live:—

"O men eternal, the minds of this day salute you, but do

not follow you. Their function is no longer yours. They have business with the virility of the human race. *The hour which makes mankind of age has struck.* They contemplate creation directly, they observe humanity directly. They have one model MAN, and one master GOD."

"It is necessary to restore some ideal in the Human mind. Whence shall you take your ideal?"

All the wits from Æsop up to Molière, all the intellects from Plato up to Newton, all the Encyclopædists from Aristotle to Voltaire—*throw all these souls into the* "*man.*"

You will cure the middle class and found the People.

What an aim! *to make the people!* Principles combined with science, *every possible quantity of the absolute* introduced by degrees into the fact. Utopia treated successively by every mode of realisation.

They must say also to the men of the present, respecting the People and their Progress:—

"Up with you all intellects! It is necessary to construct."

To construct what?

To construct where?

To construct how?

To construct the People.

To construct the People according to the laws of progress.

To construct the People according to the laws of light.

"The progress of man by the education of minds; there is no safety but in that. Teach! learn! all the revolutions of the future are enclosed, sunk in this phrase: 'Gratuitous and obligatory instruction!'"

We conclude from the foregoing argument, and propose to establish hereafter, the following principles:—

1st. That Order or Conservatism, and Freedom or Progress, are one cause,—the equal and opposite terms of an orderly Development. The first representing the mode,—the last the essence. That on the great international scale, the first, means strict non-Intervention as against Peoples,—the Individual working out of each nation's Destiny. That, on the small scale, every standpoint of constitutional right should be made the fulcrum of movement, whereon the lever of Democracy shall be plied till every vestige of prerogative, privilege, feudality, oligarchy, and Barbarism be destroyed.

That the one cause, of which order and Freedom are the positive and negative sides is DEVELOPMENT,—of the entire national manhood. That this Development *is* Democracy, and includes Conservatism as one of its inevitable results. It contains within itself "all revolutions," past, present, and to come. But it must be a Development of a certain degree of Universality as to numbers, and of completeness as to quality, or it cannot produce that faculty of Association, which as regards communities is its most essential result. That the faculty of ASSOCIATING TOGETHER is at once the means and the result of Democracy. It is a characteristic of all true Democracies, and replaces the mechanism of centralisation, with the vital unities of an aggregate national life.

That EQUALITY is of the essence of Democracy, and the main incentive to Development, just as Development is the guarantee of Equality. That Development renders Despotism impossible, by creating the best possible conditions of social, religious, and political association, and therefore of the strongest, completest, compactest, NATIONAL UNITY. That without Equality, Representation is imperfect, the "balance" of the realm impossible, and Stability a matter, not of certainty, but of sufferance.

That Equality, or the supremacy of the COLLECTIVE REASON, in other words, that this equal voting power of the entire educated manhood of a country, combines, if not in perfect proportions, at least in the best possible proportions, the two objects of Government—Individual Freedom and National Unity. That Equality, the completion of Individual freedom, *cannot* contend with unity the completion of national life. And that the tendency of the Collective Reason always is to discover and elevate its greatest men.

That plural voting is in fact *a system of representation without election*, and belongs to the oligarchic era of national life.

That in reference to the allegation that the People would constitute a "class Sovereignty," it is a self-evident truth that the *whole People*, with its broad and multitudinous base, with its ascending hierarchies, professions, and officials; its divisions into sects, parties, localities, classes; its specialities and influences of thought and learning, of pulpit, press, platform, &c.; its individuals and sections with *multiples* of power, constitute the one complete, and if not perfect, the best and only possible balance, provided by nature for nations.

Democracy alone amongst political systems, can, like the stellar firmament, rest and move at once.

That the preparation and enfranchisement of a whole People will alone secure the objects proposed by such schemes as plural voting, and that plural voting is directly revolutionary in its tendency, because it would arm the favoured with *artificial* multiples of power, and place them as obstructives directly in the highway along which the People must inevitably march to power.

That there are four grades or eras of national life and progress, indicated by the rule of the one, the few, the many, and the all; that the governing qualities are in MANHOOD; that when that is complete but restricted, the restricted sorts of Government are justified, when complete and universal, Democracy is inevitable.

That the proportion of acres to men may accelerate or retard certain political changes. To maintain that it can do more is an abject political heresy. Statesmanship is not in the soil, but in the soul. Nothing but manhood ever ruled or ever will, whether it be the stupendous manhood of an Alexander, a Cæsar, or a Napoleon, the collective manhood of a true aristocracy, the mediocre administrative mechanism of middle-class Government, or the universal manhood of Democracies.

Always and everywhere a certain manhood rules, because it is a better manhood than that other which is ruled.

That FREEDOM is three-fold—*Material, Political* and *Religious.* Material,—free trade, and direct taxation; Political,—the franchise; Religious,—that the Church be free from State endowments or control.

That where a nation has not conquered for its

masses MATERIAL freedom and comforts, it is impossible for it to attain in any large measure either *political* freedom or *moral* elevation. "They who have not learnt Humanity, may refrain from teaching Religion."

That human nature teaches us that Goverment *by*, is always and everywhere Government *for*. That, consequently, to be *best governed*, nations must be SELF-GOVERNED; and that wherever and whenever national self-government becomes a fact, the age of "stupendous Individualities" (ruling by force or fraud and for themselves,) must of necessity pass away, and that of Royal *nations* become possible.

That a nation thus constituted in an orderly manner, of this three-fold Freedom of the Body, Mind, and Soul, has necessarily, the individual interests and interrelationships of its People so strong in themselves, so bound up one with the other, and so homogeneous as regards the outer world, as to combine all the elements of NATIONALITY in the best possible proportions, and to the utmost possible extent, constituting, also, a better and completer "CONSTITUTIONAL BALANCE" than could be invented by man.

That any nation that does not, slowly perhaps, but surely, progress towards this completed Freedom, is either stagnant or declining: that if it be not stirred by agitation, it will be smitten by adversity, or finally, by that destruction which Providence always allows to fall upon the parts, when they obstruct too long the progress of the whole.

§

But perhaps, after all, the most important and essential result of Democracy is this,—that it discards "Balancings" for Progress. The old weary Europe has always "balanced" against progress, till progress has inevitably scattered the sawdust to the winds, and carried each political acrobat and his tumbling-ground away together.

Neither within nor without the State does Democracy seek to balance artificially. It seeks not to balance State against State without, nor within, interest against interest. *It seeks to advance with and by the whole.*

As to the former species of balance, it may say, with Wendell Phillips, "If Europe leaves America to Republicanism,—well. But if she interferes, we interfere, and the right of our fellowship grasps the hand of every republican in Europe to upset every throne on that Continent."

As to the latter it says, "Make yourself into a majority, and you conquer; if not, remain a minority, and submit. And this is the end of the logic, whether it be accepted at once, or be prolonged through secession and civil war."

Democracy elects its Executive (though not its Judiciary) and its Legislative, which of course act separately without confusion of function, whilst the real ultimate supreme Unity is the People. To do less would not be representative Government, but the chaotic action of Individual units and atoms. To do more, might be called a "balance," but would be obstruction. It bids its Legislative enact the best ideas of the nation, and it bids the Executive execute whatever is already the law.

Democracy leaves the tight rope and the long pole to Diplomats who represent the partial interests and artificial forces of the One or the Few. On the one hand, it regards the "Balance" as virtual war which necessitates war taxation in time of peace, and a bloated expenditure. On the other, it discards even the speciosities of Mill, who, following Montesquieu, admits that even in so-called mixed Governments there is always one preponderating force which governs, but who seems to advocate always some "nucleus of opposition" thereto, not to temper, but to obstruct or defy it.

"I regard it ('Representative Government,' pp. 234-48) as a fundamental maxim of Government that there should be in every polity *a centre of resistance* to the predominant power in the Constitution."

"A most important principle of good Government in a popular Constitution is that *no executive functionaries* should be appointed by popular election."

Where sections govern, these things are essential; where power is universal, if there be centres of resistance, presidents, &c., will be elected by the People, and if on any great national question they veto the People, it will end in the People vetoing them. Democracy studies the past, but is not chained to it. *It is Society mobilised.*

The All govern as manhood should,—*by influences, not by mechanism.* If you want a cause or an idea to govern, get first your *locus standi* in the intellect and devotion of the solitary great. Let it leaven, if it can, the lump. Let it be free of everything but opinion, and of that, if it can conquer it. Where the Collective Reason reigns, anything that is reasonable has in itself the title deeds of Empire, and is the true legitimate. Where entire freedom is, minorities that remain minorities are like untimely births, that have not the strength to exist save as infants or imbeciles, and that had better not exist. They resemble the weak progenitors of animals who are soon conquered and destroyed, lest they perpetuate their inferiority, and hand down their weakness for ever.

And this disposition against "balancings," Democracy will always assert in the world international also. It will replace the attempted communism of Families by the solidarity of Peoples. Democracy paralyses Intervention for wrong; it could never descend to non-Intervention for the Right. Its policy will always be a moral propagandism,— and perhaps something more. It steers a middle course between an aimless intervention which is a policy of idiotcy, and a policy of non-Intervention, as much without heart as without head, which is a policy of Cain. *A just intervention* is the natural result, amongst Peoples, of the habit and power of association.

These seem to us the leading positions as to the connection between DEMOCRACY, and GOVERNMENT, and NATIONALITY, between the Man, the Institution, and the State,—established by the authority of philosophers, by political science, and by the experience of the foremost nations.

The political creed thus taught by History, Authority, and Facts, may perhaps be set forth with advantage in a categorical form, as follows :—

Q. What is Democratic Government?

A. The equal voting power of the Educated Manhood of a country.

Q. What is Manhood?

A. Of the Body, Intellect, and Character.

Q. How is this Educated (developed) Manhood to be tested?

A. *In the general* it is a question of preparedness and of consequent power. If the nation be fit for self-rule, it will be competent also to organise sufficient power to conquer it. The test of manhood is Victory. *In the particular*, Tests must not be inquisitorial, arbitrary, or debateable, but we must judge by the actual visible result of a man's energies and intellect in promoting his *own* interests, and in acquiring a stake in those of the Commonwealth. In other words, the test should be one of proprietaryship *only* as it appertains to manhood. It must be such a test as a labourer with the ordinary qualifications of manhood, namely, an average measure of industry and health, may pass. It must be a mere test of *manhood and residence.* In a true Democracy, education being universal, the average labourer cannot fail to pass such a test.

Q. What withstands this arrangement?

A. Three things: In Economics, indirect taxation, congestion of trade, and a "bloated," nay, a "Demoniac" expenditure for sectional and anti-national objects; in Religion, an established, that is, a tyrannical Church; and, in Politics, "Rights," apart from Duties, and a "Conservatism" which opposes progress, destroys power, divides interests, and makes Unity impossible..

Q. What is Good Government?

A. Any Government that combines Order with Progress.

Q. What secures Order?

A. Loyalty of the greater part of the power of the country to the Executive.

Q. And what secures that Loyalty?

A. Either a good Government and a well-informed Population, or a strong Government and a degraded Population.

Q. What is "Progress"?

A. DEVELOPMENT—of the national manhood.

Q. And how is this Manhood-Development to be secured?

A. By Freedom,—Material (or Industrial), Political, and Religious.

Q. And what are these?

A. First, Free Trade and Direct Taxation. Second, Free common Schools, Press, Speech, and Assembly. Third, non-Intervention by the State with Religion.

Q. How are these to be secured?

A. By constitutional action, where the People have a *locus standi* in the Constitution; by Revolution, where they have not. In either case, they secure one another, for neither can be won without rendering the conquest of the others more easy.

Q. What then secures the union of Order and Progress?

A. The Union of Power with Development.

Q. And what secures that Union?

A. The use of the first to promote the last.

Q. And what is the result of this?

A. Democratic Government,—again, "National self-Government." In other words, Democratic Equality.

Q. Then all good Government tends to Democracy?

A. Entirely so. When the (majority of the) All possess Unity and Power (the result of Development and Association), they will most undoubtedly use them.

Q. But if Power be used against Development?

A. "All History teaches" the result. The nation submits or resists. If it submit, the nation declines, and progress goes elsewhere. The alternative for every country that does not submit to bad Government, and thus commit the unpardonable sin of nations, is Democracy or Revolution.

Q. And for the world generally?

A. There is *no* alternative. Providence secures Progress for the whole. Statesmen may secure and Peoples may submit to destruction for the parts.

Q. What, then, is *true* Conservatism?

A. That which secures national safety by means of national Development, and considers Equality,—the natural result of Development,—as the completion of that Balance of parties and interests which every true nation represents.

Q. What is Democracy?

A. That which secures Development, knowing that Conservatism is one of its inevitable results.

Q. What, then, is the function of Conservatism commmonly so called?

A. It secures, during the minority of a nation, and in a

temporary, partial, and provisional manner, a measure of security and Unity, ***whilst the universal Manhood Development, and consequent powers of Association, are preparing to achieve Equality, and to unite Conservatism, Democracy, and Nationality in one.***

And if the question be further pressed,—"Equality—Development—Association—*of what?* what do you mean, or rather what do you not mean by manhood ?" We answer, Truth is always Catholic and absolute in conception; if not obstructed it is always gradual and conservative in action.

By manhood we don't mean the animal man, aged twenty-one.

That were to crucify Democracy between two thieves : the thief who destroys his own manhood, and the thief who would use the pretence of manhood to deprive others of their rights.

That were to base Democracy, not upon manhood, but upon Animalhood, Devilhood, or Beasthood.

"Manhood rights" is a relative term, in the eye of God and of the State.

It is only some unsafe advocate of Democracy who would challenge for man absolute rights. As regards God, man must take his stand, not upon justice but mercy.

As regards his fellow, man must get his rights by gradations as he gets fit to use and able to win them.

Right,—the conquering it for oneself : Duty,—the determination to do it to others ; these two together make up that true "Reason" which constitutes the worth of States.

The first means isolation, the second reciprocity.

The cry for right without the feeling of duty is destructive and barren. The cry for right as a means to duty, is genial, productive, and sympathic. The first without the last is disease. The two together are Life,—Conservatism and Progress. Right represents the unit. Duty is Unity.

The wish to get rights, without the wish to do right,—it shakes Earth with revolutions and Hell with laughter!

Manhood in Communities is a relative term. Before it can force recognition as a political element it must have attained such a degree of Development of character and intellect as will enable it to combine and assert itself. We need not therefore define the terms of a situation that can never exist. Individuals not developed to the average extent as to intellect and morality (or a sense of others rights), will never be able thus to combine effectually with others for political purposes. Men do not associate without trust, nor without a common intelligence of mutual interest, and if they did, their association would be ineffectual, for the smaller hostile Unities would be the stronger and the easier held together.

The quantity of the People is more, *but to conquer, their quality must be equal.*

"An usurping populace is its own dupe, a mere undertaker, and a purchaser in trust for some single tyrant, whose state and power they advance to their own ruin, with as blind an instinct as those worms that die with weaving magnificent habits for Beings of a superior nature to their own."*

And if, again, we are asked at what stage any given nation is fit for any given step in advance, and realisation of Democracy, we answer, *it is fit for it when it is able to get it.* This is the sole absolute test that other classes or interests either can or will accept of the political competency of the all,—*are they able and willing to conquer it?* By revolution or by agitation as the case may be. Væ Victis is the necessary philosophy in Politics. No Government will ever "generalise Democracy from the depths of its own moral consciousness." Governments concede when they must, and deny when they can.

The only *possible* proof of the fitness of a national manhood for self-Government, is general development and powers of association. *When these exist they are the power and the means and the right.* The national *Industries* must be developed to allow of a certain general diffusion of ease and culture. The national *Intellect* must be so developed as to comprehend the means and necessity of organisation. The national *Character* must be so developed as to present the conditions of confidence, and to teach the necessity of self-restraint and of mutual trust.

When this is done, or nearly done, middle (or middling) class government will get its "crick in the neck." Its adherents will *then* extol the rights

* State Tracts, 1688-1702, p. 225.

divine of minorities, and leave off being very enthusiastic about Democracy. When Democracy was yet afar off, they would of course glorify the power of the People, and for two reasons. First, because they help the middle classes to power, and second, because the middle classes combining with the upper against the People, are supposed to be powerful enough to prevent a *further* "degradation of the franchise."

Power is the vindication of Right. The History of political Equality in old nations is usually thus. Labour accumulates Capital. Commerce establishes a third power in the nation. It stimulates the intellect and the invention. It opens up a career for manhood, and offers a premium for talent. It is the carrière ouverte for the many. The forces spread by self-interest. Labour is gradually associated in the rewards and in the *power* of capital. It becomes gradually the owner of capital. It then unites with it in political ambition. It demands power and will have it.

Such is generally the beginning of the People's Power. It is indeed essentially so in America, for there labour oftener invests in land, and *Democracy is territorial,* and has the natural Conservatism and stability of Land ownership *conferred upon about two and a half millions of farmers,* in addition to the natural progressive qualities of Democracy.

Inasmuch as one complete nation can now be said to exist, which is also the only Democracy, (having now completed its freedom and vindicated its authority) it is necessary to show from its example, first, to what extent the question of Democracy is no longer empirical—that it is a *science;* and, second, that the theory of Democracy is perfect, and its march irresistible and irreversible. Clearly it behoves us all to study that which is not American Destiny only, but world-Destiny.

The whole question of Democracy will then be treated of according to AUTHORITY, ARGUMENT, AND PRECEDENT.

Authority ; the opinions of the Fathers, and of Political thinkers since.

Argument.

Precedent, that of America.

We shall also consider the state and prospects of Democracy in England.

In any given country, that which is virtually Sovereign, must bear the blame of disaster, or reap the glory of success.

America is the chief examplar of Popular Sovereignty.

But inasmuch as any given country may, and *that* country does possess, very peculiar political conditions, it is necessary to examine the theory as well as the practice of Democracy,—to consider the argument a priori, as well as a posteriori.

The question, therefore, divides itself into the universal and the local: the abstract and the concrete.

Whether, then, we investigate the theory of Democratic Government, or its application in any given country, it is in respect of these three terms or qualities—Progress, Stability, and Unity, that we seek a verdict. And we shall find as we proceed, that they are included in the more precise expressions, "Manhood Development, and Faculty of Association."

We contend that the Theory of Democracy is absolute and unassailable. That its adaptation to any given Country is a question, not of the worth of the Principle, but of the nation.

As Hegel tells us, "what constitutes the State is a question of advanced science."

"Questions of political form," says Carrel, "have their data in the state of Society, and nowhere else."

Montesquieu (Esprit des Lois) also lays it down, that "every Government is composed of two distinct elements, its nature (structural identity), and its principle (or passions)."

"Whereupon," adds Napoleon III, "it follows that a Government can be a strong one only as its principles are in harmony with its nature."

And Aristotle contends that:—

"Government is nothing else but the arrangement of individuals in a state, and the propriety of every arrangement or composition must depend on the *number* and *nature* of its materials.

"The best Government is the best arrangement, and the best arrangement is that in which the materials to be arranged are the best fitted both to receive and to preserve.

"Of all political errors, the greatest is that of thinking that the institutions of one people may be safely communicated to another, differently endowed and circumstanced."—*Gillies' Aristotle*, pp. 234-7-376, v. ii.*

Or, to recur to the profound and quaint simplicity of the earliest authority, we are informed, in the Republic of Plato, of the truth upon which the matter stands :—

"Do you know now, said I, that there is somehow a necessity that there be *as many species of men as of Republics?* Or do you imagine that Republics are generated somehow of an oak, or a rock, and not of *the manners of those who are in the city.* * * * If, then, there be five species of cities, the species of souls in Individuals shall be likewise five. Why not?"—*The Republic of Plato*, book viii, p. 387.

Republics, then, depend upon men and their manners. We are thus admonished of the necessity of forming our opinion of both :—

"Whosoever cannot define the good by reason, separating the idea of the good from all others, and as in a battle, piercing through all arguments, eagerly striving to confute, *not according to opinion, but according to essence*, and in all these, marching forward with undeviating reason; such an one knows nothing of the good itself, nor of any good whatever, but if he has attained to any image of the good, we must say he has attained to it by opinion, not by science, that in the present life *he is sleeping and conversant with dreams*, and that before he is roused he will descend to Hades, and there be profoundly and perfectly laid asleep. By Jupiter, said he, I will strongly aver all these things."—*The Republic of Plato*, book 7, p. 379 (Taylor's Translation).

* It is important throughout to bear in mind the character of the translation here used. It has been characterized as "faultless and faithless," the latter because it was written with a view to make Aristotle appear to favour *monarchy*.

*** We insert some passages from Hugo, for the power, splendour, and truth that is in them, although, as at pp. 61 and 80, it seems doubtful how his philosophy deals with the mightiest element in man,—the spiritual. "To deprive religions of Hell, and to be brother to the damned," is perfectly allowable to so illustrious a member of a church that has excommunicated the best of mankind.

DEMOCRACY

NO LONGER EMPIRICAL.

"La Politique c'est la fatalité" (destiny).—*Napoleon* I.

"The human caravan has, thanks to 1789, arrived on a high plateau.

"The nineteenth century has an august mother, the French Revolution. It has that powerful blood in its veins. As for its source, it is beyond man. The mysterious gestations of progress succeed each other according to a providential law.

"*Revolution* will be the name of civilisation, until it can be replaced by the word *Harmony*. To deprive religions of hell, and societies of the galley; to be brothers to the wretched, the serf, the fellah, the prolétaire, the disinherited, the banished, the betrayed, the conquered, the sold, the enchained, the sacrificed, the prostitute, the convict, the ignorant, the savage, the slave, the negro, the condemned, and the damned,—yes, we are thy sons, Revolution!"—*Hugo.*

"*There is nothing in the world so sound as American society*, with its intimate union of all classes, its general diffusion of property, its common schools, and its free religion. The danger of communism, or of anything like a war of classes, is never felt, and even strikes were almost wholly unknown till the Legal Tender Act multiplied them by causing a frightful derangement of prices.

"The local institutions also are perfectly healthy, and form in themselves, and by their effect in training the political character of the people, the sheet anchor of the constitution.

"The manhood of the new nation would bring with it no doubt many new difficulties, but the past will never return. Feudalism, Primogeniture and State Churches were left behind for ever.

"That the victory has been won, not by a man, but by the nation, is your glory, and the pledge of your salvation. The Cromwell of this age is an intelligent, resolute, and united People."—*Goldwin Smith.*

"Every American is in some sense a patriot and a person of cultivated intelligence. No such wide diffusion of the ideas, tastes, and sentiments of educated minds, has ever been seen elsewhere, or even conceived of as attainable."—*J. S. Mill.*

CHAPTER III.

DEMOCRACY

NO LONGER EMPIRICAL

"The suppression of the aristocratic and Democratic rebellion of the slaveholders will in itself be the defeat of our foreign enemies, and our triumph will be shared by *our foreign friends who are fighting the battle of liberal principles and equal rights in the Old World. The existence of a strong, rich, prosperous Republic is a persistent revolutionary fact.*"—*North American Review.*

"There remains, on the one hand, that rupture which the *Catholic principle* inevitably occasions, and on the other, the requirement that *the units* of the State in their individual capacity should rule, that all Government should emanate from their express power. *This collision* (between Government and individual will) *is the problem with which history is now* (A.D. 1830) *occupied.*"

"We have now to consider the French Revolution in its organic connection with the history of the world.

"Liberalism as an abstraction (the right of individuals to govern) emanating from France, traversed the Roman world. It became bankrupt everywhere. *Religious slavery* held that world in the fetters of political servitude. For it is a false principle that there can be a revolution without a reformation. These countries sank back into their old condition. Napoleon could not coerce Spain into freedom. Here it must be frankly stated that with the Catholic religion no rational Constitution is possible."

"A share in the Government may be obtained by everyone who has a competent knowledge, experience, and a morally regulated will. Those who know ought to govern.

"These are the principal phases of that form in which the principle of freedom has realised itself,—for the history of the world is nothing but the development of the idea of freedom." —*Hegel*, pp. 472, 468, 476.

Democracy, as a theory, has always been acknowledged perfect.

Democracy, as a fact, has always been on its trial,—always until now condemned as incomplete, if not left for execution. There are various issues on which the verdict may be taken.

First. Does it as much, or more than any other polity, promote the *general* diffusion of material, intellectual, and religious advantages?

Second. Does it tend to make *an intenser nationality?*

Third. Does it promote *Individual* greatness, heroism, culture, and Genius? or is it that the system which gives a chance to the All, quenches or mitigates the aspirations of the Few?

Or, to vary the test, does it secure a strong, an honest, and a stable *Government?*

Or, again, does it secure Industrial, Political, and Religious *Freedom?*

How much, then, of this great question of Democracy can now be argued from precedents and upon evidence, and what portion of it, if any, is empirical?

The past, whether of Greece, Rome, France, England, or elsewhere in the Old World, tells us, from different standpoints, that without manhood Development sufficiently general in diffusion, and good as to quality, Democracy pure can*not* be.

What does America tell us?

It tells us that a mixed manufacturing and territorial Democracy—chiefly the latter—has stood through all changes of fortune and numbers, a veritable and a progressive Democracy; Education universal; Competency universal; remarkable for its love of peace and ability to carry on war; for its love of the arts, and devotion to the national ideal.

What America does *not* tell us is, how Democracy will stand the strain when, ages and ages hence, her territory will be filled to overflowing, and the population will be pressed back upon itself into numerous and crowded cities *to such an extent* as to raise the old questions of over population and over production, and to outvote the population settled upon the land. This problem has often been solved before *without* Democracy.

American Democracy now answers even that in part, for the great cities have responded to the awful pressure of the crisis, as well as the wide plains.

Still, in as far as America does not settle the question by a fact, it is still one of opinion and not of fact, and we are left to maintain in theory only what no thinker (not even Mr. Mill) doubts, namely, that if the educated national manhood would not, by force of numbers, give to the working classes *a preponderance of class interests,* Democracy is then in that, as in all other respects, the best polity.

But further, if Democracy will not answer in a crowded commercial and manufacturing Community, then no possible system will answer, for all others have been tried and failed. We must therefore adhere to Democracy—the only system in this respect untried,—or declare Governmental science a failure, and that Progress must drift the world to chaos.

It comes, then, to this, that all other systems

having failed in all circumstances in which they *have* been tried, and Democracy having succeeded in all circumstances *but the one in which it has not been tried,*—shall we conclude that there is *no* system that can meet the case, or that Democracy will meet it ?—that this contingency in universal Government is an oversight or a failure ; and that neither Democracy nor any other system can provide for it ?

The Territorial Democracy of America partakes of the advantages of aristocracies, whilst it avoids the dangers of Democracies. It is not a territorial *aristocracy* ; it avoids immobility, obstruction, and servility. It is not a Democracy only of serfs or manufacturing workmen ; it has the responsibility of ownership and the stability of land.

And the best grounded fears of such as do not hate, but merely *doubt,* American institutions, are thus expressed, but some time since, by Hegel :—

> "North America will be comparable with Europe only after the immeasurable space shall have been occupied, and the members of the political body shall have begun to be pressed back on each other, and so to form a compact system of civil society."

But as the space to be filled up is immeasureable, we cannot wait for it ; and if Democracy be *thus far* the only complete system that we contend it is, and if self-Government be the destiny of all political communities, we must dismiss such fears as unworthy of students or believers, and we must trust the system we cannot in theory impugn, and which has worked hitherto through infinite troubles and storms. Hegel says, elsewhere, that "History ends with Europe." We contend that the History of the People begins with America.

Unless the nature of Man is without a plan, and his faculties created for confusion and chaos, *we must trust Manhood,* and believe that the educated national manhood *must* be better than sectional manhood to govern nations.

A priori we should have argued that as all Government is a government of manhood, so the aggregate manhood *may* govern, and that the natural progress of Society *must* come to this unless it can be proved that there exists some immutable and indestructible barrier of race, caste, or capacity.

But now America supplies the argument *a posteriori* and of fact.

There can of course be no question that Democracy, pure and simple, of School, of Church, and of Assembly, conquered nature, solitude, and savages. That it formed a League, and an association, and also an organic and fundamental law, under which, as a national constitution, the Americans lived for seventy years with ever increasing prosperity, and but for Slavery—unitedness also. That during this time it got over the war of revolution, and the "one-horse war" of 1814. That a Republic has at last been founded and maintained. That it has flourished not only on pastures and tillage, and over a continent of vast spaces and area, but in cities of dense population.

So much is not empirical, but fact.

For four years, since 1860, "empirical" reasoners contended that the Union,—the Republic, has failed. But they reckoned without their republic. Some, scarcely to be called reasoners of any sort, carefully pointed out the natural boundaries of at least three new empires,—those boundaries being formed by the Mississippi and the Ohio, the mightiest agents, almost, in perpetuating the *Union* of the whole.

§

The chief friends of Democracy are Christianity, Political Economy, and History. Let us ask of the latter its verdict on the last two hundred and fifty years.

Can Democracy construct? was demanded in the year 1600, under other auspices. The attempt failed in England because society was not prepared for it, and because the Bishops, the Aristocracy, the Church, and the King combined against it. But America has answered the question by two centuries and a half of such construction as the world has not seen elsewhere.

The Edifice has not been assailed by any excesses of Democracy, but by a consolidated Oligarchy, the equal and essential foe of national Unity, and Individual right and value.

Democracy was at one with the national Genius, and it created the national Constitution. But the hour had struck when its principles of Federal Republicanism, Freedom, and nationality, must complete their triumph, or go down;—as the Richmond papers said,—"down, down, down to perdition."

This Oligarchy found, we say, the ground *pre-occupied* by its adversary; and it found the nation content, and its principles but too successful.

It found Conservatism and Democracy one. To redress the Balance, it allied itself with Revolution.

Can Democracy destroy? That, therefore, became the question, and Democracy for its life must answer it. Conservatism, Freedom, Progress, Nationality, were on the one side, and from the other a Bureaucracy of Felons cast down before God and the People the gage of battle.

Can Democracy *concentrate?* Is it an unit, a nation? Can the All become as one as the Few?

Must, for ever, Individual Development and Right, be sacrificed to "administration?" Must the man always renounce some of his rights, that the nation may be made and kept?

That is the question which America now settles for the All, there and everywhere,—now, for the first time in History, and for all the future. The Peoples, by an instinct, universal and profound, acknowledge it, and from every stronghold of Despotism in the world, tyrants strained their weary bloodshot eyes, and shuddered for the issue.

Democracy created—progressed—maintained. Must it now become a Despotism to keep its Unity, or can it by its Unity destroy Despotism?

"Democracy," in truth, pities the fears of its friends and derides the hopes of its assailants. Political science bids the one despair, and the other believe.

Democracy pronounces the issue false and vain. It says, that "there is not nor can be conflict between Individual Development and national Unity and strength." That the more of the first the more of the last. That an educated Democracy goes from glory to glory, and from strength to strength. That had its intellect outgrown its morality, and listened to compromise and Slavery, *there* had been danger and death, but that Democracy in arms for its own principles and ideal, for the completion of Individual freedom, the vindication of a national morality, is a thing upon which the shadow of Death cannot pass.

Here then is the central Truth of Democracy and Conservatism,—of the broadest based national Unity, and the completest national Strength,—THAT INDIVIDUAL DEVELOPMENT AND NATIONAL LIFE ARE ONE.

As to America, the danger is, not when a nation takes, but when it refuses to take, the next appointed step. When Will does not equal Destiny. When Fear cripples Justice. When "I dare not" waits upon "I would." America took the step. She agonises for the Purple of the People, and will have it. She is the Royal nation.

Democracy in America had two foes, Oligarchy and Materialism. Both hindered Development and both made association an object of conspiracy against progress. The first had been imposed upon the past by the necessities of order; the second was born of the vices and wickednesses of the hour. The first, the Puritan race quitted Europe to avoid; the second they will have always with them.

Materialism and Oligarchy met in the South. The two brought forth Slavery, as Sin and the Devil brought forth Death.

Materialism communed with Democracy in the North. The result was, according to the natural laws,—a neutralisation, a compromise, and an undoing, and the unmaking of the nation went on for fifty years. Opposite and equal forces contended, and have destroyed between them neither less nor more than fifty years of the nation's life. As Carlyle once said of some such other scene:—It is "*not* comic."

But there were already born within her the principles of her resurrection and political redemption,—Free Labour and Abolitionism.

Democracy, borrowed from its mother, Christianity, the principles of the higher life and law, but these rested on the broad natural human forces and interests of free labour done and free wages paid, and upon the fact that the good and the bad cannot dwell together in amity.

The meaning, present and eternal, of this conflict, is that Free Labour, Democracy, and Christianity,—the Body, the Soul, and the Spirit, of the American nation, are destroying the oligarchy of the South, and opening up the future for themselves and for all men. The serpent wreathed itself around the world-Champion of Democracy; *its Head is crushed* there, let its folds be disentwined throughout the world!

Now that the North has satisfactorily beaten the South, many good tall fallacies about the "natural superiority of oligarchies" are dead and buried.

For in every age have imbeciles of every kind, imputed their imbecility to systems which they have failed to understand, or attempted to foist their idiotcy by turns on nature, necessity, or God. The capacity, however, of Democracies for progress, is, though not indefinite, as large as the Human soul, and practically illimitable.

Oligarchy, on the other hand, is always and everywhere "a company limited." Whatever the polish or power of the few, they can never supply to a nation the interests and incentives of self-Government, nor can those who are governed by deputy ever reach the dignities or responsibilities of those who govern themselves.

At first sight the dilemma urged by De Tocqueville, following, but rather exaggerating Aristotle, is, to a true Democrat, somewhat appalling. It would seem almost as though a certain quantum of "love and glory, of culture, genius, faith, honour, and love of Republic," were allotted to each nation, of which, if the few have much, the many must have little; of which, if the many have much, the few will have less!! As if the founders or revolutionizers of States must ever choose between Institutions which will produce either an ordinary dead level of Humanity, or a few hot-house giants, at the expense of a nation of dwarfs.

We are, however, somewhat reassured in theory, when we find Aristotle teaching that equality and liberty will increase with improvement in education and manners, and that the many may become, politically, not only richer, and wiser, but *nobler* than the few; when we learn from De Tocqueville, that the organisation of this Democracy in Christendom is undoubtedly the greatest political problem of our age; and from J. S. Mill, that in great crises the "mediocre" many always choose the truly great for leaders; till at last we permit ourselves to conclude with Pascal, that "mankind is a man that never dies, and that is ever advancing towards perfection" and that, after all, man is not really a being to be thus absolutely moulded, to honour or dishonour, by "Institutions." It is not privilege, or political position that gives, in this dispensation, assurance of political manhood to the Peoples, but Christianity and Human nature, if only not obstructed by institutions, may breed in every soul the rudiments of national strength, and the love of Fame, of Beauty, of Goodness, and of Glory.

Moreover, as far as all these good things may be wanting in American representative men, let us remember the frontier life of a vast proportion of Americans, the rough but grand energies developed in the contest with nature, the strong infusion of the wild Irish element, the newly free German element, and such ingredients also as the Slave-drivers of the Red River.

Much is attributed to system which belongs to manners and circumstances, much to Democracy which belongs to the woods and the clearings.

Energy here comes to the front, not, as yet, polish, or philosophy, nor traditions. What, moreover, if it should turn out, *as we contend it has,* that with these universally diffused good qualities, Democracy combines also on the whole the best Governing qualities, and as great, if not greater men than other systems?

As to the ingredients of Congress, many gentlemen are maltreating Democracy who would be better employed in reading the American Constitution, and in studying the effect of such little enactments as this,—that every representative shall, "when elected be *an inhabitant of that State in which he shall be chosen.*" (Art. I, sec. 2.)

But after all, is not Protestantism (the reassertion, in a partial sense, of the *Individual* rights of the Soul), as well as Christianity, Democratic? Were not Napoleon, Cromwell, Gustavus Adolphus, Washington, Jefferson, and the Adams, democrats? Had Romans no "love of glory," and of the Republic? Have the French (a Democracy of eighty years) none? For what did the Ironsides fight, for what did Milton and Cromwell diplomatise? Where did nation ever grow so mightily in manhood as the Americans, before cotton and slavery, and a cotton and slavery-born oligarchy, crossed their path?

And their last crowning victory of Democracy? The North is the Puritan. He believes in God, Human nature, and Country, and is not above working, praying, or fighting for them. The South believes in oligarchy, and fought for an independence that would intensify and eternise the rights of the few and the wrongs of the many,—throughout the world in theory, and in fact over a vast slave empire.

The North,—the Republican,—the Puritan, contend for the *completed* rights of the Individual, —against that Materialism and Slavery which ate together into the heart of the nation for sixty years. The North *so* fought that all the "chivalry" of oligarchic countries cried out against its fighting, with an exceeding bitter cry.

And the bitterness to theorists is that these Democrats do by some mistake overcome the Oligarchy, and that, strange to say, the "love of comforts" has not withheld them from "the love of glory and of the Republic!"

This does not exactly agree with the attributes imputed by De Tocqueville to Democracy, namely, "the employment of the moral and intellectual activity chiefly in the production of comforts, and the acquirement of the necessaries of life, and of the greatest degree of enjoyment."

Still less accommodating are such facts as the "Christian" and the "Sanatory Commissions,"—societies of colossal dimensions, and which with lavish expenditure, and a total disregard of "comfort," and an ambition wholly beyond the mere "love of glory," fought on fields of carnage the battle of God, against cold, thirst, hunger, want, irreligion, and despair.

Thus does the first and the only Democracy answer the words of theorists, and the arms of oligarchs. Such fallacies as "over-production" and "over-population" may be safely left to destroy *one another* in the future.

But now that the Republic is fairly reconquering Unity, empirical reasoners against it will subside upon the old peradventures of a future growth of faction or denial of negro rights, or of some possible or impossible severance, forgetful or ignorant of the fact that no single factor of material or national Unity is wanting to America, that slavery (or oligarchy), the only alien element, is perishing, and that allianceship between the two halves against outsiders, would precipitate a reunion which every conclusion of political science guarantees.

So much for nationality. The world must now acknowledge that Democracy can make a complete nation.

Nor can it refuse now to make the comparison it has challenged between the *relative values*, Individual or Social, of Oligarchies and Democracies. Let any whose system can boast a wider base, or a higher or completer Unity, assail the bulwarks of the latter. Others must watch and wait, and learn, and follow.

The American experiment settles, amongst other things :—

1st. That Democracy has proved its case. That a royal nation exists and is definitively constituted. That it exists by virtue of *Individual* competency, intelligence, heroism, culture, and religion, which are not only a basis, but *the only safe basis for national Unity.*

2nd. That that *fact* involves the verification of the theories of Aristotle, consciously or unconsciously quoted by Penn and others, as to the Collective Reason, and explodes the delusion that a whole People can be a mere class interest.

3rd. That inasmuch as Democracy must soon or late, prevail everywhere, and cause every community either to pass through a revolution or to fall into complete dissolution, certain duties are devolved upon all citizens everywhere,—the chief of them being *to prepare the People by education for Democracy, and to see to it that no traitorous or foolish schemes for plural or fractional voting* are meanwhile foisted on them to create distrust, weakness, and revolution hereafter.

Democracy has been tested in battle against the strongest and subtlest of oligarchies, and it answers all the purposes of Government;—Security, for having the broadest base, its base cannot be broadened. Intellectual Power, for the People always elevate and follow their greatest men. Honesty, for when Equality governs, payments will be equal.

That was always the theory of Democracy. It is now the leading revolutionary and conservative FACT of the world's politics.

DEMOCRACY

MUST BECOME UNIVERSAL.

"*Fortune never interposes in the government of this world;* and we may be convinced of this truth by the Romans, who enjoyed a continual series of prosperity when they regulated their conduct by one invariable plan, but suffered an uninterrupted train of calamities when they acted upon different principles. There are a set of general causes, either moral or physical, which operate in every monarchy, and either raise and maintain it, or else involve it in ruin. All accidental conjunctures are subordinate to these causes; and if the hazard of a battle, which, in other words, is no more than a particular cause, has been destructive of a state, some general cause presided, and made a single battle be the inevitable ruin of that state. In a word, *the tendency of the main principle draws after it all the particular incidents.*"—*Montesquieu's Works*, v. iii, page 135.

"Progress may be safely left to the passions and the blindness of those (ruling) classes, even although warned of the result.

"Since a human race has appeared upon earth, it must attain all the development which it is possible for it to attain on earth.

"There is but one world possible,—a thoroughly good world."—*Fichte* "Vocation of Man" pp. 146, 150, 183.

"It is over with us, the multitude are enlightened."—*Volney*, "Vision of Priests and Despots."

"Every combination of ashes returns to ashes. All those granites, oligarchy, aristocracy, theocracy, are promised to the four winds."—*Hugo.*

"True History, henceforth *charged with the education of the royal infant, the People*, will study the successive movements of *Humanity*.

"*Humanity no longer possessed, but guided.* The legions of light drive backwards the hordes of flame. Planets become spectres. The flaming pleiad of men of brutal force descends deeper and deeper into the abyss, and in the deep heaven of the future, azure, henceforth rises in radiancy the sacred group of true stars."—*Hugo.*

"A regard for their own security *compels all free states to transform all around them into free states* like themselves; and thus for the sake of their own welfare, *to extend the empire of culture over barbarism, of freedom over slavery.* Soon will the nations, civilised or enfranchised by them, find themselves in the same relation towards others; *and thus of necessity* by reason of the existence of some few really free states, will the empire of *civilisation, freedom, and with it universal peace*, gradually embrace the whole world."—*Fichte.*

"When schism and faction abound in a state, it is near its ruin, and ought to be invaded."—*Institutes of Timour.*

Chapter IV.

DEMOCRACY MUST BECOME UNIVERSAL.

"Woe be to us should their fatal cry of Liberty reach the ear of the multitude. If all men are equal where is our *exclusive right* to honours and power? If all men are or ought to be free, what becomes of our *slaves*, our vassals, our property? If all are equal in a civil capacity, where are our *privileges of birth* and succession, and what becomes of nobility? If all are equal before God, what is to become of the *Priesthood?* Let us sound the alarm to Kings. Let us divide the People. Let us excite their apprehensions respecting the power of this free nation."—*Volney.*

"When a nation modifies the electoral qualification, it may easily be foreseen *that sooner or later that qualification will be entirely abolished.* There is no more invariable rule in the History of Society, for after each concession, the strength of the Democracy increases, and its demands increase with its strength."—*De Tocqueville*, p. 67, v. 1.

"It is the vocation of our race to unite itself into *one single body*, all the parts of which shall be thoroughly known to each other, *and all possessed of similar culture.* * * * And this is the first point to be attained in the endless path on which Humanity must advance. Until this shall have been attained, one nation or continent must pause on the great common path of progress, and wait for the advance of the others, and each must bring as an offering to the *universal commonwealth*, for the sake of which alone it exists, its ages of apparent immobility or retrogression. When that first point shall have been attained then, without farther interruption, without halt or regress, with united strength and equal step, *Humanity* shall move onward in a higher culture, of which we can at present form no conception."—*Fichte*, "Vocation of Man," pp. 141-2.

"Future History approaches. Historical effigy will no longer be the man-King; it will be the man-People.—*Hugo.*

The first practical successful solution of the Democratic problem is the one great step towards its universality.

Let but the first Democratic nation stand, and it must draw all systems to it.

For,—not land, or peculiar material conditions, but *manhood is the basis of Democracy.*

Wherever manhood is, there may be manhood Development. Wherever manhood Development is muliplied, there is manhood Association. Whereever developed manhood associates, it wins Equality. And manhood, developed, associated, and equal, is Democracy. Inasmuch as Democracy makes the strongest Unity and intensest concentration of power, it cannot be successfully opposed *by arms.* Inasmuch as it is a question of Development, all free *opinion* is destined to help it.

That Democracy shall become universal, arises from the nature and necessities of man, and the necessary grades and epochs through which individual and national life has to pass.

Without manhood Development there is no nation.

Where manhood Development exists to a certain extent, and subject to a certain organisation, there a nation exists.

Manhood Development either ceases or extends.

If it ceases the nation expires.

If it increases, it becomes more generally diffused in quantity, and more elevated in quality.

But with that state of things Individuals inevitably learn to associate together,—they acquire unity.

But Unity and Numbers are strength, and a

strength that constantly increases itself in a greater ratio.

And strength will always (with or without revolution) win for itself Equality.

And manhood Development and Association result in Equality, which is Democracy.

The process may take years, or ages, but the result is inevitable. If any given nation abandon the advance, and cease the Development of Democracy, the forces of progress but transmigrate to other nations more worthy. Labour leaves the land, and manhood society.

If Humanity is not to progress towards Democracy, it cannot progress at all. If it is not to progress, it must be stayed by the same hand that launched it on its career.

The logic of politics is absolute, or it is nothing.

Either the rule of the one is best, or the rule of the all. Either we must trace our steps backwards to autocracy, or onwards to the People. If responsibility educates; if Government *by*, be always and everywhere Government *for;* if right divine, which sometimes by necessity hedges Kings, goes over, when the necessity is gone, to the side of the Peoples,—then, as surely as history, progress, God, exist, and as the All are of more value than the Many or the Few, so surely, soon or late, in all countries and with all Peoples, will altered conditions of national Life transfer the rule accordingly.

There is no single atom either of the Theory, the History, or the Practice of Democracy, that we need either doubt or evade.

No! The Theory of Democracy is no longer "empirical." It rests on facts. If not yet an entire and perfect chrysolite, so pure is its water, so well has battle ground its facets, that other lights must pale beside it.

The tendency of progress and civilisation is altogether to throw down barriers and to bring men and ideas together. The only possible check to Democracy would be a system of Isolation.

And the very compromises of Democracy, during "the era of compromise," from 1777 to 1833, confirm our argument,—for the great rebellion was directly and inevitably occasioned by the untruthfulness of Democracy to itself, yielding for a time to the blandishments of materialism and a mock Democracy, while oligarchy and slavery grew and strengthened.

Since then the vast resources and intense Individuality of Democracy have done their work. Democracy found its leaders, and the army its generals. The administrative organisation of the Republic has controlled the one and wielded the other, without weakening or diminishing either. Centralisation and Unity have worked together, not in spite of, but by means of, a proper independence of States.

Why, then, should we doubt or hesitate? Destiny has put to Democracy a series of tests,—the last of them searching, exhaustive, and *conclu-*

sive. "Can Democracy emigrate, colonise, unite; repel Despotism from without, sooth disunion within, extend over a vast continent; surrender materialism and ease, extemporise an army and fleet, beat down a rebellion localised by climate, intensified by slave-interests and oligarchy, ramifying through the country by intrigue and party interests, and seeking in every state alliances on the plea of State rights. Can Democracy, in the face of this last and final trial, still crown its nationality without disowning Freedom, and regenerate and purify itself, while contending with a third of the empire, led by the ablest of its then acknowledged Statesmen?"

But one conclusion now is possible. That conclusion this book attempts to work out, through all its parts. That the collective Reason and the universal Will are not perfect, but the best possible Institutions. That "class Popular Sovereignty" is as much a chimera and a delusion as is the figment that Democracies do not love glory. *That the whole of a nation voting equally by its educated unstained manhood, is formed and specially created by nature,—necessity,—God, to control its own Destiny,* and to lead on the van of the future. That such a nation makes of its contending forces the mean,—progress; and becomes, as it were, that new thing upon the earth, A NATIONAL INDIVIDUALITY, with functions (as far as possible) perfect, complete, and reconciled.

§

So entire should our faith now be in these results, that we should be prepared to say of America or any other nation that thus fairly and fully tries Democracy, "if Democracy cannot save it, it is not worth saving,—it cannot be saved;* the time has come when it ought to be destroyed. Its blood must be poisoned; its heart rotten; its functions gone; its whole anatomy an anachronism. By what right cumbers it the ground on which other nations are waiting to grow and multiply? Let it go as other false nations have gone, howling and shrieking to its Gods. 'Nationalities' were made for man, and not men for nationalities."

Dynasties, Feudalities, ancient corporate obstructions in Church or in State, may stand in the way, but Equality and Manhood will at last get their feet upon the necks of them. This result must be as general as the nature of man is uniform.

Plural voting is as much a thing of Feudality and Privilege as any relic of Barbarism. It may be possible in feudal Societies. It is impossible elsewhere.

It is a simple, stark, staring, blank truism, that the Progress of virtue, civilisation, and religion, leads infallibly, in all ages and countries, towards or to *Democracy*, and it is neither logical nor possible for the victorious Demos to consent to fractional voting.

Where the majority are unfit to govern, they are, nevertheless, in a progressing country, preparing for Democracy. *It is a question, not of principle, but of instalments.*

* Of course Democracy involves entire freedom of religion.

Where the majority is prepared and fit to govern, the policy that would deny to *them* their rights, and refuse to *itself* the strength of their adherence, is a policy of Barbarism and Suicide. It sacrifices the country to party, puts back the whole for the sake of part, and postpones man to measures. Such a policy simply forfeits for the Government the moral and material support of the greatest number,—the wisdom of their councils, and the weight of their adherence.

Statesmanship admits everywhere and always the principle of Democracy, and hastens to reduce it to practice as fast and as far as Education has given the People self-restraint, and (with the power of acquiring property) a sense and habit of responsibility.

In numbers,—*cæteris paribus*—there is safety and conservatism. To maintain that the educated All ought not to govern, is only to proclaim to the world that the few who may be in possession, have already rendered *their* class dangerous to the interests and rights of the nation.

§

The Monitor came round the corner!—and already, whatever might be the fleet of the future, it was sufficiently clear what were the fleets of the past.

And deeper and deeper to the heart of the world presses the conviction that Democracy is coming round the corner! *Governments founded upon the Few can run no fair race, can fight no equal battle, with Governments founded upon the All.*

To those who worship force, the voice of the people begins at last to sound like the voice of God. To those who regard History as an organic whole, and recognise in the evolutions of centuries the working of ONE eternal will,—to such, the conclusions of the French philosopher are but a truism, and the progressive and irresistible development of social equality is indeed a "divine decree."

If Europe will not accept Democracy, so much the worse for Europe. As Barbarians are to Oligarchies, so are Oligarchies to a true Democracy. Democracy is not now a principle to be investigated. It converts or destroys. It is an influence which in peaceful times will carry on the peoples that can adopt it beyond all attempt at rivalry, and which, in times of war, will grind its adversaries into powder. Democracy, or "the New Zealander," will visit in turn every Capitol in Europe.

We say, "the peoples that *can* adopt Democracy," for Democracy overcomes Oligarchy *only by appropriating the truths and the forces it represents.* Thus Democracy embraces all the elements of political science.

Let us have done with dilettanti Democrats. *Power* governs. If power be with the One, the Few, or the Many,—it is where it ought to be. So much the better for the One, the Few, and the Many, but *so much the worse for the All.* They are not where they ought to be, and the *nation* is not where it ought to be.

Woe! woe! to the nation that anticipates too much its manhood. It will find that the first law of Earth, as of Heaven, is *order*; that the People that will not learn, *cannot* rule; that to the victors, always and everywhere, are the spoils; and that Victory involves force, organisation, and self-restraint,—always sooner possessed, and easier won and wielded, by the smaller Unity.

But there is, perhaps, a greater Woe to the nation that prolongs too much its minority,—that will not, or cannot (Priest-bound, Tradition-bound, or Devil-bound), *take* its manhood. It will fall back into the ruck of nations, and be nothing and nowhere in the world-race. It will breed families, and not men, and send the circles of its life-blood in and in towards extinction. The nation that forestalls its greatness, will be *taught* by the sword. The nation that declines the progressive glories of Democracy,—will *rot*.

§

Before the People can rule themselves, they must submit themselves to the double victory of education and religion;—they must have the rule of others' intellect, or of their own; the law of God, or else of some sort or other of "Better men." The result expresses the value of the nation.

Given, the proportion of educated Christian men to the population, and you have the value (relative and positive) of that population, and also its fighting, and its peaceful progressive qualities. If there be none such, there is no *nation*. If there be few, the nation is barbarous. If many, civilised. If the majority, it is a Democracy. The UNITY of the collective Reason and Will is the only complete and absolute Unity, for that alone is a complete Unity in which *the Units are individually complete and thoroughly equipped.* There alone can no revolution enter, where the reason and the interest of all do rule. Sectional interests may be general injuries. The universal or the necessary can alone be the warrant of the absolute.

Whatsoever cause has availed itself of this secret of power in *developing and organising all available intellect,* has succeeded as far as success was possible. The results are certain, as far as the power can be used.

Christianity, wielding not only the intellect, but the conscience and imagination, and working not only with the Few but with the All, is the only complete instance of *an appeal to the whole and to the All.* What were its successes until Constantine, certainly a murderer—probably a hypocrite, chained religion like a dead body to the State!

China has used it, and by her select bureaucracy, the result of her universal competitive system, has ruled for twenty centuries a third of the human race.

Rome papal used it, and from all classes she enlisted those battalions of intellect that so long mastered the world.

The *Chancellerie Russe* has given the world startling proof of what an aristocracy of talent can do.

The French Revolution used it, and it intensified an impulse which will yet complete the circuit of the globe.

The world knows well the meaning of "the open career," as the necessities of Society carry the soldier, the lawyer, the diplomatist, the writer, or the artist, victoriously to the front.

As long as Democracy had had no actual representative; as long as no People had arisen able to bear its Cross, and take its Crown; as long as national manhood seemed a *lusus naturæ*, and "Republics" were Republics of Slaves;—so long might "Patriots" assassinate order without bringing Liberty to Life;—so long might

"The hive of Roman Liars worship the Emperor-Idiot."

So long, even after age upon age of trial, must the People subside from their Cromwells to their Stuarts.

And now, at last, when a nation has arisen with valid claims to be also a Democracy, nothing but a gulf wide as the Atlantic,—nothing but such armies and fleets as the great Republic has created—could have kept the helots of reaction from intervening to crush a nation that determined at last to be wholly and truly a nation; to vindicate the honour of its Democracy by arms; and to void out Slavery, the reductio ad absurdum of Oligarchy,—the excrement of fifty years of crime!

It remains then,—since this rivalry truly international has got to be fairly worked out—to welcome the FIRST MANHOOD *of a* NATION, and to test its future and that of the waiting world of common men, not by the frantic outcries of the worsted few, nor by the old blasphemies about rights divine, but by PRINCIPLES, plain and simple, of political science, and by the FACTS, as we *see* them, in the History and Life of this American nation.

It is the "system positive," with a vengeance. For no light half so bright and searching ever beat upon cause or nation before. Nevertheless, Democracy *is* justified of her children.

DEMOCRACY:

AUTHORITIES.

"Any form may be kept together by extreme force, but that is good which flourishes by its native energy."—*Aristotle.*

"The People at large may always quash the vain pretensions of the few, by saying, we collectively are richer, wiser, and nobler than you."—*Aristotle.*

"Consider, if a man should in this manner appoint pilots of ships *according to their valuations* (property), what would be the consequence. They would, said he, make very bad navigation, and is it not in the same manner with reference to any other thing or any Government whatever?

"*Oligarchy* would then seem to have this which is so great a fault. . . . But such a city *is not one, but of necessity, two.* . . . Always plotting against one another. 'By Jupiter,' said he, 'it is in no respect less.'"—*Republic of Plato.*

"The end of man, or that which is prescribed by the eternal or immutable dictates of Reason, is the highest and most harmonious development. . . . The individuality of power and development."—*Baron W. von Humboldt.*

"The masses which can never be corrupted, should be the constant source from which all power should emanate."—*Napoleon III.*

"The all of A, how much less is it in the eye of A than the all of B in the eye of B."—*Bentham.*

"When does a People stop,—when it ceases to possess Individuality."—*Mill.*

"The inevitable might of the thoughts of the million."—*Wendell Phillips.*

"Whatever may be the facts under which, in the different countries of Europe, such an organisation (a lasting political system) takes place, or the political forms guiding it, *the basis it must rest upon is universal, and if necessary, compulsory Education.* In the more enlightened places the movement has already nearly reached that point. Already it is an accepted doctrine that the State has rights in a child as well as its parents, and that it may insist on Education; conversely also, that every child has a claim upon the Government for good instruction. After providing in the most liberal manner for that, free countries have but one thing more to do for the accomplishment of the rest."

"That one thing is to secure *intellectual freedom* as completely as the rights of property and personal liberty have been already secured. Philosophical opinions and scientific discoveries are entitled to be judged of by their truth, not by their relation to existing interests."—Pp. 386-7, vol. ii. *Draper's Intellectual Development of Europe.*

Chapter V.

DEMOCRACY:

AUTHORITIES.

"To make the People fittest to choose the chosen, and the chosen fittest to govern, will be to mend our corrupt and faulty education. Noble Education, in all liberal arts and exercises, . . . communicating the natural heat of Government and culture more distributively to all extreme parts."—*Milton.*

"*It is in a Republican Government that the whole power of Education is required.*

"Virtue may be defined the love of the laws and of our country. This love is peculiar to democracies. In these alone the Government is intrusted to private citizens."—Vol. i, p. 43. *Montesquieu.*

"Peace and moderation is the spirit of a Republic."—*Ibid.*, p. 167, vol. i.

"There is no great share of probity necessary to support a monarchical or despotic Government: the force of laws in one, and the Prince's arm, in the other, are sufficient to direct and maintain the whole; but in a popular state, one spring more is necessary, namely, *Virtue.*"—*Ibid.*, vol. i, p. 25.

"Is it not almost a self-evident axiom that the *State should require and compel the education*, up to a certain standard, *of every human being* who is born its citizen. To bring a child into existence without a fair prospect of being able, not only to provide food for its body, but instruction and training for its mind, is a *moral crime* against the offspring and society; and if the parent does not fulfil this obligation, the State ought to see it fulfilled, at the charge, as far as possible, of the Parent."—*J. S. Mill*, on "Liberty," p. 189, &c.

"*To learn* is the first step; to live is but the second. It is beautiful on this sombre earth, during this dark life, short passage to something else, it is beautiful that force should have right for a master, that progress should have courage as a chief, that intelligence should have honour as a Sovereign; that conscience should have duty as a despot; that civilisation should have Liberty as a queen; that ignorance should have a servant, *Light.*"—*Hugo.*

In considering the old authorities, it is well to remember, as Montesquieu reminds us, that "Aristotle wanted to indulge sometimes his jealousy against Plato, and sometimes his passion for Alexander," and that "Plato was incensed against the tyranny of the People of Athens."

One of the most striking and instructive facts is that from epoch to epoch, not only the same lines of thought, but often the very same words (as translated), are employed and repeated by those Hierarchs of thought,—so comparatively few indeed,—whom it is necessary to consult on this question.

The Perfection of the Democratic *Principle* has not been questioned by theorists until the present time. Save in America and France, its practice is generally relegated to a future, when Capital and Labour shall, more or less, have adjusted their disputes by combining their advantages in the labourer, but Mr. J. S. Mill, by way of alternative to Popular Sovereignty, though not perhaps with a view to an eternal postponement of it in England, recommends a graduated scale of suffrages according to education and wealth.

It is, however, believed, that with whatever intention proposed, the People that should once adopt this sliding scale of Manhood, would have to reach Democracy through revolution.

Political theorists used to be divided into believers in the rule of the one, the few, the many, and the all.

Amongst living nations they are now mostly divided into two parties.

Those who trust no class at all, and those who trust none but the universal People.

1st. Those who believe in no class and would guard against all. Who object to Democracy pure,—to Popular Sovereignty, not because it is *Popular* Sovereignty, but because it is, they say, *class* Sovereignty, and who seek political safety in any artificial balance of votes and interests.

2nd. Those who trust the People.

Amongst the first class the only great representative advocate is Mr. J. S. Mill.

To the second, really belong all the authorities from Socrates downwards.

It is almost as impossible to find a great man who does not trust the People, as it is to find a great People that does not trust its great men.

Socrates denounced the evils of oligarchy, and Aristotle, though recommending a compromise therewith, enunciated principles which lead straight to Democracy pure, whilst his definitions of Democracy ("to constitute a Democracy, the many who are masters of the Government must be poor") would not apply to the state of Society in America, or to any state where political economy is understood, or the rights and interests of all are attended to.

If the theorists of old be compared with those of to-day, the former appear the more scientific, and consistent, and courageous. They believed more in the man, and less in his chattels. They mistrust pure unmixed Democracy, for in Greek and Roman Democracies, from four-fifths to eleven-twelfths of the People were Slaves, and they evidently did not anticipate the time when the majority would be in circumstances of ease.

Thus, from Aristotle until J. S. Mill, the two ideas of *Popular Sovereignty,* and *popular disqualification through poverty,* pervade, more or less, all theories of politics.

Socrates derided the idea of "valuation" of a voter. Aristotle attributes political "prerogative" to wealth, and certainly neither foresaw the (approximate) annihilation of poverty. But Mill (J. S.) in an age when machinery invented since 1816, does the work of five hundred millions of men, and when the labourers of all *living* nations are being lifted more and more from the earth, comes forward with mongrel theories of plural voting, to counteract ignorance and Democratic class Sovereignty, theories which, if accepted, would go far to prevent the attributes of manhood from ever in our day being properly recognised.

We now consider the principle of the SOVEREIGNTY OF THE PEOPLE;—

1st, as treated of by the fathers of political science, and therein chiefly as affected by the elements of Poverty and Ignorance, which are the only elements in respect of which, until lately, the principle has been doubted, and we shall show how even such writers as Mill resolutely maintain the Principles of Democracy pure, whilst propounding divers plans for its perpetual denial.

We shall afterwards give the reasons why the Sovereignty of an educated nation secures the three objects of Government,—Progress, Stability or Conservatism, and Unity.

The Principle of Popular Sovereignty is directly asserted by Aristotle. Herein he is one in theory with Penn, although almost all the world's history rolls between them. Christianity was really the basis of the principle of Democracy, and the motive power for its realisation, but it required the mighty equalising agency of the printing press, it required English isolation from Europe, before Popular Sovereignty could be established,—it required the completer isolation of America from England and Europe, ere Penn could found in fact the principles which the mighty Grecian thus propounded :—

"In what portion of the State the Sovereignty ought to reside."

"The People at large, how contemptible soever they may appear when taken individually, *are yet, when collectively considered, not perhaps unworthy of Sovereignty.* It is a trite observation, that those entertainments where each man sends the dish most agreeable to his own palate, are preferable to those furnished by the most sumptuous delicacy of individuals. The People at large are allowed to be the best judges of music and poetry. *The moral and intellectual excellencies of the multitude* thus differ from those of a wise and virtuous man, as the beauty of a fine picture does from the beauty of individuals, of whom some have features more perfect and beautiful than those of the picture; yet the picture, collecting only excellencies, and always avoiding deformities, will be found *more beautiful and more perfect than any original in nature,* with whom it can be compared. The excellencies therefore of that complex entity, the public, may sometimes surpass those of the most accomplished Prince or most virtuous council."—
Aristotle, b. 3, pp. 214-15. (Gillie's Trans.)

"The safety of every free Government requires that the major part of the citizens should enjoy a certain weight in the administration . . the people, collectively considered, are capable of discharging functions of which, in their individual characters, they seem altogether unworthy. . . . Such is *the absurdity resulting from the supposition that those who are superior in one particular, ought to be entitled to a superiority in political society,* in which mankind have assembled *in order to club their respective advantages,* and to direct their various but united efforts to one salutary end and purpose; and in which *the People at large may always quash the vain pretensions of the few, by saying, we collectively, are richer, wiser, and nobler than you.*"

"The arguments in favour of the judgment of the many, we have already had occasion to explain; and in favour of their justice, *the many are less liable to corruption than one man or the few,* in the same manner that a large lake is less corruptible than a small pool. If we deal therefore impartially with Kings, Magistrates and People. . . it must be acknowledged, that in communities consisting of such members, a republic is better than an aristocracy, and an aristocracy than a monarchy."—*Ibid,* pp. 218, 222, 230.

§

We contend that notwithstanding Aristotle condemns Democracy, together with Oligarchy and Tyranny, and extols the "Republic," as destroying the evils, and retaining the advantages of both, and as a state in which "the prerogatives of the few, and the rights and liberties of the many, are duly respected and impartially maintained," yet if attempted to be applied to the actual state of Society in democratic America, where education and production are free, his own principles and definitions are inconsistent with these "prerogatives of those wealthy few."

For he says (vol. ii, p. 329):—"To constitute an oligarchy, the few who are masters of the Government, must be rich; and to constitute a Democracy, the many who are masters of the

Government, must be poor: for it is only when both circumstances concur in these Governments, that their respective characters are strongly impressed, and their opposite genius fully displayed."

He also says (v. ii. p. 340) that:—

"Those mixed Governments which incline most to the side of oligarchy are commonly called aristocracies, because *morals and education* seem to have a natural connection with wealth." That "when (p. 341) with regard to any one object, the respective laws of these distinct forms of polity are inconsistent, neither of them is to be employed, but a new law is to be framed holding a due middle between them." That (p. 343) "any form may be kept together by external force, but that is good which flourishes by its native energy." That (p. 345) "excess of wealth spurns the authority of reason, and extreme poverty debases the character." That "a certain mediocrity is necessary to equality, equality to friendliness, and friendliness to security. It is plain, therefore, that *the best commonwealth is that in which middling men most abound*, and prove, at least, superior to either of the extremes." That a republic "*abounding in the middle ranks*" is least likely to fall under the tyranny of one man, and least likely to be subverted.

Again (p. 348), "the political arrangement of every State must always depend on the prevailing inclinations of that party which is predominant; and the preponderancy must consist in quantity or quality; *quantity* denoting number, and *quality* the distinguishing excellencies of the upper ranks; *birth, wealth, education, the love of glory, and of the Republic. If the popular party exceed more in quantity, than they are excelled in quality, Democracy must prevail.* The first and best kind of it, if the majority be husbandmen and shepherds, the last and worst, if tradesmen and manufacturers."

Aristotle further contends that next to a community of husbandmen, a nation subsisting by pasturage is the fittest for being formed into a democracy.

He also teaches that the more Society is improved, and education perfected, the more equality will prevail, and the further will liberty be extended. Also that the stability of Government depends

(v. iii, p. 373) chiefly on :—1st. Respect to age and experience. 2nd. Distribution of honours and offices according to merit. 3rd. Education accurately adapted to the pattern of the commonwealth.

From these quotations we get the following conclusions respecting the politics of Aristotle :—

1st. He concedes the principle of *Popular Sovereignty.*

2nd. He concedes also its practicability if Poverty and Ignorance can be put in a minority. *Poverty* is the main cause of the deficiencies of Democracy. Pure *morals, education,* and *public spirit,* are qualities which usually accompany a competency, and which in his time rendered the Oligarchic element essential.

3rd. That a preponderating middle class is the safest and best for the State.

4th. That the main reason why Aristotle attached so great importance to the preponderance of a middle class, was that ignorance and poverty were then supposed to attach to the lower many whom it debased, and who were deprived of a love of glory, culture, and genius. Democracy has changed all that since Aristotle. Moreover, where Equality really prevails, it tempers the failings of the "middle classes," as known in England. The *essence* of middle class advantages, as claimed by Aristotle, was "equality," as promoting "friendliness," and therefore "security."

5th. That pursuits connected with the soil are the best fitted for Democracies. How is this proved by the "territorial Democracy" of America!

There is, then, at least one country in the world qualified, according to Aristotle, for a pure Democracy.

It is the country, namely, where Popular Sovereignty, Loyalty, Education, Love of Country, a vast middle class, and property, universally diffused, and illimitable fields for agriculture and pasturage, all combine to make Democracy natural and inevitable.

That Country is America. The latest and completest Development vindicates the most ancient philosophy.

§

But to illustrate yet further the connection between universal competency and popular Sovereignty and power, we will quote the political Economy of James Mill in contrast with the results of the American census. Mr. Mill says :—

"Universally, then, we may affirm, other things remaining the same, that if the ratio that Capital and Population bear to one another remains the same, wages will remain the same; if the ratio which Capital bears to Population increases, wages will rise; if the ratio which Population bears to Capital increases, wages will fall.

"If the condition of the great body of the People is not easy and comfortable, it can only be made so by one of two methods; either by *quickening* the rate at which *capital* increases, or *retarding* the rate at which *population* increases.

"*This general misery of mankind* is a fact which can be accounted for upon one only of two suppositions; either that there is a natural tendency in population to increase faster than capital, *or that capital has by some means been prevented from increasing so fast as it has a tendency to increase.*

"This, therefore, is an enquiry of the highest importance." —*James Mill.* "Political Economy," pp. 28-30.

It will suffice here, without examining the causes which *have* "prevented the natural increase of Capital and wages," to state the result established by the American census,—that although Population increased rapidly, and there is a vast immigration, capital there increases more than three times as fast as Population, and that this is due as much to the freedom of man and of his labour and invention, as to cheapness of land.

Thus let Freedom of Land, Labour, Schools, Press, and Religion; let also Direct Taxation prevail,—and wages and savings (Capital) increase at an unheard-of ratio. Let the average wages of a free nation be raised, and the average education rises with them.

Hence we are led to this conclusion,—*that wherever labour is really free, there Democracy will soon prevail; that wherever labour and land are not free, whether by unwise laws of parochial settlement, unjust tariffs, taxes on invention, unjust patent laws, corn laws, unjust and complicated land laws, laws of primogeniture, or otherwise howsoever, there Oligarchy and Oligarchic interests are the criminal cause of the social and political incompetency of the People.*

The fact of the Progress and Unity, and consequent strength of Democracies, and the counterpart weakness and divisions of Oligarchy, is indeed maintained by Socrates:—

"And do they not then make laws, marking out the boundary of the *Oligarchic constitution*, and regulating the quantity of Oligarchic power according to the quantity of wealth, more to the wealthy, and less to the less, intimating that *he who has not the valuation* (property) *settled by law is to have no share in the Government?* . . .

"Consider, if a man should in this manner appoint pilots of ships, according to their valuations (property), but never intrust one with a poor man, though better skilled in piloting, what would be the consequence? *They would*, said he, *make very bad navigation.* And is it not in the same manner with reference to any other thing, or any Government whatever?

"Oligarchy would then seem to have this, which is so great a fault. . . . That *such a city is not one, but of necessity two*; one consisting of the poor, and the other of the rich, dwelling in one place, and always plotting against one another. 'By Jupiter,' said he, 'it is in no respect less.'"—*The Republic of Plato*, Book viii, p. 397. (Taylor's Translation.)

Guizot (on Civilisation) insists on *Individual Development* as the great Factor of States, and on *increased production and more equal distribution.* The following are condensed extracts:—

"On the one hand, an increasing production of means of power and prosperity in Society; on the other, a more equal distribution among individuals of the power and prosperity provided.

"Is this all? Have we exhausted the natural and common meaning of the word civilisation?

"Another Development of Individual life, of man himself, of his faculties, sentiments, ideas.

"Two facts then are comprised in this great fact. . . . the progress of Society and of Humanity.

"If we examine the nature of the grand crises of civilisation . . . it has always been of individual or social development; always facts that have changed the internal man, his faith, his manners, or his external condition, his situation in relation with his fellows."—*Guizot on "Civilisation."*

Baron W. von Humboldt gives us the following as to ancient and modern Individuality, Freedom, and Diversity of conditions:—

"Antiquity captivates us above all by that inherent greatness which is comprised in the life of the Individual, and perishes with him,—the bloom of fancy, the depth of thought, the strength of will, the perfect oneness of the entire being, which alone confer true worth on human nature."

"The grand point to be kept in view by the State is the development of the powers of all its single citizens in their perfect individuality."

"The true end of man or that which is prescribed by the eternal and immutable dictates of reason, and not suggested by vague and transient desires, in the highest and most harmonious development of his powers to a complete and consistent whole: freedom is the grand and indispensable condition which the possibility of such a development presupposes; but there is besides *another essential*,—intimately connected with freedom, it is true,—*a variety of situations*."

"Their individual vigour, then, and *manifold diversity*, combine themselves in originality; and hence, that on which the consummate grandeur of our nature ultimately depends,—that towards which every human being must ceaselessly direct his efforts, and that on which especially those who design to influence their fellow men must ever keep their eyes, is the *Individuality of power and development*.

"Just as this individuality springs naturally from the *perfect freedom* of action, and the *greatest diversity in the agents*, it tends immediately to produce them in turn.

"The grand leading principle, towards which every argument hitherto unfolded in these pages directly conveys, is *the absolute and essential importance of human development in its richest diversity*."

Milton, upon the advantages of a free commonwealth, and on the necessity of a high class education to the maintenance of the Commonwealth, maintains that—

". . . A free commonwealth is not only *held by wisest men in all ages, the noblest, the manliest, the equallest, the justest Government*, the most agreeable to all due liberty and *proportioned equality*, both human, civil, and Christian, most cherishing to virtue and true religion, but also plainly commended, or rather enjoined by our Saviour himself."—*Milton*, "Ready and easy way to establish a free Commonwealth," p. 645.

"Good education and accurate wisdom ought to correct the fluxible fault, if any such be, of our watry situation. To make the People fittest to choose the chosen, and the chosen fittest to govern will be *to mend our corrupt and faulty education*."—*Milton*, ibid., p. 650.

"And if the people, laying aside prejudice and impatience, will seriously and calmly now consider their own good, both religious and civil, their own liberty and the only means thereof, as shall be here laid down before them, and will elect their knights and burgesses able men, and according to the just and necessary qualifications (which, for aught I hear, remain yet in force unrepealed, as they were formerly decreed in parliament), men not addicted to a single person or House of Lords, the work is done; at least the foundation firmly laid of a free commonwealth, and good part also erected of the main structures."

"The whole Freedom of man consists either in *spiritual or civil liberty*. . . The other part of our freedom consists in the civil rights and *advancements of every person according to his merit:* the enjoyment of those never more certain, and the access to these never more open, than in a free commonwealth. *Both which, in my opinion, may be best and soonest obtained, if every county in the land were made a kind of subordinate commonalty or commonwealth.**

"They should have here also schools and academies at their own choice, wherein their children may be bred up in their own sight, to all learning and *noble education;* not in grammar only, but in all *liberal arts and exercises.* This would soon spread much more knowledge and civility, yea, religion, through all parts of the land, by *communicating the natural heat of government and culture more distributively to all extreme parts*, which now lie numb and neglected, would soon make the whole nation more industrious, more ingenious at home; more potent, more honorable abroad. To this a free commonwealth will easily assent; (nay, the parliament hath had already some such thing in design) for of all governments a commonwealth aims most to make *the people* flourishing, virtuous, noble, and high spirited."—*Milton*, ibid., pp. 648, 654, and 655.

"I doubt not but all ingenuous and knowing men will easily agree with me that *a free commonwealth* without single person or House of Lords is by far the best Government if it can be had."—*Milton*, ibid., p. 647.

And Montesquieu, whose writings on the Spirit of Laws, and on the causes of the corruption of the Roman Republic, are of the profoundest, thus descants, in his first volume, on the true principles and characteristics of Republics :—

"The principle of democracy is corrupted, not only when the spirit of equality is extinct, but likewise when they fall into a

* A forecast of the United States!

spirit of *extreme equality*, and when each citizen would fain be upon a level with those whom he has chosen to command him, —to debate for the senate, execute for the magistrates, and decide for the judges."—P. 143.

"Democracy hath, therefore, two excesses to avoid; *the spirit of inequality*, which leads to aristocracy or monarchy; and the spirit of *extreme equality*, which leads to despotic power.

"As distant as heaven is from the earth, so is the true spirit of equality from that of extreme equality; in the former men are equal only as citizens, but in the latter they are equal also as magistrates, senators, judges, or masters.

"The natural place of virtue is near to liberty; but it is not nearer to excessive liberty than to servitude."—P. 146.

"As those who govern (in a free State) have a power which in some measure, has need of *fresh vigour* every day, they have a greater regard for such as are *useful* to them than for those who contribute to their *amusement*.

"They have not that *politeness* which is founded on indolence. An absolute Government produces indolence, and this gives birth to politeness."—P. 417.

"Their laws not being made for one more than for another, each considers himself a monarch.

"In a free nation, it is very often a matter of indifference whether individuals reason well or ill; it is sufficient that they do reason: from hence springs that *liberty which is a security from the effects of these reasonings*.

"But in a despotic Government, it is equally pernicious whether they reason well or ill; their reasoning is alone sufficient to reach the principle of that Government."—P. 418.

"The character of the (free) nation is more particularly discovered in their literary performances, in which we find the *men of thought and deep meditation*."—P. 419.

And Napoleon, with more detail and equal emphasis, explaining his entire approval of Republican Principles, declares that it is essential to them that *the whole People without distinction* should take part in the elections.

In this opinion almost the entire French and American nations have now for seventy years concurred.

These Principles are, as Napoleon says, entirely Republican. That they are not, in their pure and simple shape, entirely suited to the French, is the fault, not of Napoleon, but of the French.

It is only a consistency of formality and narrow-mindness, that blames him for securing fixity of tenure where tenure has always been fixed, and where the Rhine and not the sea, is boundary. In France, if Napoleon does not rule, Rome will. But that the People are with Napoleon, and that he is as democratic a leader as France is prepared for, cannot be doubted.

"The first wants of a nation are *Independence*, *Liberty*, *Stability*, *the supremacy of Merit*, and *the enjoyments of life equally diffused. The best form of Government would be* that under which every abuse of power might in any case be corrected; under which, without social disturbance, without effusion of blood, *not only the laws*, *but the head of the State might be susceptible of change;* for one generation has no right to subject to its laws generations to come.

"In order that the *Independence* of a nation be secure, it is necessary that the Government be *strong;* and that the Government be strong, it behoves that it should *enjoy the confidence of the people*, that it should be in a condition to maintain a numerous and well disciplined army without exciting outcries against tyranny, and that it should be *able to arm the whole nation without fear of being overthrown by it.*

"To be Free, freedom being only a consequence of independence, it is necessary that *the whole people*, *without distinction*, should *take a part in the election* of the representatives of the nation; *that the masses*, *which can never be corrupted*, *and which never flatter or dissemble*, *should be the constant source from which all power should emanate.*

"In order that the *enjoyments of life be equally spread* amongst all classes, it is necessary not only that taxation should be diminished, but also that the Government should wear an aspect of *stability* which shall tranquillise the minds of men, and warrant a dependence upon the future. *The Government will be stable when institutions are not exclusive*; that is to say, when, without favoring any class, they are tolerant of all, and, above all, are *in harmony with the requirements and the desires of the majority of the nation. Then will merit be the only passport to success, and services rendered to the country the only ground for rewards."—Louis Napoleon Bonaparte.* "Life and Works." Political Reveries. Vol. i, pp. 169-170.

§

Mill, the last, and perhaps the most resolute, as well as most careful of all writers on the nature of Government, so emphatically asserts, and so clearly explains, the advantages of Popular Government, that it may be assumed that the theory of popular Government is so far sufficiently vindicated. Yet he maintains as strenuously the principle of a graduated suffrage, and insists upon the dangers of an alleged popular class sovereignty as incident to pure democracy. Unless then these arguments can be set aside or overruled, the cause of pure Democracy will not have been established, but on the contrary, will have suffered in his hands.

Let us first show shortly the gist of his reasoning on the advantages of Government by the many :—

"*Freedom and Variety of Situations.* . . . Europe is in my judgment wholly indebted to this plurality of paths for its progress and many-sided *Development.* . . *Individuality is the same thing as Development.* . . . . When does a People stop? When it ceases to possess Individuality. . . . The only unfailing and permanent source of its improvement is Liberty, since by it there are as many possible independent centres of improvement, as there are Individuals."—*Mill on Liberty*, pp. 130, 114, 126, 127.

"We have now, therefore, obtained a foundation for a twofold division of the merit which any set of political institutions can possess. It consists partly of the degree in which they promote the *general mental advancement* of the community in intellect, virtue, and practical activity; and partly of the degree of perfection in which they *organise* the moral, intellectual, and active *worth already existing.*

"And the one indispensable merit of a Government is that its operation on the people is favorable or not unfavorable to *the next step* which it is necessary for them to take in order to raise themselves to a higher level.

"It is then impossible to understand the question of the adaptation of forms of Government to states of society, without taking into account not only the next step, but *all the steps* which society has yet to make.

"The ideally best form of Government is that in which *the sovereignty or supreme controlling power in the last resort is vested in the entire aggregate of the community*. . . . It is both more favorable to *present good Government*, and promotes a better and higher form of *national character* than any other polity whatsoever.

"Its superiority in reference to PRESENT WELL-BEING rests upon principles of as universal truth and applicability as any general principles which can be laid down respecting human affairs. Human beings are only secure from the hands of *others* in proportion as they are *self-protecting*; and they only achieve a high degree of success in their struggle with *nature*, in proportion as they are *self-dependent*.

". . Whenever it ceases to be true that mankind as a rule prefer themselves to others, from that moment Communism is the only defensible form of society.

"If we now pass to the influence of the form of Government upon *character*, we shall find *the superiority of popular Government over every other* to be, if possible, still more decided. This question really depends upon a still more fundamental one, viz., which of two common types of character is it most desirable should predominate—the *active* or the *passive* type?

"There can be no kind of doubt that the passive type is favored by the Government of one or a few, and *the active self-helping type by that of the* MANY.

"The striving, go-ahead character of England and the United States is in itself the foundation of the best hopes for the general improvement of mankind."—*J. S. Mill*, on "Representative Government," pp. 33, 37, 43, 55, 59, 64.

Thus much, then, is clear from *authority*. All the writers we have quoted, from Socrates downwards as far as Mill, either represent the advantages of Democracy as unquestionable, or its evils as depending on some removeable cause, such as ignorance or poverty. Mill, however, will have it that when these are dispelled and replaced by education and competence, there still exists the fatal objection to that equal voting of the All which is Democracy; namely, that however good may be the class, it is still a class, and that excelling in votes and in numbers, it must of necessity swamp all other classes.

We contend that this cannot be, because in a true Democracy there are no longer "classes," but *the nation.*

We believe in Human Nature, as intended for social, political life, and that the generally educated manhood of a nation is likely to do less wrong than any other attainable form of Government.

And it seems to us that all authority and argument, except Mills', maintain that Manhood may and *ought* to rule, if it be educated,—that is, if it is a symmetrical manhood, fitted by development for association in political action.

It is true that De Tocqueville thus exposes what he considers to be the weak point of Democracy :—

"We must first understand what the purport of Society and the aim of Government is held to be.

". . . If, in short, you are of opinion that the principal object of a Government is *not* to confer the greatest possible share *of power and of glory* upon the body of the nation, but to ensure the greatest amount of enjoyment, and the least degree of misery to each of the individuals who compose it,—if such be your desires, you can have no surer means of satisfying them than *by equalising the conditions of men* and establishing democratic institutions."—*De Tocqueville,* 140-1-2, v. ii.

Apart from this "power and glory" of which the great Repulic has now shown the world enough, it is indeed difficult to say what advantages M. de Tocqueville does *not* attribute to Democracy.

He says it seeks the greatest possible happiness of the greatest number—that its officials cannot easily combine against the People—that it excels in public spirit, in notions of right, in respect of the law, and in the universal activity it promotes,—that it is endangered rather by its strength than its weakness, and that it has a secret tendency to promote public prosperity notwithstanding private vices and mistakes, and to produce advantages never thought of, whilst in aristocratic institutions there is a secret propensity which, notwithstanding the talents and virtues of rulers, leads them to contribute to the evils which oppress, and does injuries even when not intended.—*Ibid.*, v. ii, p. 120, &c.

But elsewhere he rebukes the idea that nations cannot be masters of their own Destiny, and declares that it tends only to make "feeble men and pusillanimous nations."

We leave this part of the subject, quoting a bit from Bentham on the sort of mechanical nonsense talked about the advantages of a constitutional Balance, of a mixed Government, and about the danger of manhood rule to property, as though *property* could suffer from an increase of *proprietors* :—

"Talk of *balance*, never will it do. What mean ye by this your balance? Know ye not that when forces balance each other, the machine is at a stand? Well, and in the machine of Government, immobility, the perpetual absence of all motion, is that the thing which is wanted? Know ye not, that since an emblem you must have,—since you can neither talk nor attempt to think, but in hieroglyphics,—know ye not that, as in the case of the body natural, so in the case of the body politic, *when motion ceases, the body dies?*

"So much for the *balance*,—now for the *mixture*. Good;—this notion about mixture, so long as the respective natures of the several interests are kept out of sight. A form of Government in which the interest *of the whole* is the only interest provided for, in this form behold the *simple* substance. To this add a power employed in the interest of one *single* person, and a power employed in the interest of a *small knot* of persons;—in either of these cases you have a mixture;—well, compared then with the simple substance, when and where can be the advantage of this mixture?

"The all of A, how much less is it in the eye of A than the all of B in the eye of B? When you have solved this problem,—then and not before, say that universal confusion and destruction of property would be the result of universal suffrage.—*Bentham*, "Plan of Reform," pp. 51-3, 118.

The great representative fact of the existence and stability of Democracy in America, is a guarantee to Democracies everywhere, that there may be a future for them, but it is also a warning, that to rule they must first obey; that education, loyalty, and self-restraint, are the conditions of their existence,—in fact, that if the All are to govern the State, they must (in the general), first be qualified to govern,—each of them,—himself.

Granted, then, the principle of human progress, all other forms of Government than this Government for and by the all, are but compromises between order and progress, whereby the People submit for a while to the one, the few, or the many, for the sake of the necessities of the present, or the fears of the past.

Naturally, therefore,—inevitably, the oligarchies and the people of all countries are at issue about the American "experiment."

All ideas tend,—as representatives of all races are emigrating,—towards the continent of the People.

Association of ideas, or of forces, will necessarily decide the matter for Europe. If oligarchies cannot prevail upon Democracies to commit suicide by warring against the Great Republic, a conservative progress will gradually lead them after it on the inevitable road. If oligarchies can succeed in launching People against People, the principle of ASSOCIATION will still prevail. But it will then become a revolutionary propagandism, and present the leverage which will upheave every throne, and unsettle every Government in Christendom.

DEMOCRACY:

ARGUMENT ON AUTHORITIES.

"It is said we shall have safeguards, and Mr. Stuart Mill, a political philosopher, has busied himself in discovering what those safeguards are to be. I can conceive no employment less worthy of a philosopher or statesman than to advise this House to give away political power in order to devise means of getting it back again."—*The Hon. Robt. Lowe,* May 3rd, 1865.

"Their laws not being made for one more than for another, each considers himself a monarch."

"In a free nation it is very often a matter of indifference whether individuals reason well or ill; it is sufficient that they do reason: from hence springs that liberty which is a security from the effects of their reasonings."—*Montesquieu.*

"The form of Government usually termed mixed, has always appeared to me a mere chimera. In all communities *some one principle* of action may be discovered which *preponderates over the others.* When a community really has a mixed Government, that is to say, when it is equally divided between two adverse principles, it must either pass through a revolution or fall into complete dissolution."—*De Tocqueville.*

"The political arrangement of every state must always depend on the prevailing inclination *of that party which is predominant.*"—*Aristotle.*

"The form of Government assigned to a particular stage of Development *must* present itself."—*Hegel.*

"The superiority of popular Government in reference to present well-being rests upon two principles of as universal truth and applicability as any general propositions which can be laid down respecting human affairs. The first is, that the rights and interests of every or any *person* are only secure from being disregarded *when the person interested is himself able, and habitually disposed, to stand up for them.* The second is, that the *general* prosperity attains a greater height, and is more widely diffused, in proportion to the amount and variety of the personal energies in promoting it."—*J. S. Mill*, on "Representative Government," p. 54.

Chapter VI.

DEMOCRACY:

ARGUMENT ON AUTHORITIES,

CHIEFLY IN REFERENCE TO THE HERESIES OF MILL.

"Every distinct development of character is capable of its peculiar excess, and to this it constantly tends to degenerate. If, then, an entire nation has adhered *to some certain variety of development*, it comes in time to *lose all power of resisting the preponderant bias* to this one peculiarity, and along with it all power of regaining its equilibrium. Perhaps it is in this that we discover the reason of such frequent changes in the constitution of *ancient states.* Every fresh constitution exercised an undue influence on the national character, and this, definitely developed, degenerated in turn and necessitated a new one." —*Baron W. von Humboldt.*

"The estate goes before the steward, the foundation before the house, *people before their representatives,* and the Creator before the creature. The steward lives by preserving the estate; the house stands by reason of its foundation; the representative depends upon the people, as the creature subsists by the power of the Creator."—*Penn.*

"Responsibility educates, and politics is but another name for God's way of teaching the masses ethics, under the responsibility of great present interest."—*Wendell Phillips.*

"Not that depositaries of power will not, but that they *cannot,* misemploy it. Democracy is not the ideally best form of Government unless this weak side of it can be strengthened." —*J. S. Mill.*

We quote Baron Humboldt here, because he fears a "preponderant bias, or undue influence" on national types, conveyed through the sameness of Government education,—the very thing which Mill most insists upon, and because Humboldt himself insists that "absolute freedom," which is something very like equality, is the great promoter of *variety* of conditions. He seems to contemplate either State education of an elaborate kind, or education in a despotic state of society under control of a Despotism.

The difference is curious. Mill says, "Let the State educate, but avoid a majority class preponderance by plural voting." Humboldt says, "Do not educate by the State, or you will create a special bias which will degenerate into extremes."

We now leave the domain of authority and proceed in the first place to combat Mr. Mill's new objections to Democracy pure, and the precautions he proposes against ignorance and the class interests of a numerical majority. In some respects he herein follows Aristotle, although in a state of society entirely different. He also fears that a general mediocrity is incident to Progress; but a mediocrity that means a general diffusion of comforts and knowledge, that discovers and promotes its truly great men, that is compatible with an intense nationality, and that can combine a revolution with a reformation, in such an apocalypse as America has just shown the world,—such a "mediocrity," we say, is an argument not against, but for Democracies.

Mr. Mill must be tired of being always stupidly and mechanically praised. It appears to us that he has pursued one line of argument which begins with universal means of development, and ends with the universal vote-power, and that other line of argument anent conservatism, till the greatness of the interests at stake and the untried conclusions it then involved, startled him into compromise and "graduation."

Surely he should have been at home in this greatness. He should have trusted nature and God. He should have seen that a true national manhood is the *mean* of progress and conservatism. That if so many good and amiable and educated men do shrink from public life, perhaps, after all, they are best in the bosom of their families. That in the revolutionary energies of the "All," the conservative instincts of the many, the God-given leadership of the few, the oneness of the Presidential executive, and the universality and power of his constituency,—we shall find the necessary virtues of all systems, whether Democracy, middle-class rule, oligarchy, or autocracy, and that in a true People thus expressed, led, and organised, there is a function that has *yet to be explained* to the politicians of this generation.

The remedies he would apply are certain simple education tests, to keep out the most ignorant, a general right to cast votes for individuals who are not candidates for any particular place ; and a system of plural voting as the right of those, who by academical tests, or a rough money test, may be supposed to be more learned and politically competent.

To the first there is perhaps no objection if it can be rendered practicable.

The second is admirable, if possible.

To the latter there are objections both as to Principle and as to Practice.

Amongst them are :—

1st. That Society in England is prepared to wait or to advance by degrees, until education shall beyond all doubt have qualified the all as citizens. There is no need for experimentalising upon the English constitution with a measure of such new and tremendous power as one for plural voting.

2nd. Education will undoubtedly prepare the all for power quite as fast as they will demand it. Mr. Mill himself insists upon it that the citizens of the only democratic country are all in some sense both "Patriots and cultivated." He als admits the connection between "these qualities and democratic institutions."

3rd. To establish a plurality of voting power would be to create a more scientific and dangerous instrument of Despotism and obstruction than has hitherto been invented for the enemies of mankind.

4th. England is already the country of corporate and feudal obstructions of all sorts against the popular advance. These have to be attacked and carried in detail, and the storming of them will be ample "graduation." It seems *now* as though they could never be carried without the impetus of *revolutionary* energies. To implant fresh obstructions in the constitution itself, would arouse not the mere revolutionary energies of the People fresh from contact with the soil and with reality, but revolution itself.

5th. The working classes cannot form a *preponderating class* unless, 1st, their power exceeds the power of the other classes, and 2ndly, unless they combine as a class for class objects, instead of as citizens with citizens.

In reference to the first postulate, *numbers* never have constituted, and never will constitute power in any permanent sense, until they deserve to do so. Numbers are not power without organisation, and there can be no organisation without a common platform, and in a country like this, that platform must be one of intellect and morality.

In reference to the second postulate, there are no democratic class objects of an unfair, unjust, and improper sort, which education and intercourse will not demonstrate to be injurious as sectional, and unattainable as injurious. The Few have attained class objects throughout history, but it has been under cover of the general ignorance.

To put one man at nothing and another at one may for the time be necessary. To admit the education, and yet to put one man at three and another at one is illogical. It both denies and affirms manhood. It blasphemes and drivels in a strophe.

We refuse to believe that any man who admits

the conservative effect of education,—that the popular power can only become efficient as it is organised by education,—and that to judge of political capacity and honesty is no affair of recondite science, but of mere common sense, will also deliberately affirm that the educated citizen is not competent to use his manhood, so fearfully and wonderfully made, for the rudimentary rights and equal functions of political life.

But our categorical answer to this "preponderating," and "swamping," and "plurality" business is:—

6th. That in all Government whatsoever, some one principle and power *must* preponderate and swamp. That to try to avoid it by handicapping the national manhood, is to mistake the principles and the possibilities of Government, and the needs as well as the patience of nations; is to organise revolutions and call that a balance, and to guarantee the deluge by contriving dams against it.

7th. Democracy, or the *equal* voting power of the all, is that towards which the whole world gravitates.

That which gives unity to Government is a single preponderating power, and there can be no true Government without it.

And we have seen what has been the *warrant* of the various powers that have preponderated.

The power of the one is justified by the necessity of order:—of the few and the many by the same necessity, tempered more and more by right, as gradations of the all have been admitted. Throughout history, other classes have preponderated from necessity,—*the people alone can preponderate by fitness and right.*

8th. But this preponderance of the People is only a preponderance of the all against privileges and abuse. *It is in reality a Balance,* and the only righteous balance possible,—the balance of the multiple of numbers against all the other multiples, as hereafter explained,—the God-created balance of a great and true nation!

Alas, in mistrusting the People, Mill misses and would mar the last sublime and only true and complete unity.

The all would indeed "swamp" and "neutralise," and "preponderate,"—over the abuses, vis inertiæ, and corruption of the *sections,* but they would create the People one and indivisible.

We denounce then Mr. Mill's plan as a plan for the eternal subordination of the masses. Unless it secure that, it must secure revolution or destroy the country.

Though wide as the poles asunder in moral intent, he works in one line with the cause lately called "The South," for he works for that which is in its nature and essence, *oligarchic.*

And a *nation* he would never have, but an artificial *balance of classes,* waiting the furnace of revolution to purge and fuse them.

Let the wheat and the tares grow awhile together, till the People are graduated into fitness. *That* may make a nation. Mill would only make a *judgment.*

And all because, forsooth, the common people are not fit to say whether A. or B. is fittest to represent them !

We say, on the contrary, that ten thousand sober common Englishmen, listening in public assembly to A. and B., are *better* fitted than the same number of M.A.'s, B.A.'s, or LL.D.'s, millionaires, bankers, esquires, or tailors, to pronounce on the qualifications of the said A. and B. as public men. But if education is wanted yet further to prepare them, they can better afford to wait than to have battalions of political enemies, with multiples of political power, marshalled across their path. Those who impute class antagonism to the people, must not admit it against them.

Prepare the People for the vote : universalise it ; and then protect them in it.

Nothing tends so much to remove this disqualification of ignorance as the incentives supplied by a sense of freedom and responsibility conferred by a share in the Government. As Wendell Phillips teaches,—" responsibility educates ;" and Mr. Mill himself insists that—

" Among the foremost benefits of free Government is *that education of the intelligence and sentiments which is carried down to the very lowest* when they are called upon to take a part in acts which directly affect the great interests of their country. Unless substantial mental cultivation in the mass of mankind is to be a mere vision, this is the road by which it must come.

" Almost all travellers are struck by the fact *that every American is in some sense both a patriot and a person of cultivated intelligence* ; and M. de Tocqueville has shown how close the connection is between these qualities and their democratic institutions. *No such wide diffusion of the ideas, tastes, and sentiments of educated minds, has ever been seen elsewhere, or even conceived of as attainable.*"—*Representative Government*, pp. 156-7.

But Mr. Mill proceeds to say that "this is nothing to what we might look for in a Government *equally democratic in its unexclusiveness*, but better organised in other important points." Further, that "no one but a fool, and only *a fool of a peculiar description*, feels offended by the acknowledgment that there are others whose opinion, and even whose wish, is entitled to a greater amount of consideration than his."

In other words, Mr. Mill considers *that* a Government "equally democratic in *unexclusiveness*" as the American, where the scholar, for instance, or the banker, shall have two or more votes for one of the laborer's votes!

This, again, involves two questions: 1st, what the laborer would feel; and, 2nd, what the State has to decide as to this supposed overwhelming class power of an equal-voting Demos.

At present the laborer looks upon the suffrage as a right to be won by economy and industry for the individual, and by agitation and political progress for his class; and he knows that those next above him have but lately won their vote, after a national struggle. But to be openly and scientifically appraised as but half or three-quarters of a man; to be told that another who knows Latin and Greek, and has got over the ass's bridge, is three times as able as himself to decide whether Mr. Smith or Mr. Jones would be the best M.P., or whether we should go to war for Poland, or be imprisoned for Church Rates,—this would lead to deep-seated class hostility, would evoke class agitation, and make the workmen declare that they indeed would not be such "fools" (they might quote Mr. Mill, and say, such fools "*of a peculiar description*") as to submit to the valuation.

With regard to "ignorance," in the sense in which the argument relating thereto was used by Aristotle, we need not further refer to it. Modern Democracy completely cuts away that ground, and Mr. Mill is one of the foremost in insisting on its extirpation.

Democracy says that a nation cannot be democratic till it is educated. The nation must prepare and wait. Mr. Mill says, let us take the nation as it is, and graduate votes to education, &c.

Democracy says that the whole equal voting educated manhood of a nation can alone fulfil its destiny, and can alone secure (amongst other things) the objects proposed by such schemes as plural voting; and further, as has been already stated, that plural voting is directly revolutionary, for it arms those who already possess natural multiples of power, with *artificial* ones also, and places them as necessary antagonists directly in the march of the People.

The ancient objection of "ignorance," then, has been transformed into a question of "graduation." It is now asserted that "quality" must balance "numbers,"—that "preponderance of classes" must for the first time be avoided, or that, as the stock phrase now is, the People must not be allowed to "swamp" their betters.

We prefer Aristotle to Mill and to the Tories. We repeat with Aristotle, that when "quantity" joins "quality," "Democracy *must* prevail," and with De Tocqueville,—that if the natural preponderating power is withstood successfully, the result is "revolution or dissolution,"—that the obstruction is overthrown, or the country destroyed.

§

But as pointed out before, this is not so much a question of argument as of power. The men with multiples of influence and power are always sure to prevent the access of the People to it, until the latter are prepared to conquer these smaller and compacter hostile unities. Power is only conquered by power, and by a power greater or better organised. When the People can conquer it by public opinion, it will always be safest to give it them.

Nor can we forbear remarking on the inconsistency of urging plural voting as the "only alternative to universal suffrage."

Mr. Mill wants to see all men prepared for citizenship. He urges on the State to allow no man to grow up without education. A universal education is a universal citizenship. Universal citizenship and suffrage is the goal of political progress: it unites interest and right, conservatism and progress;—and yet this universal competency of citizenship is to be rewarded by a comparative disenfranchisement!

The heresy of Mill resolves itself into *a disbelief in equality,*—that it is not possible without producing tyranny, in other words, that it is not possible. To meet this theory of danger, he would make equality impossible. He would make inequality an institution, and expect the all to accept their degradation. He would bind over the People in sureties to wage eternal electoral war, for he would urge on development, and promote association, and when these have brought forth their inevitable offspring—Equality, he would say to the People, "now you are getting dangerous, come on to my patent graduated sliding scale, and let us see how many parts of a man you are entitled to be considered."

This is to inaugurate revolution with a vengeance, for it creates the power and then denies its use.

The answer to all this is clear.

In the inevitable course of human nature there are no contradictions. You cannot execute a strategic movement upon necessity, nor outflank Destiny.

Up to a certain point those classes which possess the multiples of power—high class education, oratory, learning, culture, wealth, birth, &c., will by excelling in quality neutralise mere numbers.

After a certain point the quality of the Demos will improve,—better developed, he will the more closely associate, and as his "quality" comes up to the standard of the more favored classes, and as, exceeding in quantity, he equals also in *quality,* then at the same time that his preponderance is secured, the evils attending it are removed.

Therefore the all cannot attain a class preponderance till classes, in the bad sense, have ceased, and there remains instead of them a completed nation.

The attempt to institute plural voting, this only alternative with universal equal suffrage, must begin and end in exasperation, distrust, and suspicion.

Mr. Mill's own theory of moral and mental "development," contradicts the scheme. If the man valued the vote, passion, and a sense of injury, would ensue from this graduated scale of manhood. If he did not value and use it, so given, where would be the "Development?"

If it is an obvious fact, that "Free Government educates the intelligence and sentiments of the very lowest,—makes him a patriot, and widely diffuses the ideas, tastes, and sentiments of educated minds to an extent neither seen nor conceived of elsewhere," it is neither conceivable nor right, that individuals so qualified should submit to be constituted politically the third or the ninth part of a man. Such qualities, forced into opposition, would become dangerous precisely in proportion as they would otherwise be conservative and valuable.

With such admissions neither the *ignorance* nor the *numbers* of the Demos can serve as a plea for plural voting.

§

Plural voting is also a scheme which would unite a most diverse and powerful opposition.

If the scholar is to have twice the voting power of the workman, would the wealthy man have twice that of the scholar, or would the B.A. in the garret or the shop outvote his landlord or his master? In the first case, the class power would be overweighted as against the artisan class. In the second, property would oppose the scheme.

Moreover the educated and wealthy classes have already a "plurality" of influence upon the franchise. The money power, the social power, the writing power, the speaking power, the preaching power, the newspaper press. The forum, the pulpit, the exchange.

Never before was a system so well contrived as that of English representation, to represent minorities.

A majority of a section has ruled England since Cromwell.

What is the result?

Five-sixths of our People are declared unfit to vote.

Large, religious, and powerful majorities are not only unrepresented, but *they are outraged.*

It is only when the People are grasping power, that the value of minorities is discovered.

Again as far as Conservatism consists of *prejudice*, of mere likes and dislikes, sentiment or passion, it depends not upon knowledge or ignorance, but obviously and notoriously on whether one is *in* or *out* of the pale of the Constitution. Outside, one rages against the barriers; inside, one pities, despises, or neglects the disqualified. To make men conservative, qualify them.

Nor would this feeling stop here. It intensifies as the outside recedes, and the innermost penetralia is reached. They who "simper in gilded saloons" have generally not been used to them. In his progress from the outer world to the political holy of holies, the Demagogue naturally becomes a parasite. It is high intelligence or stern principle alone, that comprehends what is true Conservatism and true Democracy, and thus combines and adheres to both.

Moreover, to a great extent, *poverty is itself a qualification.* It is more a qualification than a disqualification. If the question be "the right men in the right places,—merit and not influence," the masses would vote for merit, the families would vote for "influence." In other words, each would vote for its own interest. With regard to war, the masses would incline against it, it means taxation, the few for it, it means employment, and also lavish expenditure, and a continuation of class monopolies of all sorts. On the other hand, the national honor is safe with the People, who would vote, fight, and pay in a just cause. We have had more than a century of frequent fighting for Bourbons, Legitimists, and Popes, for Austria and Turkey, and against Nations, Republics, and Progress generally. We should have had another war now for slavery, and against another Republic and Nation, if the million had not kept the peace which the oligarchy attempted to break. Further, war draws the working man for the militia, and trenches on his necessities, to promote extravagance in naval, military, and civil services.

The working man would vote for free trade, peace, and economy.

The candidates of the few vote for imposts on trade,—have sons, brothers, and relations in the services and the embassies, discharge their Hudsons for their Elliots, and give their sympathies and influence to despotism and laissez faire.

Manhood always recognises manhood. That is the sum of the whole matter. It is the intelligence, disinterestedness, and determination of the whole People, one and indivisible, that the tyrannous few, now and always, fear. The more plenary and complete the manhood of a leader, the nearer does he come to a certainty of popular favour. *For the universal and the all are in natural and inevitable unity.*

We have said that poverty is a qualification, and wealth the contrary. Man has five objects of attention and carefulness,—his person, his family, his property, his country, his God. As property increases, thought and care for *it* increases, and must increase, till respectability hangs like a millstone upon manhood. The rich man's family are often provided for by the State. His country requires expensive services, and the church rewards a timely zeal with a place for his sons in a costly religious establishment. It were as easy for this average rich man, with his riches, to regard the interests of the all, as for a camel and his hump to pass through the eye of a needle.

The position of the rich man tends to lead him against the State, save as to the promotion of a certain irresolute security,—that of the poor man identifies his and its interests. In a word, the rule of the all cannot be a monopoly.

On the other hand, when the working man sees that he has a property in the Government, the imperial powers of governing within him tend to become developed and exalted into a passion. The idea of the State fills his political horizon. *He* is the Government.

After all, political influence always has been, and always will be, rather weighed than counted.

Concentrated voting would be undue influence, and bribery made easy.

Nor is it to be forgotten that the pleas of majority-tyranny are good only as affecting questions of rights of *property.* But rights of the *person* are as varied and important. Everybody possesses and understands them. They belong to no class. Everybody, therefore, should vote upon them equally.

And different localities involve a variety of counterbalancing interests. As an old writer says :—

"Because this must be said in behalf of human kind, that common sense and plain reason, while men are disengaged from acquired opinions, will ever have some general influence upon their minds; whereas *the species of folly and vice are infinite, and so different in every individual,* that they could never procure a majority, if other corruptions did not enter to pervert men's understandings, and misguide their wills."—"A Discourse on the Contests between the Nobles and Commons in Athens and Rome, &c." *State Tracts*, 1688-1702, v. iii, p. 227.

Nor is any depth of intellect or variety of learning necessary for the suffrage. The requisite is not statesmanship, but to appreciate statesmen; often, only to decide which of two candidates is the more honest and capable.

It was the opinion of Cavour ("Dicey," p. 81) that the right to the suffrage depends on three moral qualifications,—independence from bribery, intelligence to judge of fitness of candidate, and the possession of a stake in the preservation of social order. For appreciation of statesmanship, we contend not only that the People are not incompetent, but that they have a special political instinct and competency. As for independence, we know that the all cannot be bribed. And every average educated workman would have stake enough in the country if only unjust laws did not prevent his acquiring it.

All the authorities go to this.

When Socrates contends against the expediency of "valuation," it is because it would produce very "bad navigation" of the State, and he swears that it would make the city not one but two. When Aristotle objects to Democracy only because ignorance and poverty characterised it, the inevitable inference is, that with competency comes greater concern for the public weal, and that with education comes a better understanding of the mutual interest of citizens. When Fichte, and Mill, and Guizot, and Humboldt declare that individual development is the great object of Government; when Napoleon says that to be stable, institutions must be free and men equal; and when Milton insists on an educated Democracy and on Liberty and apportioned Equality,—then we say, from each and all we gather that *development* and *equality*, which produce one another, are the factors of national and individual advancement, and the objects of all enlightened Government.

Ideas of Government and development seem to the thoughtless only to clash. The one means a universal free and intelligent action, the best guarantee of the other,—of the unity of the whole, and subordination and adjustment of the parts.

"The whole" is a great word, and but little understood yet. "The parts" was the cry of the old dead world,—old and dead because, not having unity, it could not perpetuate life. The parts of a man,—his intellect without his character, his body and work without his soul. The parts of a State,—the one instead of the nation, or the few or the many without the all. Political equality is another name for unity, and without unity "nation" is but a "geographical expression."

So much for fears respecting equality felt by men possessing multiples of power. So much for right relationship to the State of those who, as individuals, can never be equally powerful with their *betters*, and who, by association, can never become too powerful for the public good.

To our mind, to doubt equality as a principle, as it would prevail in a true Democracy, is to doubt manhood.

Without development a State dies. With equality denied to development the State is destroyed.

The simple and decisive question is, "Are men prepared to trust or to distrust the People and manhood?" This is the great divider of parties.

Thus said Jefferson :—

"Call them Liberals and Serviles, Jacobins and Ultras, Whigs and Tories, Republicans and Federalists, Aristocrats and Democrats, or by whatever name you please, they are the same parties still, and pursue the same object. The last appellation of Aristocrats and Democrats is the true one, expressing the essence of all."

DEMOCRACY:

EQUALITY THE ESSENCE.

"But for Equality in Democratic communities the passion is ardent, insatiable, incessant, invincible: they call for Equality in Freedom; and if they cannot obtain that, they call for Equality in slavery. They will endure poverty, servitude, barbarism,—but they will not endure aristocracy."

"This is true at all times and especially true in our own. All men and all powers seeking to cope with this irresistible passion will be overthrown and destroyed by it. In our age Freedom cannot be established without it, and despotism itself cannot reign without its support."—*De Tocqueville.*

"A love of Democracy is a love of Equality."—*Montesquieu.*

"The *equality* of citizens which commonly produces an equality in their fortunes, *brings plenty and life into every part of the body politic*, and extends them throughout the whole."—*Ibid.*

"The most favorable position which man can occupy as member of a political community has appeared to me to be that in which the most manifold individuality and the most original independence subsisted, with *the most various and intimate union* of a number of men,—a *problem which nothing but* THE MOST ABSOLUTE LIBERTY *can ever hope to solve.*"—*Baron W. von Humboldt.*

"Their deliberations, in which every man shall decide whatever he decides for himself, and not for one subject to him whose sufferings will never affect him;—deliberations, according to which *no one can hope that it shall be he who is to practise a permitted injustice, but every one must fear that he may have to suffer it;* deliberations which *alone deserve the name of legislation,* which is something wholly different from the ordinances of combined Lords to the countless herds of their slaves;—these deliberations will necessarily be guided by justice, and *will lay the foundation of a true State.*

"By the establishment of *this only true State* (where equality and justice prevail) the possibility of FOREIGN WAR, at least with other true States, is cut off. This law concerning the security of neighbours is necessarily a law in every State that is not a robber-State. That a whole nation should determine, for the sake of plunder, to make war on a neighbouring country is impossible; *for in a State where all are equal,* the plunder could not become the booty of a few, but must be equally divided amongst all, and *the share of no one individual could ever recompense him* for the trouble of war. Only where the advantage falls to a few oppressors, only from savages or barbarians, *or from enslaved nations.*"—*Fichte,* "Vocation of Man," p. 143-5.

Chapter VII.

EQUALITY THE ESSENCE OF DEMOCRACY.

"The very essence of Democratic Government consists in the absolute sovereignty of the majority."—*De Tocqueville.*

"A love of the republic in a Democracy, is a love of the Democracy; as the latter is that of Equality.

"Though *real Equality is the very soul of a Democracy,* it is so difficult to establish, that an extreme exactness in this respect would not be always convenient.

"The love of Equality in a Democracy limits ambition to the sole desire of doing greater services to our country. Hence distinctions here arise from the principle of Equality. All inequality in Democracies ought to be derived from the nature of the Government, and even from the principle of equality."—*Montesquieu,* v. i. pp. 52-3-7.

"The moral authority of the majority is partly based upon the notion that there is more intelligence and wisdom in a great number of men collected together than in a single individual.

"*The Theory of Equality* is in fact applied to the intellect of man, and human pride is thus assailed in its last retreat."—*De Tocqueville.*

"The People collectively considered are capable of discharging functions of which in their individual character they seem altogether unworthy.

"The People at large are yet, when collectively considered, not perhaps unworthy of Sovereignty. The excellencies of that complex entity, the public, may sometimes surpass those of the most accomplished prince or most virtuous council."—*Aristotle,* b. iii, p. 222.

"*They will no longer endure any among them who cannot be satisfied to be on an equality with others,* and so to remain. In order to protect themselves against internal violence or new oppression, all will take the same obligations."—*Fichte.*

We now proceed to carry the argument a step further, and to show that Equality is of the essence of Democracy. This principle means, from the point of view of the Individual,—the completest state of Freedom. From the general point of view it means that the best possible balance of the State is that arrived at by the *political* equality of the All, *together with those intellectual, social, and moral inequalities, gradations, and influences* which will always remain.

Democracy involves Manhood-Development and Association, but one cannot fail to perceive that as these together constitute unity and strength, —the power to combine for common objects,— national self-interest must soon or late accomplish the next step—Equality.

This is the theory; and also the fact in the only Democracy that yet exists.

That which other forms of Government attain by force, and by the suppression, more or less, of the universal will and intelligence, Democracy seeks to attain by directly opposite measures,—by stimulating the one and organising the other. The formula is the "universal intelligence fully developed, and the universal will fairly and fully organised." *In a word, the rights and values of the individual make the nation.*

And if the hopes of Democracy be not for ever a chimera, these positions respecting it will be established in argument, as they have been by the life of the American nation.

Democracy is that kind of Government which

most completely combines the spirit or motive power, with the organisation or machinery.

It has been pointed out that this is the excellence of Democracy, *that it unites manhood and organisation.*

And we here repeat that the excellence of this union chiefly depends upon :—

1st. Political Equality,—the absence of sectional or class jealousies and weaknesses, the formation of *a mighty uniform preponderating power*, consisting of the aggregate manhood, with no law-made causes of contention. Equality is essential to this uniform power, because otherwise *classes* must preponderate, and can never be balanced, nor can manhood be at one with manhood, or identical with Government.

2nd. That this *equalily is in reality a balance,* and the true natural balance. The all having a voice,—the many and the few, natural or artificial multiples of power.

3rd. That this equality is *the mightiest agent in manhood-development,*—that it promotes the greatest and completest variety of conditions of life.

4th. That it is *the only completion of freedom* as between individuals. It unites man with man.

5th. That it is the only guarantee of freedom as against the State. It is the sword and shield of the People.

6th. That *inequality* therefore divides into classes, destroys the natural national balance, obstructs development, and arrests the march of freedom and union. That plural voting would present to prerogative, privilege, and abuse, a new and inveterate Swiss guard, which, paying itself in kind, *must destroy or be destroyed by the People.*

Inequality is the cause and the result of barbarism, contention, tyranny, disunion, and weakness. Equality is the crown of political achievement: it can only result from an aggregate educated national manhood,—it alone can make a complete nation.

The natural working of development and of associative powers must bring equality, unless there be an arrest in the national progress.

Without equality there must be inequality, and inequality is oligarchy, and oligarchy without the warrant of necessity, is tyranny and confusion.

Equality alone can protect a nation from a return to this barbarism.

Government organised upon a basis of a graduated inequality, *intended to be permanent,* would be a conspiracy against manhood, and, amongst systems, a new, and scientific, and most infernal machine of tyranny.

It is at once the test and triumph of Democracy, that development and unity assist and complement one another. The best units make the completest unity; and that is not the best unity, or the completest system of Government, which is incompatible with the completest development of individuals.

It is admitted, without argument, that individual development is promoted by freedom, education, and variety of forms and conditions, and that association depends upon development. Equality is also admitted to be the essential principle of Democracy, but the new controversy is *about its meaning*; whether it means *an equality of classes or of individuals,* a balance of power to protect class interests which the majority would assail, or absolute political equality. And if the former, then of two things one,—either those interests are against manhood, and ought to be destroyed, or manhood is not sufficiently educated to value them. The remedy is, not to deny manhood, but to educate it.

Any other interpretation of equality sins against national unity, as well as individual right. It sins against national unity because it divides into classes instead of promoting homogeneity, and against individual right because, when the average citizen is sufficiently educated to choose a representative well, it is a wrong to give another citizen, who need do no more, twice his electoral power. It is to maintain the rights of parts and sections against the whole, and is in principle the same denial of the rights of the all, which has just received an eternal quietus in America.

We have already seen that the education required by the two interests which have to be consulted, namely, the individual and the nation, must be an education which does not clash with freeedom, and which consists of Free School, Press, Church, and Assembly.

§

Individual development thus generally promoted amounts, in fact, to Statesmanship. It possesses self-restraint. It comprehends and discusses the history of its country, and the tendencies of its principles. It calculates causes and results. It knows how to combine, and anticipate, and organise, and associate. It confers that universal consentaneity of thought and sentiment which, especially in national crises, thrills through the mind and heart of the million, and makes it as one man.

But to arrange for so complete a development of the national manhood is of necessity to arrange for equality or revolution. To arrange for permanent inequality is to arrange for the permanent debasement, not of the franchise, but of man. Rather it is to guarantee and *legitimate* revolution.

Equality requires that there be no clashing minor sovereignties, whether of sections, minorities, or States,—that the People be sovereign. A People thus constituted will be taught by intelligence to combine for truly national objects, and will be enabled by the franchise to root out those laws which interfere with the laws of production and of economics.

And this three-fold panoply of *universal vote-power*, *universal interest*, and *universal intelligence*, tends to render faction itself an advantage, causing it to stir without commanding the whole, whilst it converts to the commonweal those "stupendous individualities" which are apt, in other dispensations, to supersede the general will.

Until the present epoch, the basis of a true

Republic was wanting, and Aristotle, whilst pronouncing that " the best commonwealth is that in which middling men most abound," laments that "a Republic founded on the salutary principle of mediocrity and a just equality had been in his time indeed a rare phenomenon."

Further, "promotion of means and conditions favorable to the next step in national progress, and to all future steps," depends chiefly upon leaving human nature unhampered with the forms, interests, and castes of corporate and privileged bodies descended from the past. But an organised inequality of votes would be the most formidable corporate obstruction that could be created.

The essence of all proposals for a permanent inequality is distrust of human nature. Equality, on the other hand, declares that human nature is to be trusted ; that the best and completest "balance" is the virtual and national one of numbers against influence, wealth, genius, and organisation,—of localities against localisation,—*of the universal and profound self-consciousness of an educated and self-governing People,* —and that the average action of *such a nation* is better, wiser, and more virtuous than that of any part of it.

It is evident that manhood is the one harmonious, conservative, progressive governing power of the world, and that manhood-development is the only statesmanship that is not a compromise or an expedient. Where the Collective Reason reigns, it points out infallibly the Collective *Interest.*

The problem of which Democracy demands the

solution is, *how to promote individual development, and diffuse and stimulate it to a certain point*, and how to organise and consolidate individual forces.

For it is obvious that beyond a certain point, individual development and character guarantee *national* progress and unity, *because they guarantee individual progress and co-operation.* And the point in question is reached and passed *when a certain quality of education and morality has reached a certain amount of general diffusion.*

The right to define "what is a State," and in whom shall reside its sovereignty, must be either a right divine of kings and of privileged classes, or a right which *may* reside in the whole community.

If the latter, then the only remaining question is one of instalment.

Right divine of personages and classes once abandoned as barbarous, there can be naught of *principle* in the matter of exceptional qualification. It is rather a question of time, place, and preparedness.

This granted, all exceptions, on principle, are arbitrary, and therefore the *onus probandi* lies upon those who suggest them. This is the gravamen of Mr. Gladstone's Democracy.

But "right divine" wrested first from the one by the few, and then from the few by the many, is now led forth to do its last duty.

Through each stage, as manhood has spread and rights have broadened downwards, necessity and fear have checked the advance and the extension.

Necessity,—the unrepresented were not "qualified;" fear,—lest they should become so. And thus the right divine has widened with the qualifications, till necessity again asserts that the *million* are not qualified, and fear suggests that, when qualified, they will act as a class. A higher wisdom would reply,—"Injustice and ignorance make 'classes;' justice and education make nations."

In England, the Family Governments have restricted the qualifications by restricting education. As a class, world without end, have *they* always acted, and now, according to Mill, by a "valuation" of the poor man as a fraction of the rich man, and according to Grey by admitting him *as a class* or guild, each element that is *possible*, of mistrust, alienation, and class feeling, would be imported into the question,—to make of every concession a defeat, and to suggest to the conquerors the question, by what natural or constitutional right, the power to dispose of the destinies of the whole, is thus deposited in the hands of the parts.

§

Necessity is warrant enough for the practice of anything; but for the *theory* of oligarchy, or permanent inequality, there is in the universe but one logical stand-point,—a natural and permanent inequality of class and race: the incapacity of the multitude to judge ordinary political problems: the natural, and necessary, and permanent inferiority of the serving races: the natural and essential superiority of the ruling races.

That stand-point the South reached, and Democracy met it at the bayonet's point.

The South had the courage to assert with the distinctness of a theorem, and the aplomb of a courage entirely immoral, that only principle which can vindicate oligarchy;—that God has *not* made all nations of one blood; that the Black is essentially an inferior race, that the rule of the few there is unavoidable. But *all* oligarchies mean *that* or a mere temporary compromise; or nothing.

Said Stephens, of the Rebellion, "Let the North maintain that all men are equal, we maintain directly the opposite doctrine." We maintain that negroes were born to be slaves to us. That we shall be always superior to them. That man in politics is essentially and eternally unequal. "Even as one star differeth from another star in glory."

This doctrine of course impugns the truth of the Scriptures, and the justice and therefore the existence of God. It shakes the whole system of morals and philosophy. It challenged the *ultima ratio.* This issue the world waited for a long time, and it is well that the South raised it. The fool hath said in his heart, there is no God. And we know that the fool is the only absolutely fatal personage,—to his own side of the question or the strife.

Glory be to God that the representative South *did* at last reach the ultima ratio of infidelity and oligarchy, that it might be worthily met by the ultima ratio of freedom.

All other contests between the rights of the few and the all have been but preparations for this final test. And the question about an educated Democracy if not treated as a mere question of time, is but a compromise, a quibble, and an evasion,—if it be not a confession and admission of the *principle* of Democracy. ARE THE SOULS EQUAL? Are the educated multitude competent in morals and in judgment? If they are, then soon or late, the *Governments* and representations will be equal. If not, then all efforts of Democracy are vain and vicious struggles in an impossible cause.

If the mental and moral capacity of the average individual be competent to political problems, then one soul is as good as another in political theory,—there is an end of argument, and it is a question only of preparation, of education, and of how many of the future rulers of the world, are at any given epoch ready for their inheritance.

If on the other hand, inequality and natural incompetence are the law and the bond of strength and unity, the South should have proved it, for never again will oligarchy be bound together by equal inducements. What says Burke?—"In such a People the haughtiness of domination combines itself with the spirit of freedom, fortifies it, and renders it invincible. Such will be all masters of all slaves who are not slaves themselves." And such doubtless they are, but there were not 200,000 of them when the war began. How has Destiny burlesqued this war for inequality!

§

Such are the opposing principles, and the one party or the other, holds a right,—imprescriptible, indefeasible, eternal,—to reign. A right from God, —from nature, necessity, destiny, law, or by whatsoever other name, man, whether in reverence or imbecility, images to, or conceals from himself, the essential forces of the Unseen.

We say then that *here is an end of argument.* On the one side is a party whom nothing but defeat and destruction will convince. On the other a party that begins with the fundamental rights of Human nature,—That traces the tap-root of Democracy back through time and change to creation.

We take, therefore, the Individual MAN, and say to him, " Education, Freedom, Religion, these " are thy wants. The first to develop thy faculties, " the second to prove and exercise thy powers, the " third to give thee motives of self-restraint and " elevation, ideas of charity and duty, stronger and " higher than the present life. With these thou " art, if needs be, King, Emperor, Statesman, President, for thou art indeed a man governing thyself,—fit to govern others. Fit to be the autocrat, because fit to be of a true Democracy."

We add to this man, a few others, with the like equipment, and find, for like reasons, a fit and proper oligarchy.

We add to these few the MANY, and again, the ALL, again with the like equipment, and behold a middle-class rule or a Democracy. If we do not find that, the fault is with the men or with their training,—with God or the system. Either the proper natural *men* are not there, or the education, the freedom, or the religion, are not there. In the latter case, the Government, or the previous Governments are to blame, in the former,—but there we stop, and let Atheists alike to God and to Adam,—go on to anarchy or extinction — meanwhile groping through earth and nature for a warrant they will ever find, for any *permanent* rule of the one or the few, or any permanent incapacity of the equal governing all.

Well, we carry this process out till we are met, —not by a principle, but by the limitations of *necessity* itself. Unity is a necessity. Democracy is (soon or late) a necessity. The all cannot speak, the all cannot vote at once, or Democracy would destroy unity. The "One" must not long rule alone, for he would absorb the nation in himself. Hence the All must speak and act by degrees, and by delegates or representation, and so progress and order, theory and right, are in the way to be reconciled.

And what is all this, but the very actual history of the making of the American nation and Democracy?—two hundred years, compressed in about as many words and seconds. Americans are a nation and have searched out *unity*. Americans are a Democracy,—they will have their representation complete. *All nations will follow them.*

In "man" are the forces, and they will out. Men who cannot *see* the necessity of a gradually completed representation, may *feel* the ultima ratio of revolution, destroying them and their phantasies together. In politics there is no finality but with the all. Democracy is the goal of progress. The fate of selfish and perverse oligarchies, if not their blood, will be upon themselves or upon their children.

§

What then is the difficulty?

It is not the unwieldyness of numbers, for the principle of representation disposes of that.

It is not the difficulty of organisation, for the only Democracy that has tried it, has developed powers of association never yet equalled even in small communities.

"Let Americans," says Mill (on Liberty), "be left without a *Government, every body of Americans is able to improvise one,* and to carry on that or any other public business with a sufficient amount of intelligence, order, and decision. This is what every free people ought to be; and a people capable of this is certain to be free."

So much for Democratic Organisation.

Nor is it want of ability and penetration in the advocates of oligarchy. It is simply the old solution,—prejudice, or fancied interest.

If the many cannot profit as do the few, by freedom, education, and religion, *how many* are the few that can profit by them? *At what point* is it that the addition of one educated, religious, and free soul, makes order, anarchy?—makes that which was proved true before, seem false again?

"What makes *this* doctrine plain and clear?" Why it is just the two hundred pounds a-year supposed to go or come by the change, or else it is mere prejudice,—the sheer imbecility of men without manhood, or of logicians without faith.

Meanwhile the world will not be persuaded that there is truer philosophy in dividing a nation into "valuations," classes, and interests, and in seeking to balance and adjust their ever shifting forces, than in trusting the natural balance and compensations of a free and true nation.

Permanent "Graduation" is oligarchy, and "oligarchy without the warrant of necessity is tyranny and confusion." "To make the People fit to choose" is the problem, in representative countries, as put by Milton. To choose between two or more would-be representatives is a feat not beyond a common intelligence. There is then no warrant for this graduation,—for this permanent inequality of classes.

Once admit on philosophic grounds this unhappy contrivance, and there would be a free fight over every step of graduation, and whenever it might be proposed to alter it for the benefit of the all, it would be a nucleus around which a specious conservatism would rally against them the abettors of every infamy, and the interested in every abuse.

"By Jupiter," say we, with Plato, let *our* city or republic become not thus permanently two—each part "always plotting against the other,"—but gradually and then for ever one.

Democracy is *a power and a system*, a life and an organisation of life. Manhood-equality represents both, without contradiction and without alloy.

DEMOCRACY AND NATIONAL UNITY.

"The grand point is the development of the powers of all its single citizens in their perfect individuality; it must therefore pursue no other object than that which they cannot procure of themselves, viz., security, and that this is the only true and infallible means to connect by a strong and enduring bond things which appear at first sight contradictory,—the aims of the State as a whole, and the collective aims of all its individual citizens.—*Baron W. von Humboldt*, "Sphere and Duties of Government," p. 184.

"*Each individual national genius* is to be treated as only *one individual, in the process of Universal History*, which is the exhibition of the divine absolute development of spirit in its highest forms. The forms which these *grades of progress* assume are the characteristic national spirits of history; the peculiar tenor of their moral life, of their Government, their art, religion, and science. *To realise these grades is the boundless impulse of the world-spirit*, —the goal of its irresistible urging; for this division into organic members, and the full *development* of each is its idea. . . . Universal History exhibits the *gradation* in the development of that principle, whose substantial purport is the consciousness of Freedom."

"The State is here *a living universal Spirit*, but which is at the same time the self-conscious spirit of the individuals composing the community."

"The essential condition and distinction in regard to various phases of Democracy is, *what is the character of the individual members?*"—*Hegel*, pp. 258, 260–2.

"Individuality will be a term of greater comprehension, and *nations* free and enlightened, *will hereafter become one complex individual*, as single men now are. The whole species will become one grand society, one individual family. . . A new age will make its appearance, an age of astonishment to vulgar minds, of surprise and dread to tyrants, of emancipation to a great people, and of hope to the whole world."—*Volney*.

"*True union* is such a harmony as makes all the particular parts, opposite as they may seem to us, concur in the general welfare of the country in the same manner *as discords in music contribute to the general melody* of sound. . . Prosperity which alone is true peace.—*Montesquieu*, v. iii, p. 65.

"A People cannot rise but by a principle or by a man."—*Mazzini.*

"The People in combination with men of genius, this will be the Voltaic pile of civilization. The mysterious dynasty of men of genius."—*Hugo.*

"In the reality, in the highest power of the People, they are solely in the man of genius; in him resides the great soul. All the world is surprised to see the inert masses vibrate at his slightest word. Why wonder? That voice is the People's; they speak in that man, and God with him. Then it is we may truly say, 'Vox populi, vox Dei.'"—*Michelet.*

"The mighty genius of Athens has made as much of an imperceptible city, in two or three centuries, as twelve nations of the middle ages in a thousand years."—*Ibid.*

"Germany, who in the seventeenth and eighteenth centuries was groping about to find herself, has at length discovered herself in Goethe, Schiller, and Beethoven; it is only since that period that she has been able to aspire earnestly after unity."—*Ibid.*

"One of my grandest ideas was the agglomeration or concentration of the same geographical nations which had been divided and portioned by revolution and politics. Thus there were in Europe though scattered, more than thirty millions French, fifteen millions Spaniards, fifteen millions Italians, thirty millions Germans. I wished to make of each of these peoples one simple body of a nation. It is with such a cortége that it would have been grand to advance to prosperity and the benediction of ages. I felt myself worthy of that glory."—*Napoleon I.*

Chapter VIII.

DEMOCRACY AND NATIONAL UNITY.

Individuality and nationality.

Powers of association and nationality.

The people and great men.

"When a Prince puts his confidence in the People,—a man of courage, &c., himself,—he will never be deserted by them." —*Machiavel.*

"The People are extremely well qualified *for choosing* those whom they are to intrust with part of their authority. They have only to be determined by things to which they cannot be strangers, and by facts that are obvious to sense. They can tell when a person has fought many battles, and been crowned with success; they are therefore very capable of electing a general. They can tell when a judge is assiduous in his office, gives general satisfaction, and has never been charged with bribery: this is sufficient for choosing a prætor. They are struck with the magnificence or riches of a fellow-citizen: no more is requisite for electing an ædile. *These are facts of which they can have better information in a public forum than a monarch in his palace.* But are they capable of conducting an intricate affair, of seizing and improving the opportunity and critical moment of action? No; this surpasses their abilities.

"Should we doubt of the People's *natural capacity in respect to the discernment of merit,* we need only cast an eye on the series of *surprising elections made by the Athenians and Romans,* which no one surely will attribute to hazard.

"We know that, though the people of Rome assumed to themselves the right of *raising plebeians to public offices, yet they never would exert this power*; and though at Athens the magistrates were allowed, by the law of Aristides, to be elected from all the different classes of inhabitants, there never was a case, says Xenophon, that the common people petitioned for employments which could endanger either their security or their glory."—*Montesquieu,* v. i, pp. 11 and 12.

Three axiomatic truths express and define the effect of Democracy on nationality.

The first is, that the more of freedom and

equality there is in a nation, the more numerous, complex, intimate, and harmonious the inter-relations of individuals, and the greater their development.

The second is that indicated by De Tocqueville, that wherever freedom increases, "the faculty of association must increase in the same ratio."

The third is, that the People in crises always know and appreciate their great men.

Here, then, is the creation and increment of power by freedom: its combination; and its effective unity.

Nothing can resist a force thus always new created, thus combined, and thus wielded, but such a compact, unyielding, impregnable phalanx of prerogative, privilege, and ignorance, as in resisting *Democracy*, must also destroy the *nation*.

Life and freedom,—motion and power, must be taken together for better or for worse;—

> "Those," said Montesquieu, "who expect in a free State to see the People undaunted in war and pusillanimous in peace, are certainly desirous of impossibilities; and it may be advanced as a general rule that *whenever a perfect calm is visible, in a State that calls itself a Republic, the spirit of liberty no longer subsists*."

That the aggregate national manhood constitutes the universal national spirit, and also assumes naturally and necessarily a certain outward form and organisation, is a truism, but a truism ill-understood. It follows from it, that until the universal manhood is prepared by education, and admitted to power,—there can be no complete national Unity.

That Democracy, or the rule of the equal voting entire national manhood, conduces to the intensest and completest national unity, is also a truism, but until lately no such nation existed, and its existence involves a new world of fact and theory.

National unity is threefold,—material, intellectual, and moral. It corresponds to the three elements of manhood,—of the body, mind, and character.

National manhood bears the same relation to national unity, that manhood does to individual life.

If this requires demonstration, we have only to consider what are the complete national unities,—the formal and essential conditions of a complete national life.

A complete nation has complete and sound its *material bases* (unity of race, language, boundary, and climate), its *individuality* (or unity of ideas and character, and institution), and its *organic functions*, or its Legislative and Executive.

In respect of *individuality*, Democracy guarantees to the nation its natural symmetrical growth and character, preparing for it the most favorable conditions of development in Free School, Press, Church, and Assembly. "Individuality is development."

In respect of the *organic functions* of a democratic State, the People, by an equal and universal act, create the Legislature, and the Executive is an absolute impersonation of their will.

The People,—the whole national manhood—create the institutions. There is therefore the greatest attainable certainty (apart from the question of the excellence of the creation) that the creature and the creator will be at one.

In all other systems the institutions are made, not by the all, but *for* and *by* the one, the few, or the many. The inference is obvious.

In reference to the intense *Executive* unity necessary to Democracies, and secured by the American Government, the Emperor Napoleon III. has the following profound remarks :—

"Whatever Government a nation gives itself, whether monarchical, constitutional, or republican, *one of its first and fundamental wants is the spirit of combination.*

"In a monarchical and aristocratic country, the spirit of combination results from the existence even of those great traditional bodies which receive and perpetuate the idea of former administrations.

"But to enable a chief of the democratic Government to give *unity* and consistency to public affairs, he must have a system, and be armed with the necessary means of adopting it. The national representation, possessed of its immense rights, and holding the budget in its hands, is always in a situation to moderate and to restrain the system, and to put a boundary to its encroachments, if they become contrary to the real or apparent interests of the country.

"In electing a President for four years, the United States are aware, in the first place, what system they are raising to power, and they are afterwards certain that this system will be frankly carried out and tried for four years, without any impediments arising from the ministers empowered to apply it, whatever this system may be, whether peace or war, banking, liberation, or slavery, protection, or the annexing a new State.

"If after having rendered the President responsible for the acts of his Government, the American constitution had imposed on him *the necessity of receiving his ministers from the hands of a parliamentary majority,* although these ministers differed from him on many subjects, or even had totally different ideas, the constitution would sullenly, and as it were, regretting that she granted them, rob him of the means of fulfilling duties imposed. It is a manifest truth which will not admit of argument, that *to be responsible you must be free, so that the ministers of the President of the United States are the objects of his direct and free choice,* the depositaries and organs of his ideas, which they know, they accept, and they obey,—are disengaged from all political responsibility towards the chambers, and entirely *covered by the responsibility of the President,* whose views they only record and carry out.

"Such ideas and such facts are, as we have said, *an elementary and fundamental necessity in democratic countries,* where the chief of the Government who is empowered to direct public affairs upon his own responsibility, should be armed with the necessary authority for effecting his projects.

"It is surprising that Monsieur de Tocqueville, who has studied the Government of the United States, should not have perceived as the result of his meditations the spirit of so simple and so wise an arrangement."—*Louis Napoleon Bonaparte.* "Life and Works," vol. ii, pp. 392, 393.

§

The result of the ideal best Government would be, industrial, political, and religious freedom, securing universal distribution of comforts and universal mental activity, *and crowning all this with an intense and invincible feeling of nationality, and aspirations after glory, greatness, purity, and God.*

Does Democracy, which does everything for the individual, do as much as any other system of polity *for the State?*

Securing freedom, and competency, and progress, does it also inspire loyalty to order, to greatness, to genius, to the ideal, and to God?

If so, there is in addition to individual success and culture,—national unity, and national greatness, and the problem of Democracy is completely solved.

We have shown that Democracy transcends all other polities as far in regard to the *higher* qualities of national life, as it transcends them in providing comforts and competence, and a political sphere for the greatest number.

Democracy and nationality mutually support each other. It is the most assured conclusion of political science. The most complete performance of vital individual functions *must* produce the most perfect aggregate unity, and the highest kind of life. The greater the proportion of individuals amply developed and equipped, free and trained to every variety of interest and aptitude of exertion, —the greater the number of such individuals in a State, the more complete their inter-relations,—the stronger, the truer, the intenser, the resulting *national* individuality or unity.

The American nation *has* thus become "one complex individual, as single men" were formerly, and the consequences are proportioned to such a state of things. The American nation is the completest vital organic unity in existence, and the idea of American nationality is the greatest secular power of any age or country.

A complete nation is necessarily a complete Democracy. For it is a nation of completely equipped men, who have known and conquered their rights. And Democracy in its turn is a chief factor and guarantee of nationality, for it binds up the whole in unity of interest, sentiment, and action.

In Democracies individual intercourse is more equal, thorough, and universal, and therefore the nationality is more homogeneous,—more completely an Individuality.

A true Democracy is the rule of the All, and is therefore a Popular Unity.

Democracy makes its own laws, and tends therefore to Loyalty,—again a unity.

Democracies possess extraordinary powers of association, and *thus* tend to unity.

In Democracies the Church is free. It teaches mankind the virtues of conservatism and self-restraint, and gives them the motive power of progress, whilst itself shares none of the perils of party and unites with no faction.

In true Democracies the will of the People tends to express itself through *one man*, the elect of the People—in crises always elected to do *a certain work*,—responsible to the People alone, and therefore with authority one and indivisible. This direct concurrence and universal fiat of the All, expressed upon each great national question, as in the order of Providence and of a People's History it arises, and enacted by one man, elected for the purpose, and upon whom all responsibility centres, appears to be *the very highest position, form, and expression of unity, intelligence, and power.*

It is in these respects that we are driven again and again to consult the only working model of Democracy, as seen in America.

§

Of the two processes which constitute the history of the American nation, the first, *the tendency of States to a national conglomerate,* is no new thing in politics, and but marks an era in the life of that nation. The second, *the tendency of progressive civilisation, education, and freedom, to Democracy, and of such Democracy to unequalled national unity,* is a phenomenon of direct, unique, and universal interest.

The principle of this tendency is indeed but a truism, yet it has in America reached so advanced a stage, and wrought on so vast an area, as to strike the world as a new principle and power.

The science of Politics is the science of Human Nature—and something more. There are material elements in politics, and there is also the Infinite—God's will, developing.

"The One, the Few, the Many, and the All. Freedom and order. The universal People's will, and the universal will of God. How to reconcile Liberty with Necessity, or orderly Development with Destiny which represents the final consummation?" The one and the all are, as ruling powers, the only fixed quantities. The few, and the many, are either instalments and compromises, or quackeries, delusions, and names.

The theory of Democracy is catholic and unassailable. The practice exists only in the United States of America. The possible failure therefore of Democracy *there,* would only subject the world to new cycles of revolutions, and to other circles of vicissitudes, of which the only certain things would be the torment and desolation of the process, and the ultimate triumph of the principle.

The true conservatism of the world was therefore concerned to see this fight fought out fairly and to the end.

The wondering and enquiring world saw, in America, certain forces contending on the *widest scale,* and urged on by *intensest passions,* with the *most inexorable resolve,* and on questions of *universal interest.*

That the strength of an EDUCATED and prosperous DEMOCRACY, which is also a nation, was till lately, amongst political equations, an unknown quantity, added to the interest of the question by adding to its uncertainty.

Democracy must be justified of her children. Each theory of Government has its own raison d'être in the conditions of the age and the peculiarities of race. Democracy is good when the all (or the majority) are good. Oligarchy is good when only the few are good. Autocracy is good when the one is good. We need not point out which theory is narrow, local, temporary, partial in ideal, and perilous in practice, nor which is glorious in principle and grand in universality and strength. We contend that to this "universality," Democracy combines also the intensity of Autocracy. Necessity may justify the rule of the one or the few, but fatuity itself could not insist on the perfectibility of a class, and deny that of the race.

In the one case the guarantee of the commonweal is the *intelligence and virtue of the few;* in the other, it is that of the many or the all. In Democracies public virtue is intelligent self-interest. Inasmuch as men are apt to be the most intelligent about their own interests, an educated Democracy is a better guarantee than an educated Oligarchy, and inasmuch as it is an universal one it is the strongest also.

§

But the question of individuality as well as of unity, depends much upon the relations between the People and their natural leaders. Because the latter are not only the advanced guard of truth in science and of morals, but they alone can master the will, and command the faith of a nation in crises.

The *experimentum crusis,* therefore, of Democracy is this,—Can the many submit themselves on occasion to the guidance of the ONE or of the few, who, in supreme moments of national existence can alone work out the national salvation? In other words, *can freedom confer on a nation that intense unity,* without which a nation cannot weather certain crises?

The great law of intellect and genius is *inequality.* The great law of national right is equality. We contend that nature makes the equation, in a Democracy where the all possess the equal voice and right to distinguish those whom nature has crowned their masters.

Equality develops Individual forces and self-reliance. Can it also with all its learning learn in stress of battle this one great lesson of strategy and statescraft, namely, unity? The all in the one, and the one for the all? Can it choose its leaders well, and follow them?

So far from doubting this, we believe that a true Democracy develops a special faculty of selection. The natural leaders of our race will always be few. They are the natural aristocracy. To recognise them requires intelligence and disinterestedness, and the universality of Democracy guarantees the one, whilst education would guarantee the other. The masses have a natural power of recognising their great men. What says Mill hereon?—

"No Government by a Democracy or a numerous aristocracy, never did, or could rise above mediocrity, except in so far as the sovereign many, have let themselves be guided (*which in their best times they always have done*) by the counsels and influence of a more highly gifted and instructed one or few. . . The honor and glory of the average man is that he is capable of following that initiative."—*Mill on "Liberty,"* p. 119.

And from the opposite extreme of mental character (Hugo), but with perhaps more intuitive profundity, we meet with the following exposition, and indeed glorification, of men of genius as related to the People, and of the intimate relations and loyalty of the People to them.

"No one can foresee the quantity of light which will be brought forth by letting the People be in communication with men of genius. This combination of hearts will be the Voltaic pile of civilisation. *We know of nothing too lofty for the People.* The People are a great soul. *They throw themselves passionately into the beautiful.* . . . The transfiguration of enthusiasm operates. . . The multitude, and *in this lies their grandeur, are profoundly open to the ideal.*"

"Contact with the beautiful agitates ecstatically the surface of multitudes, sure sign that the depth is sounded. All the teachings are due to the People. *The more divine the light, the more is it made for this simple soul.*"

"People! the author, God, dedicates geniuses to thee."

"True History explains how Francis II. succeeds to Henry II., &c., but not how Watt succeeds to Popin, and Fulton to Watt. The lamp which smokes on the opaque frontage of royal accessions hides the starry reflection that the creators of civilisation throw over ages. Not an historian of that series points out the divine affiliation of human prodigies, that practical logic of Providence."—*Hugo.*

The problem is two-fold: to discover the ideas, and to obey them; to discover the men who, being greatest, serve most and best the age. Men there are in every age, sent by God to lead it. If *they* lead it not, it is unled. *This is the root and justification of the autocratic principle*: necessity,—the necessity of leadership. But there is another necessity,—that of the followers; the aspirations and the wants of the million-headed and million-hearted people. Age after age,—nation after nation, have the People been put back to school to misfortune, because they were not prepared, as an entire People, to learn the lessons, or to deserve and accept the progress and the glory set them or won for them by their leaders.

And until one true nation had done this, the best influence of nation upon nation was unemployed, and the world yet waited for its first great step.

Therefore if a People cannot or will not recognise the men meant to connect epoch with epoch, and each stage with the next, other nations are promoted over them to urge on the universal result.

"The People and the Men," unless they act together, the *form* of Government is failure, or revolt, or a despotism. If the men are not the natural leaders, there is despotism and miscarriage. —Neither a true oligarchy nor a true People, but anarchy instead of Democracy, and Devil's unction for the Lord's anointing. The People comprehend, but must act through their *leaders*, and we claim that an instructed Democracy is the only means possible whereby these two can be united for the greatest commonweal.

If there be an overwhelming physical force and weight of institutions against the People, then the nation halts, until false systems are overthrown or destroyed. What an instance of this, in 1776, when the great commoner stood alone for the People of both hemispheres, against a dastard Oligarchy scrambling for privilege, and an imbecile king, holding desperately on with all the soul he had, to Prerogative! What an instance, again, the era of dead lock and compromise, before the late war in America!

No Oligarchy ever did, or ever can, either maintain itself or lead the people, *unless it lead the People towards Democracy.* And we know of no Oligarchy in history that was not more intent on remaining an Oligarchy than on leading the People from itself.

The natural kings of the earth lead its common

people. The relations between *them* are eternal. There is no other progress.

Let, then, the People acquire the power to choose the men, and the men will conquer for them the path into the future. Let education also be universal. Then will the best thoughts of the best men of the past, and the energies and will of the great men of the present, become the common property of the People. And where the universal progress is not overshadowed by sectional or exclusive interests, this is the natural, the necessary, and the inevitable.

§

There are three passions or vital creative forces in the Universe; the first is the passion of God for Souls. The second the passion of the sexes The third the passion of the People for Genius.

First, Creation. Next, the family Unity. Lastly, the Unity of parties, communities, and nations.

The People can only unite and advance under a principle or a man.

God loved and created man. From the one sprang the All. Love replenishes and perpetuates creation, and prepares from an union of souls the minor family unities that prepare for nations. Genius presides over the making of nations and the propaganda of truth, and prepares by the arts and sciences the material media of international and world-wide Union.

The universal reason of a People, and the intuitions of genius, bear somewhat the same relation to the ideal and the infinite. The relationship between genius and the People is a sacred and intuitive passion. *Between them they procreate nations.*

The *universal reason* corresponds, as far as mere reason can, with *the absolute in right* and *in truth*, and the absolute is the warrant of all our aspirations and of all our advances,—whether for this world or that which is to come. This correspondence is the basis of Democracy and of Belief.

The *universal interest*, also, is the *absolute right.* "God and the People" is the ultimate expression of this fact, for God rules the People by his lieutenants,—the Prophets, the Priests, the Lawgivers, the Warriors, and the Martyrs, through the ages.

Common sense tells us that the foregoing must be the conditions of the highest national unity. America,—the only country of "equality of conditions," tells us that they are so.

So much for this momentous four-fold truism, that development qualifies for, and inevitably leads to association, that the two necessitate equality; that equality tends to level all pretensions, save those of intellect and character, and that thus Democracy tends to national unity and life.

"The vocation of man" and the vocation of men are subjects that cannot be separated. When these political and personal vocations are fulfilled, then, indeed, do progress and unity combine in the result attributed by Fichte to a complete humanity;—

"The dead heavy mass, which did but stop up space, has

vanished; and in its place there flows onward, with the rushing music of mighty waves, an eternal stream of life and power and action, which issues from the original source of all life.

"Through that which to others seems a dead mass my eye beholds this *eternal life and movement* rising in ever-increasing growth, and ever purifying itself to a more spiritual expression. The universe is to me *no longer that eternally-repeated play*; it has become transfigured before me, and now bears *the one stamp of spiritual life, a constant progress towards higher perfection* in a line that runs out into the infinite.

"The sun rises and sets, the stars sink and reappear, and all the spheres hold their circle dance; but they never return again as they disappeared. Every hour which they lead on, every morning and every evening sinks with *new increase upon the world*; new life and new love descend from the spheres like dew-drops from the clouds, and encircle nature as cool night the earth."

"The individual," says Hegel, "traverses as a unity various grades of Development, and remains the same individual; in like manner also does a People, till the spirit which it embodies reaches the grade of universality." The impulse of the world-spirit to realise these grades is indeed boundless,—the urging to its goal, irresistible.

Such is the natural course where the nation-life is not called to halt by sectional combinations against it,—where Democracy can run its career.

In the last analysis, UNIVERSALITY and UNITY are the two-fold object of Governments, and how can either be secured without the all? The interests of the universal People, by the will of the universal People, free to learn of and to follow their natural leaders;—this is the formulum of efficiency and right. Governments are good in proportion as they approach it.

"If," said Michelet, "God has placed anywhere the type of the *political city*, it was according to every appearance, in the *moral city*,—in the soul of man. Well! what does this soul do first? It takes up a fixed position, meditates there, forms for itself a body, a dwelling place, a train of ideas. And then it can act. In the same manner, the soul of a people ought to make for itself a central point of organism.

"Nationality is ever the life of the world: if dead, all would be dead.

"Let us sum up this history (of mere mechanical progress). The State, without the country; industry and literature, without art; philosophy, without research; humanity, without man."

"The spirit of nationality" (said Burke) "is at once the bond and the safeguard of kingdoms; it is something above laws and beyond thrones,—the impalpable element, the inner life of States; but anti-nationality is the confusion and the downfall of kingdoms,—it is a blight and a mildew to the heritage of the People."

DEMOCRACY IN AMERICA.

The Precedent.

"The contest began in America. Considered in its unity, as interesting mankind, the question was, shall *the reformation* developed to the fulness of free enquiry, succeed in its protest against the middle ages."—*Bancroft.*

"Soon after the reformation, a few People came over into their new world for conscience sake. This apparently trivial incident may transfer the great seat of empire into America." —*John Adams.*

"It may prove the advantage of all oppressed Christendom."—*Gustavus Adolphus.*

"The consequences of this design will be favorable to all Christendom, to Europe, to the whole world."—*Oxenstiern.*

"America is therefore the land of the future, where in the ages that lie before us, the burden of the world's history shall reveal itself. It is a land of desire for all those who are weary of the historical lumber-room of old Europe. It is for America to abandon the ground on which hitherto the history of the world has developed itself. As regards history our concern must be with that which has been and that which is. In regard to philosophy we have to do with that which is neither past nor future, but with that which has an eternal existence,—with Reason."—*Hegel's Philosophy of History.*

"America has left behind it, in its passage over the ocean, *the cerements of the feudal system, hereditary aristocracy, primogeniture, entails, and the Established Church.*

"Their fundamental institutions,—*the principle of social and political equality*, the absence of hereditary rank, of primogeniture and entails, their free Churches and common schools, are essentially those of the new, not those of the old world." —*Goldwin Smith.*

"I regret to say that I only see at the present time two Governments which well fulfil their providential mission; these are the two colossi at either end of the world. Whilst our old European centre is like a volcano consuming itself in its own crater, the two nations, Oriental and Occidental, proceed unhesitatingly towards perfection, the one at the will of one man, and the other by liberty."—*Napoleon III.*

"This *general misery of mankind* is a fact which can be accounted for upon one only of two suppositions; either that there is a natural tendency in population to increase faster than capital, or that *capital has by some means been prevented from increasing* so fast as it has a tendency to increase."—*James Mill*, Political Economy.

"126–45 increase of *Wealth* per cent. in ten years.
35–59 ditto *Population* ditto ditto."—
American Census, 1860.

"We are draining,—*we shall drain from the old world its most precious, its most important possession*,—its intelligent laboring classes. Thus emigration will change our relation to the European nations Men and money make a nation powerful. Our true policy is peace."—*North American Review*.

"50,000,000 acres of Public land appropriated to educational purposes."—*Census*, 1860.

"Here more and more care is given to provide Education for every one born on our soil. Here religion, released from political connection, refuses to subserve the craft of Statesmen, and becomes the spiritual life of the People. Here the national domain is offered, and held in millions of separate freeholds, so that our fellow citizens, beyond the occupants of any other part of the earth, *constitute in reality a People.*"

"Under the provisions of the *Homestead Act*, 1,160,533 acres of the public lands were entered during the last fiscal year." "The *Homestead Policy* was established after long and earnest resistance; experience proves its wisdom. The lands in the hands of industrious settlers, whose labor creates wealth, and contributes to the public resources, are worth more to the United States than if they had been reserved as a *solitude for future purchasers*."—*Johnson*, Message, 1865.

"Compare the slow progress of those European countries of which the wealth depends very much upon their commerce and manufactures, with the rapid advance of our North American colonies, of which the wealth is founded altogether in agriculture. Through the greater part of Europe the number of inhabitants is not (A.D. 1784) supposed to double in less than five hundred years. In several of our North American colonies it is found to double in twenty or five and twenty years. In Europe, the law of primogeniture and perpetuities of different kinds prevent the division of great estates, and thereby hinders the multiplication of small proprietors."—*Smith's Wealth of Nations*, v. ii, p. 131.

CHAPTER IX.

DEMOCRACY IN AMERICA.

THE PRECEDENT.

"The American Democracy is a territorial Democracy."—*D'Israeli.*

"The whole freedom of man consists either in *spiritual or civil liberty* . . . and advancements of every person according to his merit: the enjoyment of those never more certain, and the access to these never more open, than in a free commonwealth. *Both which, in my opinion, may be best and soonest obtained, if every county in the land were made a kind of subordinate commonalty or commonwealth.*"—*Milton.*

"Now my idea of American civilisation is that it is a second part, a repetition of that same sublime confidence in the public conscience and the public thought that made the groundwork of Grecian Democracy."

"Not only the inevitable, but the best power this side of the ocean, is the unfettered common sense of the masses.

"We are launched on the ocean of an unchained Democracy, with no safety but in those laws that bind the ocean to its bed,—the instinctive love of right in the popular heart."—*Wendell Phillips.*

"Not Democracy in America, but *free Christianity* in America, is the real key to the study of the People and their institutions. Christianity the great reality of history. In Europe Christianity was paralysed by divisions into national Churches. So that until State and Church were separated, a higher spirit was hopeless.

"The Church in the old world was therefore unable to do what the men of two centuries ago proposed, when England was in her noblest mood, for never had she been so noble as in the days of Hampden, Falkland, Milton, and Cromwell, and when she sent forth a religious band, who founded a colony in the new world. By this exodus, which brought Christianity out of the State Churches, men escaped from feudalism to the system founded upon equality and justice."—*Goldwin Smith.*

Three mighty problems, in which all Peoples and systems are concerned, are now, in the fullness of time, nearly worked out upon the American Continent.

The making of the American nation, Federation, and Democracy.

That making means the ascendency of the nationality over its two deadly foes,—materialism and oligarchy. It means the definitive victory of national unity, not only over law-made classes (the vice of the old world), but over sectional and sinister interests supported by "State" power.

It is the NEXT STEP, in the world logic of history, to the English and French Revolutions, which settled, on the carcases of Kings, the principle of the right divine of Peoples.

The English revolution failed of its direct purpose. The people could not continue in power, but they had broken the spell of prerogative, and made possible a successful contest between the few and the one, the families and the sovereign. It took England from Cromwell to the Reform Bill to get from the power of the few to that of the many.

The sea saved the English from an intervention of Catholics and Legitimists, or perhaps from an European war.

The French, without the sea, *had* their European war. Since then, the revolution has energised the empire and the empire has organised the revolution, both have been a propagandism for Europe, and French emperors have been its hierarchs or victims.

What the sea did for the English, the ocean has done for America and the world.

Three thousand miles of water, which first saved the infant Republic, have now saved the oligarchs and men-stealers of the South from extermination. They have also saved America a thirty years' war, which European Statesmen might have made into a universal war, had the Peoples of Europe allowed them.

The next step to the assertion of the representative or the national sovereignty is now taken.

The Royal nation is at last definitively constituted. The People sit at last in their own Purple,—with no equal yet in the world, and with no master save their conscience, their reason, and their God.

It is proved not only that slavery is not necessary to Republics, but that it cannot exist in a true Republic. And as for oligarchy (a form of barbarism), the voiding of it out, is an act, so to speak, of mere Republican nature.

And we need not explain here, how that nature, the temperate zone, and Republicanism, being all against slavery, the South had always to choose between secession and defeat, or concession and the gradual destruction of Slavery, and with it, of the material basis of oligarchy.

Free labour was everywhere invading, and "demoralising" the border States, and the waiting game of the North, working with the exactness of economics, and the remorselessness of Destiny, left no one chance for slaveholders, save a move further South, a re-opening on a gigantic scale of the Slave Trade, and the erection in the real South of a veritable Slave Empire.

This chance, the "Statesmanship" of Davis, and the armies of Lee, have lost to the Devil and to the South, for ever and a day.

The principle of national unity has triumphed over the licence of individuals, and even the licence of States. Secession is the reductio ad absurdum of State rights, as anarchy in that of freedom. America now presents the completest example yet of what a State should be. In complete contrast to German Federalism, it secures the full liberty of the individual, and reconciles it to the strongest expression of nationality.

"The political constitution of Germany (says Hegel, p. 455, 'Philosophy of History') involves no thought, no conception of the proper aim of a State. . . . The establishment of a constituted anarchy, such as the world had never before seen; i. e., the position that an empire is properly a unity, a totality, a state, while yet all the relations are determined so exclusively on the principle of private right, that the privilege of all the constituent parts of that empire to act for themselves, contrarily to the interest of the whole, or to neglect that which its interest demands, is guaranteed and secured by the most inviolable sanctions."

This mighty danger *is* passed for America. Instead of straining the principle of State rights to the denial of national and individual rights, and to the formation of a "constituted anarchy," it has gone naturally and necessarily on, upon its natural unities of race, language, religion, boundary, and (now of) institutions, to a Democratic empire.

The great Montesquieu thus unconsciously pronounces upon the advantages of *this* Republican Federation :—

"It is therefore very probable that mankind would have been, at length, obliged to live constantly under the Government of a single person, had they not contrived a kind of constitution that has *all the internal advantages of a republican*, together with *the external force of a monarchical* Government. I mean, *a confederate republic.*

"This form of Government is a convention, by which several petty estates agree to become members of a larger one, which they intend to establish. It is a kind of assemblage of societies, that constitute a new one, *capable of increasing by means of farther associations*, till they arrive to such a degree of power, as to be able to provide for the security of the whole body.

"It was these associations that so long contributed to the prosperity of Greece. By these the Romans attacked the whole globe; and by these alone the whole globe withstood them. For, when Rome was arriving to her highest pitch of grandeur, it was the associations beyond the Danube and the Rhine, associations formed by the terror of her arms, that enabled the barbarians to resist her. . . .

"A republic of this kind, able to withstand an external force, *may support itself without any internal corruption;* the form of this society prevents all manner of inconveniences.

"If a single member should attempt to usurp the supreme power, he could not be supposed to have an equal authority and credit in all the confederate States. Were he to have too great an influence over one, this would alarm the rest; were he to subdue a part, that which would still remain free might oppose him with forces independent of those which he had usurped, and overpower him before he could be settled in his usurpation.

"*Should a popular insurrection happen in one of the confederate States, the others are able to quell it.* Should abuses creep into one part they are reformed by those that remain sound. The State may be destroyed on one side and not on the other; the confederacy may be dissolved, and the confederates preserve their sovereignty.

"As this Government is composed of petty republics, it enjoys the internal happiness of each; and, with regard to its external situation, by means of the association, it possesseth *all the advantages of large monarchies.*"—*Montesquieu*, vol. i. pp. 165–167.

The American nation and Democracy are made.

The spirit of Republicanism will recommence its moral propagandism under all the thrones of the world, and it needs no base of operations, for its base is in every soul of man.

The loss and despair of the Oligarchic Empire is the hope and the gain of every human creature.

The question to be put to any given nation respecting the system of Government that claims to rule it, is, as we have seen, always this :—" Has it *also* promoted the *Individual Manhood-Development* of that nation,—diffused it to a reasonable extent, and raised it to a certain quality ?"

If it have not, the thing is hardly to be called " Government." If it have, one need scarcely ask about the inevitable results, national unity, progress, and conservatism. Still less need we fear that proximity, or increasing compactness of the social state can alter the problem or the result.

The first question, then, wherewith to test this great democratic precedent, is the individual ; it is the problem of the effect of an universal education and enfranchisement upon individual well-being.

The second is of intermediate powers (called, in America, States).

The third is of national unity.

The fourth is of the balance and adjustment of the rights and properties of Individual, State, and Nation.

The fifth is the problem of the safe increase of

States, in the formation and maintenance of vaster conglomerates of empire than have hitherto been practicable.

Many other questions there are which are American only, but the grand all-involving problem, both American and universal, is *the effect of the universality and equality of the basis upon the Development of individuals, the Adjustment of subordinate parts, and the Unity of the whole.*

"Universality,"—of vote power, interest, and intelligence.

"Equality,"—nothing against manhood or nationality. No law-made classes and castes against the first; no corporate obstructions or sub-sovereignties as against the second.

Religion being free, it will be purer and stronger.

Intelligence, being free in school, press, church, and assembly, the motive power developed will be greater.

Greater Stability, greater Loyalty, Material, Political, and Religious Development. The motive power and the organisation as nearly coinciding as possible. A true "Democracy,"—for *its rule is of, by, and for the People.*

These problems America has now more completely solved than any other nation. FEDERAL REPUBLICANISM is the term that best expresses the fact. It combines the three principles (so constantly alleged to be contradictory) of Equality, Adjustment, and Unity.

Respecting these principles, it may be alleged in detail that the "Freedom" of the American citizen is not at present equalled;* that the activity and self-reliance of his intellect is a proverb; that their provisions for education and religious teaching are unrivalled; that their powers of association were one of the special themes of De Tocqueville, and are unique; that the public life of the People is equally energetic, the highest offices rewarding personal ambition; and that the road of civilisation is always open to the People, and the next step in national progress always agitated, and often settled *beforehand*, and decided by the entire nation for itself in the presidential and other contests.

Further, not only is this war an unequalled test and triumph of moral principle, but it is in one aspect a struggle of national against sectional sovereignty, the result of a widening and intensifying of the sentiment of patriotism during the last epoch. Its nationality is thus "completer." It is also "stronger," inasmuch as individual freedom is now also completer. Americans know and elevate their best men. They unanimously reject all theories of Church endowment that would make religion an accomplice with class jealousies, despotism, or reaction. Their dependence on the Collective Reason has become more entire and direct.

* "The 'tyranny of opinion' in America in the midst of a dangerous civil war, appeared to him very like the freedom of opinion which other countries enjoy in time of perfect peace." —*Goldwin Smith*, Jan. 22nd, 1866.

Their battle was and is against treason to the will of a constitutional majority. Their national unity has proved itself equal to the greatest strain that was ever applied to an administration. The temporary submission to mediocre Presidents in the era of compromise which the desperation of Slavery enforced, and the treason of factions permitted, is an exception that proves the rule.

These considerations are indeed amplified elsewhere, but it suffices here to say that that which had been a priori a *truism*, is, a posteriori, a *fact;* that Democracy, of all systems, develops the qualities of manhood most freely and amply, that where nature is left unshackled, she works best; that the freest Government calls forth the best qualities, that the best qualities make the best men,—the best men the best citizens,—the best citizens the best community; that, in fine, the triumph of *Individuality*, with its interconnections free and infinite, is also the triumph of *Nationality*, —"that the most complete Democracy is also the completest, intensest, and strongest of nations."

§

But leaving these positions, most of which are now admitted, and all of which are getting more undeniable every day, we address ourselves to that which may be considered the *crux* as regards this working model of Democracy, namely, the question of the *conservative* effect of republican principles and institutions.

The bases of DEMOCRATIC CONSERVATISM in

America are two-fold,—*natural and artificial*, arising from harmony of the institutions with the national life, and from the free conditions of that life.

According to Montesquieu and common sense, there is in every nation "a general spirit upon which power itself is founded," and where constitutional forms agree with the national principle and passion, and allow of ready modification by an orderly expression of the national will, *there* Government can be strong, and the nation conservative, and yet progressive.

American conservatism is both natural and artificial, essential and formal. The first depends of course upon a continued right direction of public opinion. The second upon a continued coincidence between the executive and public opinion.

We shall see, and *this is the great lesson, that as power and opportunity recede from the nation* to its representatives, and from them to the representatives of States, they lose true conservatism and true Democracy together, and tend more to weakness, conservatism and anarchy.

The American People, whose passion is equality, have conquered it and deserve it. *With it alone is the mean of conservatism and progress.*

It is the pretence of the old politics where the People and the Government are never identified, that good Government depends upon an elaborately arranged and accurately adjusted system of check and counter-check, to keep in balance or mutually to destroy or neutralise the opposing selfishness and follies *of the People.* In other words, that national unity cannot rest upon the *nation.* The American constitution adopts the principle of a balance, but applies it, not as against the People, *but as against officials.*

The history of the American Government and People shews throughout, *that the People have been the true Conservatives,* that the checks have been useless or worse, and that where they have been dispensed with, they have been dispensed with by conservatives for evil, and by the People for good.

The American system will not entertain the possibility of standing armies of soldiers or of priests to cajole or coerce the People. That system endeavours, not even to oppose the national will by official machinery, but simply to make sure of an adequate unanimity. It seeks and bows to the collective wisdom equally and adequately expressed.

And here again simplicity and nature bear away the palm. The executive is but the arm of opinion, lengthened through four years, and the People are the constitution. Both are destroying the treason of a minority, aimed alike against Democracy, public opinion, conservatism, and themselves. Public opinion and the executive can only quarrel when the President or Vice attempts, during his four years term, to cast off his opinions and his party, and to repudiate the platform for which he has worked and conquered, or when some new and startling question arises in dispute. In either case public opinion could instantly combine against its instrument, and secure his extinction at the earliest constitutional period, if not before. In the latter case public opinion would express itself as it has often done, through its representatives and by convention, but in completer fashion than in other constitutional countries, where the representation is on a narrower base.

It may be objected;—"This is indeed an unchained Democracy." We answer, such is the boast of Americans. The nation depends on ITSELF. It can neither be pulled down nor kept up by its servants. And as cosmopolitans we may rejoin —"If it should deserve destruction, let it be destroyed; if it is worthy of life, let us appropriate the elements of its immortality."

And the tendency of this Democracy, is to become more Democratic.

How then, it is asked, does this *natural* conservatism of the American nation show itself? We answer this question by asking and answering another.

What *is* the actual American Government?

It has its supreme Legislative, Executive, and Judiciary. It has also its Balances, simple, natural, and inevitable, between the Individual, the "States," and the Nation. *But the actual supreme Legislative* has been the People's Convention, "tempered" with the electoral college. The sovereign People declare by Press, Platform, and Convention their will. They instruct their candidate, and his political existence, as well as honour, binds him to them, although in theory they elect not him, but his electors. And what is this "balance of the Constitution," this system of check and counter-check by a supposed indirect election?—nothing! The electors are mere "conduit pipes,"—trustees with the trust dictated from hour to hour. The electoral college neither "tempers" nor even "hampers" popular action. The election of President is virtually *direct.* And mark! *It is the People—the nation—that began and carried on this war against Slavery.*

And how about *the Senate,* which is supposed to be a mainstay of "conservatism," and another item in the check system? Why the two-fold answer is this,—*The People* fought for this Senate power, by fighting for free institutions in new States (two senators for each State). The People conquered. They got the majority. But until they got it the senators were, in almost all divisions, the chief supports of a slave-system, at once immoral, anarchical, and destructive.

As for the *House of Representatives,* their term is shorter, they depend more upon the People. The northern section was more outspoken than that in the Senate, and truer to the right.

Thus we see that the People, the true Democracy, adhere to the Constitution, and "Conservatism" was so excessive as to identify itself with destruction, anarchy, and rebellion. The Conservatives would have retained Slavery and embraced destruction, because "Slavery is in the Constitution." They rent the Constitution, and declared war against the nation, because they despaired of identifying Slavery (oligarchy and barbarism) with either. They overrode all the Slave States' Constitutions, because to wait for constitutional action would have been fatal to their plans.

And the supreme *Judiciary?* It left the People, and declared that negroes are not men. It was sufficiently "tempered," to parody the *mot* of the Revolution, to declare that "robbery is property," and to identify the judgment seat with a felony which deprived of their dearest rights four millions of souls! The Chief Justice was the arch-thief of the Republic. The People appealed to the *ultima ratio* of nations against his decision.

§

For schemes of partial interest, or of difficult comprehension, no doubt, Oligarchy is best adapted. But such schemes are not to the interest of the universal People, and therefore cannot be really conservative. The universal reason of the universally instructed People is, and must be, *the least defective expression of the will of God.* A People that only endorses a policy already transacted is not free, and is conservative only as imbecility or nonentity is conservative. A People that has its affairs done for it in secret conclave, can have but little volition and less character, and is scarcely yet a nation.

The English people could not feed on the strong meat of Cromwell, and were put back to the offal of the second Charles. They did not support Chatham in his thoughts of peace for America, and reform for England,—they were put back through two wars against the American Republic, and one long war, of near a generation, against the French People. When their training is complete, they will follow their leaders to power,—know what is, and what is not, their foreign policy, and leaving it to others to reign by whatsoever *forms*, will see to it that they themselves govern.

As pointed out before, it is the very universality of power, and will, and education upon which Democracy is based, that makes its executive at once the intensest unity, and the safest of all systems.

There is no grander moral spectacle than the appeal of their future rulers to the American People. The universal conscience and intellect are stirred to the depths. Parties are matched against parties on definite platforms and projects. Leaders descend into the arena and canvass the States, discussing, *not what has been* a policy already secretly enacted, and then for the first time revealed, but what ought to be the work of the next four years of the People's servants.

The general and excessive tendencies of American *statesmen*, during the Slavery era, to Conservatism are powerfully illustrated by the proceedings of the famous Committee of Thirty-three, in 1860. It consisted of one from each State, and was to consider the perilous condition of the country. It met again and again; resolved and re-resolved; rescinded, confirmed, and abandoned; proposed an immense number of resolutions, and rejected all that tended to settle anything or present distinct issues, and affirmed about half a dozen propositions, such as—that it is improper for Congress to abolish slavery,—that certain things should not be interfered with,—the most emphatic conclusion being that "no amendment against Slavery shall originate with non-slaveholding States, or shall be valid *without the assent of every one of the States!*" (See p. 25, Report No. 31.)

Thus the delegates of every State but five would have "conserved" even Slavery.

Let us, then, not be deceived by vain words. There is a point where "conservatism" becomes corruption, just as there is another point where progress becomes mania.

To conserve forms that are not adapted to the spirit is to ensure their violent destruction.

To conserve evil principles of Government is to appeal to the ultima ratio of revolution, or to drive progress from our shores that other nations may use it to pass us in peaceful competition or to destroy us by war.

The function of Conservatism is to reject what is premature in opportunity or bad in principle. To postpone unjustly or too long ensures perpetual barrenness or premature decrepitude, and puts to the nation the alternative of the destruction of its politicians or of *itself.*

The Americans tolerated an excessive Conser-

vatism till the land stank with it, and the spawn of its putrescence went up over all their institutions. These politicians would have destroyed the nation with their conservatism, and so by war the nation destroyed *them.*

Nations that go back, perish. A policy of retrogression is a policy of despair. A policy of stagnation is a policy of suicide. The essence of Conservatism is progress, but in the right direction.

And thus deeper down and more elementary than any written proviso whatsoever, is *the conservatism of religion, intelligence, prosperity, and political equality,* guaranteed by human nature to all those nations that shall, like America, have the sense and the daring to trust her.

§

There is one kind of Conservatism which partakes both of the natural and artificial, namely, the spirit of reluctance with which any project would be entertained for the alteration of the form of the Constitution,—a *natural* reluctance to meddle with the *artificial* formulum of their liberties agreed on by their Fathers. Thus, as Mr. Everett said, it was at the time of the Reform Bill admitted in England, "that the United States possessed in their written Constitution, and in the difficulty of procuring amendments to it, *a conservative principle unknown to the English Government.*"

American Democracy is Conservative by reason of the following *artificial or constitutional* arrangements. We repeat, the advantage and the aim is, not to limit the People, but to check one branch of Government by another, and to correct the views of extreme sections of the People by the general mass :—

1st. There is the great constitutional check in the limitation of the granted powers of Congress, and in the exactness of the written Constitution.

2nd. The constitutional law of change and amendment of the Constitution. Thus Draper says :—

"For the permanency of any such system, it is essentially necessary that it should include within its own organisation *a law of change*, and not of change only, but change in the right direction,—the direction in which the Society interested is about to pass."

Reservation of rights to States require a majority of *States* for alterations in the Constitution.

3rd. The organisation of the Senate as their representative, two for each State, whatever its size or population.

4th. THE SUPREME COURT is a check on unconstitutional Legislation, whether by acts of Congress or by Sovereign States. It sits in judgment on both.

In seventy-one years preceding 1860, there had been but four Chief Justices of the United States, and the fourth was then on the bench. They are not, as such, members of the Cabinet, nor displaced with political changes, nor have they any such office as the Speakership of the Upper House in England, with vast official influence and patronage.

5th. Owing to the peculiar state of Society,

members of the LEGAL PROFESSION, there so active, numerous, and powerful, constitute, says De Tocqueville, "*the most powerful existing security against the excesses of Democracy*, whilst Democratic Government is favorable to the political power of lawyers, who constitute the only enlightened class the People does not mistrust. Their habits of order, taste for formalities, and instinctive regard for the regular connection of ideas, render them hostile to the revolutionary spirit. They oppose their aristocratic propensities to the democratic instincts of the people, their attachment to what is antique to its love of novelty, *their narrow views to its immense designs*, and their habitual procrastination to its ardent impatience. *The American aristocracy* is not composed of the rich, who are united by no common tie. It *occupies the judicial bench and the bar*. This party extends over the whole community, and penetrates into all classes of society; it acts upon the country imperceptibly, but it finally fashions it to suit its purposes."

6th. Moreover, one conspicuous element in the Democratic conservatism of America is the FREEDOM OF WORSHIP.

De Tocqueville says of this (p. 266, v. ii) :—

"The American legislators had succeeded to a certain extent *in opposing the permanence of the religious world to the continual shifting of politics*, and Churchmen mainly attributed *the peaceful dominion of religion in their country to the separation of Church and State*. As long as religion is sustained by those feelings, propensities, and passions, which are found to occur under the same forms at all the different periods of history, it may defy the efforts of time; or, at least, *it can only be destroyed by another religion. As a nation assumes a democratic condition, it becomes more and more dangerous to connect religion with political institutions.* Political powers often depend on the opinion of a generation, the interests of the time, or the life of an individual. If the Americans had not placed religion *beyond the reach of innovators*, where could it abide in the ebb and flow of human opinions? Where would that respect which belongs to it be paid amidst the struggles of faction, what would become of its immortality in the midst of perpetual decay? In America religion is perhaps less powerful than at certain periods, but *its influence is more lasting.* The two great dangers which threaten the existence of religion are *schism* and *indifference.* In Europe the living body of religion has been bound down to the dead corpse of superannuated polity."

7th. The increased centralisation wrought in the habits and manners of the People by war, railways, canals, telegraphs, banks, &c.

8th. And the responsibility of the President, the head of the Executive, *to the People alone*, whilst yet they check one another, has an element of conservatism in it. Thus Mill confesses :—

"There is unquestionably some advantage in a country like America, where no apprehension need be entertained of a coup d'Etat, *in making the chief minister constitutionally independent of the legislative body*, and rendering the two great branches of the Government, while equally popular both in their origin and in their responsibility, *an effective check on the other.* The plan is in accordance with *that sedulous avoidance of the concentration of great masses of power in the same hands, which is a marked characteristic of the American Federal constitution."—J. S. Mill*, on "Representative Government," p. 250.

The London Times, of January 11th, 1865, adverted to the plan then proposed of having thenceforth talking ministers, heads of the executive departments, in the House of Representatives, and argued that that would raise the standard and the value of public talent, and tend to divide the responsibility, and limit the power of the President. We have already quoted Napoleon III on this point (see "Democracy and National Unity"). The change would involve many other changes, and is not now entertained. It is, however, essentially only a question of who shall be *called* President, and as long as the universal People are the *fons et origo* of power, and the constant dispensers of it, they will not be baulked by their creatures.

Public opinion will always be president of America.

9th. There are certain principles which attend a federated nationality, and which constitute a fundamental difference between the effect of great set currents of opinion in America and those which pervade the politics of all other nations. Here is a veritable nation, and also a federation of States. Elsewhere, there is not the nation, or there is not the federation, or other conditions are essentially different. Here there are the People, the State, and the States.

The Democratic and Conservative tendencies, —the eternal flux and reflux, and conflict, between the past and the future,—between the things that are and the things that have to come,—how are these tendencies and forces affected or controlled by the *forms* of the American Constitution ? What is the natural vice of Democracy ? It is to exaggerate the rights of the Individual, without reference to the necessities of order. What is the natural vice of Conservatism ? It is to exaggerate the necessities of order, as against ideal and actual right.

But the American system introduces a strange third element.

Is there any movement really wild, furious, or uncertain? It encounters, naturally and necessarily, not only the forms and the interests of national, but of State organization (always excepting the anomaly of the Slave interest). Is there any danger of a too great or despairing tenacity of central conservatism? Then the thirty-four nuclei also of vested interests and of minor sovereignties, would combine to oppose it, for they have natural instincts, so to speak, equally averse to be absorbed by the great centre, or to be swept away by a too "sovereign People."

As Mr. Everett put it:—"Each of these States is a representative commonwealth, composed of two branches, with the ordinary divisions of Executive, Legislative, and Judicial power."

Their representation by Senators is the least objectionable "representation of minorities" that could be devised.

America avoids the "constituted anarchy" of German federal politics, whilst it maintains State life and local action.

This system seems to explain many so-called "anomalies" in American politics, and to go further than human political science has gone elsewhere, towards the accomplishment of that feat which will crown some future political millennium, —the perfect reconcilement of order and progress, of indispensable forms and of abstract right.

10th. The absolute executive unity of the President is all powerful under the constitution. Also his election by the People.

11th. Representation according to population.

§

We have shown how in the mighty struggle and strain against Slavery, the *natural* conservatism *of the nation* asserted itself against official opponents, excessive conservatism, and anarchy.

We have also just seen what are some of the *artificial* conservative arrangements.

We propose now to show certain extraordinary instances of that only true conservatism,—of life, morals, and character.

For before all things there has been an intense, agonising realisation of the supreme value of the human life and soul, and *a conservatism of morality, humanity, and religion, irrepressibly developed, and incessantly, and aggressively manifested* by this Democracy during the conduct of the war.

We say that for *economy of and respect for life*, for *humanity*, and *religion*, American organisations have surpassed all others. Witness the following, from the Sanitary, and Christian Commissions, which complemented the Commissariat and the Chaplaincy in a way never before suggested.

A pair of shoes are often as good as a recruit, and to dispense with red tape, when ice, brandy, or blankets are wanted, is often to save life.

The groans of the wounded rise usually from battle fields like the roar of a distant cataract, till slowly, silence and death prevail. The rate of mortality, in January, 1855, would have annihilated our army in the Crimea by hunger, cold, and untended wounds, in ten months.

In America, the standing army was 12,000. Suddenly an immense number of wholly unskilled men rushed to arms. Large numbers of Church members were amongst them, for they believed in Government and in God. The worst and the best enlisted. Congregations have given whole companies. Young Men's Christian Associations have given regiments. The Churches sent about one-seventh of their male communicants. The Western Churches more. The Bible Classes an immense number. An Illinois regiment was officered almost wholly by clergymen. And a higher class than ordinary was the staple, and not for *any* war, but for special national service.

A great central Women's Association, with town and village sub-associations, "Soldiers Aid Societies," and "Village Sewing Circles," also upheld the cause.

The objects of the Commission were,—to choose sites of camps on scientific sanitary principles—to avoid malaria,—to drain, to water, to cook, to clothe, to regard the health, comfort, and morale,—to control and stop unnecessary waste of life,—to study and act upon vital statistics,—to remove official obstructions,—to supply surgeons with professional reading and short treatises on army diseases,—to study European military invalid systems,—establish experimental sanatoria, &c.

In the first two years the Sanitary Commission received gifts valued at nearly eight millions of dollars. Its "flying depôt" carried underclothing, bedding, towels, handkerchiefs, vegetables, condensed milk, pickles, crutches, ice, dressing gowns, fans, pads, sponges, eau-de-Cologne, mosquito netting, potatoes and onions, refrigerating cars lined with zinc and ice, needles, thread, buttons, cutlery, papers and envelopes, currant wine, &c., &c. The waggons and huge wheeled caldrons were always in reach. It established vast gardens, and also frequently swept the Western markets, to hunt the demon scurvy from the camp. It is believed that a million of men have passed through the hospitals, In the autumn of 1862, seventy thousand beds were arranged in a short time. A "railway ambulance" was devised with perfect appointments for sleep, rest, and food. It established an Hospital Directory and scheme of death records, of relations wounds, and sickness, and of dying requests, place of burial, and memorial tablets. Sickness was reduced to the ordinary civil-life ratio. *The Commission has modified history.*

California has given 600,000 dollars, placing money boxes beside the electoral urns. Insurance Companies, Banks, Railway Companies, have given princely donations. The Chicago and New York fairs each yielded about a million. *The farmers and mechanics moved with their gifts and produce, en masse, and offered them with tears and prayers.*

A convention of delegates from Young Men's Christian Associations, started the Christian Commission.

Railways, telegraphs, hotels, offices, clerks, pub-

lication societies, tracts, and Bibles were offered and used by it free of charge.

Three thousand devoted men, — clergymen, lawyers, doctors, merchants, *laboured for it even to the borders of the grave,* each man received his commission and free railway pass, a blanket and strap (to be sure of a bed), a bucket and cup, a lantern, small comforts, books or tracts. A depôt was always at the nearest convenient place, and stores for the next battle are always labelled and ready. They hurried to every field. They washed, clothed, fed, wrote for, prayed with, and advised the living, and closed the eyes of the dead.

From all corners of the Union was an unceasing influx of comforts,—to every point of the vast war horizon an unceasing efflux.

After the march, the huge cooking waggons were ready with coffee or soup. With the march went the supply waggons, and hot coffee has been served during the fight to wearied soldiers.

Scarcely a man has served without receiving Bibles and tracts, or died without the voice of promise and of prayer. Vast military prayer-meetings were held, Churches were founded, and communion dispensed.

In 1863 were distributed half a million Bibles, nearly the same number of hymn and psalm-books, one million and a quarter of small books, three millions religious newspapers, and twelve millions pages of tracts.

The revenue of Christian Commission rose the last year to nearly two millions.

Religion was thus powerfully aggressive. The song of praise has been heard to spread far and wide over the field after battle, and probably the Bible was more generally read than by any other half million of men.

At the various head-quarters there was always a soldier's reading-room, with this conspicuous notice :—" The newspapers on the files are dailies and weeklies, from your State and country. Sit down and read. The writing-table and stationery are for your use. They want to hear from you at home. If out of stamps, drop your letter in the box,—we will stamp and mail it. Those Testaments, hymn-books, and religious papers were sent to you—take one. The library has many interesting books ; find the one you like, have it recorded, and return it in five days. If you are in trouble, speak to any agent in the room ; you are the one he wants to see."

In September, 1864, Mr. E. C. Fisher, of New York, addressed the Social Science Congress at York (England), on "Military Discipline and Volunteer Philanthropy," ending with the following affirmations :—

" This Volunteer Sanitary Commission has furnished to the different armies of the Republic, since the commencement of the war, nearly four millions of pounds sterling of army necessaries, comforts, and luxuries. Its establishment, organisation, magnitude, and achievements prove three things :

"*Firstly*. The armies of the North could be rendered *incomparably more efficient* by the volunteer aid and assistance of the people, without the slightest infringement of military discipline, or interference with the constituted medical authorities of armies.

"*Secondly.* The American civil war affords the brightest example of spontaneous, and yet organised, benevolence, and furnishes an example which other nations will do well to emulate.

"*Thirdly.* The whole of the American people—men, women, and children alike—in thus rendering their armies efficient, proved conclusively that the war was not carried on, as many in Europe suppose, by the Government of a minority; but was *waged by the great mass of the citizens.* In no other way can you explain the colossal achievements of this volunteer commission."—(London Correspondent of New York Tribune, *see* "Sanitary Reporter," Nov. 1, 1864.)

The Freedmen's Aid Societies constitute another gigantic organisation too well known to require explanation. Patriotism, Religion, and Humanity are equally represented in them,—and to save a *nation* of bondsmen.

§

The spectacle of the American nation and Democracy ought to reassure the most cautious, of the final success of the Principle of Democracy, and of that particular example of it.

Without an army, with scarcely a fleet; during the Presidency of a traitor or an imbecile; divided within by a false "Democracy" uniting all who feared universal suffrage, who hated immigrant preponderance, or who would surrender principle for peace,—and divided without by a schism of thirteen States bound together in as intense and enthralling a union as interest, fear, prejudice, and Oligarchy could make. Yet over all these the nation and the Democracy triumph.

What is the secret?—for the "educated" opinion of the world pronounced a priori against the actual result.

The secret of course is that American Democracy answers near enough to the ideal Democracy. That it is a real Democracy. That it is *Democracy enough* to do what it ought to do,—assimilate or destroy its foes.

There is the three-fold bond, *universal intelligence, interest, and will,*—the knowledge, the responsibility, and the power.

There are the States with local energies, ambitions, and rewards, minding their local matters, and balancing with wholesome jealousies any tendencies of any other States to exceed their powers.

There are the individuals who compose each State, constituting also the nation, and with passion for nationality naturally overruling (save when selfish and purely local abuses interfere) those for neighbourhood and locality.

There is the Church minding her own business, "its ministers not (see New York State Constitution) diverted from the great duties of their functions by holding any civil or military offices." Thus the Church keeps her influence for that which is essentially expansive, universal, conservative, and progressive.

It concerns itself with the individual American, the individual sectarian, and if it favored the South or Slavery, it did it not in any national capacity.

There is the Territory one as Adam, with Mississippi for back bone, Ohio and Upper Mississippi for arms, grasping east and west the land; with its confluent rivers for ribs and muscles; with cities for ganglions, and the universal Democracy for nerve-essence, and brain, and soul.

It has improvised the vastest armies, and shown that the interests of rebels are sectional, vicious, and irreconcileable; it survived four months of traitorous administration, it has conciliated the Border States, is liberating the negro nation, conducted a general election with calmness amidst a political tempest, re-elected its peasant emperor, giving him the necessary powers of dictatorship whilst it remains a Republic, and has turned the greatest struggle the world has seen into its greatest blessing.

It has transcended the hopes and rebuked the fears of the great philosopher of Democracy, and has shown a life, a tenacity, a statesmanship, a conservatism, a morality, a culture, a power, and a love of glory,—a caution to Despotisms of the present, and a beacon light to Democracies of the future.

It has not created a new science, but it has shown to the trembling and to the waiting world *a developed and united* People,—*a working model of Democracy.*

Naturally, the world of the few is full of fears, blasphemies, unbelief, and despair,—the world of the many, of hopes, faith, and exultation.

The flag of the People stands. It waves at last over a ROYAL NATION.

§

American Democracy sprung from the best part of the best age of England. It has flourished in spite of and by means of every foe, especially of its last and greatest,—Slavery. It contains two elements *never before united, for long, in Democracies,*—FREEDOM and EQUALITY. The first secures it from oppression in the present; the last retains to it self-Government, and secures it from those *forms* of Oligarchy which may at last degenerate into the fact of Despotism. Equality can alone so completely prepare the individual as to make him a fitting material for the vastest international combinations.

The qualities and proportions of the great American nation are, in fact, at present, the one essential question for the future of *Democracy and Nationality* everywhere. And, strange to say, they are still to the politicians of this generation almost an unknown quantity.

The constitutional balance between the Man,

the Institution, and the Government;—the completion of freedom, municipal organisation and nationality;—the boundless area, the Federal bond, the exhaustless resources, the equal conditions of life and competition, the "Black Yankees," who may populate and work that portion, comparatively small, of territory below the temperate zone;—the unity of ideas (not forgetting the bond of a common Anglo-American literature), interests, principles, and territory; of institution, language, race, and religion;—all these conditions (working together, also, for the destruction of the oligarchic or slave element, with which they cannot coexist) combine to make,—*have made*—such a NATION as the world has not seen before, and therefore is not, as yet, quite prepared to recognise, even in the great Anglo-American Continent,—the home, we say, of that royal nation which beckons on all other nations towards the future.

Thus did Bentham comment, even in his time, on the disturbing influences of this American precedent:—

"But now, suppose the same or a similar accursed Government, with the accursed prosperity, transplanted from that blessed distance,—planted under our very noses, with no more than one and twenty miles of sea to dilute the stench of it, without so much as a single useless place, needless place, overpaid place, unmerited pension—not to speak of sinecures, —no, not so much as a peerage, to settle a borough or buy off a country gentleman—suppose these miscreants . . . and not more than half a guinea or a crown, not more than a three hours' row, necessary to enable a man to see it!

"In this case, by what possibility could the eye, the head, or the heart be shut against the spectacle of the *united nuisances* —prosperity and good government?

"There they are—but happily with the Atlantic between us and them—the never sufficiently accursed United States, living, and, oh! horror, flourishing—and so flourishing! flourishing under a Government so essentially illegitimate.

"There they are—but happily with two thousand leagues of sea between us and them—the millions of two-legged swine, with the illegitimacy and the unencumbered and undisturbed prosperity in which they wallow."—*Bentham's Plan of Reform*, p. 8.

This is about the English of all talk about Democracy not being conservative. That the disturbing cause in the late tremendous conflict was Oligarchy, and that the Atlantic may now be said to be bridged by steam, if not joined by the cable, takes nothing from the force of the above, or from its appositeness to the subject of this work.

Oligarchy, we have said, was the disturbing cause. In a deeper sense it has been the irresistible, ceaseless march of Democracy that has disturbed and uprooted all things contrary to it since the world began.

And before and after all other considerations is this one,—supreme in politics. Only as the organisation and the forms express the spirit and essence of power, can there be *formal* conservatism. Only as a four-fold freedom of School, Press, Church, and Assembly complete the development of an ever-increasing proportion of the all, is the final preponderance of universal national manhood approached, and the *right* national spirit attained. Till then, destruction may be conservative, and conservatism destructive. Manhood is Democracy, —and that must include conservatism, which tends to the completion of manhood.

The history of America is the history of manhood.

It began when a perfect manhood was first shown forth to the world.

When Rome failed to develope manhood, manhood passed from Rome, and prepared to associate against it for freedom in German woods.

England continued its story, but to mature freedom into equality it wanted a new world, and it found it yonder.

Equality must be the crown of all nations that are to continue. *How* this is to be accomplished is a comparatively trifling question.

BOOK II.

DEMOCRACY IN ENGLAND.

"Mr. Carlyle's judgment on this point (his inferences from the fact that Roman Democracy could not get on without Dictators) is like that of a man who had only known the steam engine before the invention of governor balls, and was ready to declare that its mechanism would be shattered if a boy were not at hand to regulate the pressure of the steam."—*The Times*, April 4th, 1866.

"They had institutions partly derived from Imperial Rome, partly from Papal Rome, partly from the old Germany. Our laws and customs have never been lost in general and irreparable ruin. With us the precedents of the middle ages are still valid."—*Macaulay*.

"In perusing the admirable treatise of Tacitus on the manners of the Germans, we find it is from that nation the English have borrowed the idea of their political government. This beautiful system was invented first in the woods,—'De minoribus rebus principes consultant, de majoribus omnes; ita tamen ut ea quoque, quorum penes plebem arbitrium est, apud principes pertractentur.'"—*Bancroft*, 212, v. i.

"The great constitutional theory of jurisdiction in Anglo-Saxon times was not feudal, but primitive Teutonic."—*Hallam*.

"Accurately speaking there is no such thing as a mixed Government."—*De Tocqueville.*

"After ages will moralise on the hallucination under which *an exceptional and transitional state of things, marking the last phase in the existence of an old feudal monarchy*, has been regarded, and confidentially propagated, as the normal and final state of man.

"The Liberal party represents the modern and Protestant element of the nation in its *protracted and wavering effort to throw off the remains of the feudal system*, and place society and religion on a rational foundation."—*Goldwin Smith.*

"In point of private right and freedom of possession, the English present an incredible deficiency; sufficient proof of which is afforded in the rights of *primogeniture*, involving military or ecclesiastical appointments for younger sons."—*Hegel*, "Philosophy of History."

"The descent of LANDS before the conquest was according to the custom of gavelkind, or equal partition; in the age of H. I, the eldest son took the principal fief."

"In that of Glanvil he inherited all the lands held by knight service.

"One most prominent and characteristic distinction between the constitution of England and *that of every other country in Europe* is its refusal of civil privileges to the *lower nobility.* No restraint seems to have lain upon marriage. There was a *virtual equality of rights* among all the commoners of England. The peerage imparts no privilege except to its actual possessor. There is no part of our constitution so admirable. It is to this peculiarly democratical character of the English monarchy, that we are indebted to its long permanence, its regular improvement, and its present vigor."—*Hallam's* "Middle Ages," v. ii, pp. 336—342-3-4.

CONTENTS OF BOOK II.

"The cities became so considerable that the Sovereign could impose no tax upon them besides the stated farm rent of the town, without their own consent. They were therefore called upon to send deputies to the General Assembly of the States of the kingdom. Hence the origin of burghs in the States General of all the great monarchies in Europe.

"These laws and customs so favourable to the yeomanry, have perhaps contributed more to the present grandeur of England than all their boasted regulations of commerce taken together."—*Adam Smith.*

"Tenure in villanage gradually wore out through the greater part of Europe. The time and manner, however, in which so important a revolution was brought about, is one of the most obscure points in modern history. Slavery was gradually abolished by the joint operation of the two interests of the proprietor on the one hand, and of the sovereign on the other."—*Ibid.*, "Wealth of Nations," v. ii. pp. 91-94.

"In the monarchy of the Franks, military service was soon substituted for taxation."—*Montesquieu.*

"The old English monarchy was one of a class of limited monarchies which sprang up in Western Europe during the middle ages. All had municipal corporations enjoying large franchises, and senates whose consent was necessary to the validity of some public acts; of these, the English was, from an early period, justly reputed the best. If the King dared to oppress great masses, his subjects promptly appealed to the laws, and that appeal failing, appealed as promptly to the God of battles. In the middle ages resistance was an ordinary remedy."—*Macaulay.*

"The relation established between a lord and his vassal, by the feudal tenure, far from containing principles of any servile and implicit obedience, permitted the compact to be dissolved in case of its violation by either party. This extended as much to the sovereign as to inferior lords. If a vassal was aggrieved, and if justice was denied him, he sent a defiance, that is, a renunciation of fealty to the king, and was entitled to enforce redress at the point of his sword. It then became a contest of strength as between two independent potentates."—*Hallam's* "Middle Ages," v. iii, p. 162.

Chapter I.

TACITUS TO THE REFORM BILL.

An Outline of Forms and Powers.

"It was not so much *from* Slavery as *through* Slavery that humanity was emancipated."—*Hegel*, "Philosophy of History."

"The principle of Feudal Sovereignty is the outward force of individuals,—princes, liege lords; it is a force destitute of intrinsic right. Whether the subjects of such a constitution perform their stipulated duties or not depends upon the Seigneurs being able to induce them so to do by force of character or favours.

"The supremacy implied in monarchy is essentially a power emanating from a political body, and is pledged to the furtherance of that equitable purpose on which the constitution of a State is based.

"Feudal sovereignty is a polyarchy; we see nothing but lords and serfs; *in monarchy*, on the contrary, there is one lord and no serf, for *servitude is abrogated* by it, and in it *right and law are recognised.* The barons compelled King John to swear to the Magna Charta, the basis of English liberty, *i. e.*, more particularly of the privileges of the nobility."—*Ibid.*, pp. 416-422.

"The great spiritual facts which lie at the basis of human freedom are the dignity, immortality, responsibility, and redemption of manhood. This is the Magna Charta. It is God's Charter."—*The Bible and the People.*

"Let the idea take hold of the more generous and cultivated minds, that the most serious danger to the future prospects of mankind is in the unbalanced influence of the commercial spirit."—*Edinburgh Review.*

"The mischief is when excessive wealth destroys the spirit of commerce."—*Montesquieu.*

"To cure the middle class and found the People."—*Hugo.*

"The fashion of the day, and perhaps I might almost venture to say, the vice of the day, is a disposition almost to idolise the middle classes."—*Gladstone.*

The Development and organisation of the whole as to qualities, and of the all as to numbers, is the sum of civilisation, religion, and Government.

The proportions in which the whole and the all are thus developed and organised, represent the civilisation of any given epoch, and knowing that, we know also the sort of freedom therein possible, and we know absolutely into what form of slavery the deficiencies of the period must shape themselves.

Throughout all the era when feudal chivalry was the preponderating power, those who possessed neither physical energies, nor courage, nor military genius, became of necessity Slaves. Slaves they must have been a priori, and slaves they were in fact.

This simplifies much the question of "franchises." Every system has its refuse; and the refuse are the disfranchised. The Slaves of one epoch are the paupers of another. Ascertain what is the main drift and object of an age, and the qualities necessary to a certain success in it, and those who want them most are the pariahs and failures.

In every age and country, except the advanced Democratic era, where the universal manhood is educated, and power and organisation are one, there are and must be those who have their own failures, or those of their fathers, visited upon them in political incompetence.

The millennium never having come yet, there has never yet been universal suffrage; when the millennium comes, universal suffrage will come with it, and, we hope, a good many other things.

Besides the aboriginal British, the elements of the making of this English nation, are the aboriginal German or Teutonic, the Roman, the Scandinavian, the Anglo-Saxon, and the Norman. All had their forms or organisations adapted to the necessities that created them, or to the ruling ideas that moulded them. All these types of ideas and nationality united to form our own.

In the present chapter, which only aims at such a general outline of the development and organisation of our national manhood, from Anglo-Saxon times, as is essential to an adequate view of the traditions and prospects of "Democracy in England," we endeavour to trace the successive relations of labour, land, justice, and representation.

Respecting the general scheme of the Anglo-Saxon and Scandinavian commonwealths, and of Gothic monarchies, it appears that the Anglo-Saxon differed from the feudal scheme in giving more to the freeman and to the King, and it differed from the Scandinavian in giving more to the King. In both it seemed adapted to secure an earlier and compacter national unity. The adjustment between the units of the State, the freemen, and the intermediate powers, and the Sovereign, seems to have been more complete. On this Hallam says:—

"The scheme of the Anglo-Saxon commonwealth was better than the feudal; it preserved more of the Teutonic character, it gave more to the common freeman as well as to the King. The love of utopian romance, and the bias in favour of a democratic origin for our constitution, have led many to overstate the freedom of the Saxon Commonwealth; or rather, perhaps, to look less for that freedom where it is really to be found, in the administration of justice, than in representative councils, which authentic records do not confirm."

"The analogies between the Scandinavian and Anglo-Saxon institutions are too striking to be disregarded, though some conclusions may have been drawn from them, to which we cannot thoroughly agree. If it is alleged that we do not find, in the ancient customs of Germany, that peculiar scale of society which ascends from the hundred, as a monad of self-Government, to the collective unity of a royal commonwealth, it may be replied that we trace the essential principle in the *pagus* or *gau* of Tacitus, though perhaps there might be nothing numerical in that territorial direction; that we have, in fact, the centenary distribution under peculiar magistrates in the old continental laws and other documents; and that a large proportion of the inhabitants of England, ultimately coalescing with the rest, so far at least as to acknowledge a common Sovereign, came from the very birthplace of Scandinavian institutions."

"A theory has been developed in a very brilliant and learned article of the Edinburgh Review for 1822 (xxxvi, 287), justly ascribed to Sir F. Palgrave, which deduces the hundred from the *hærad* of Scandinavian commonwealths. 'The Gothic commonwealth is not an unit of which the smaller bodies politic are fractions. They are the units, and the commonwealth is the multiple. Every Gothic monarchy is in the nature of a confederation. It is composed of towns, townships, shires, bailiwicks, burghs, earldoms, dukedoms, all in a certain degree strangers to each other, and separated in jurisdiction. Their magistrates, therefore, in theory, at least, ought not to emanate from the sovereign. . . . . The strength of the state ascends from region to region. The representative form of Government, adopted by no nation but the Gothic tribes, and originally common to them all, necessarily resulted from this federative system in which the Sovereign was compelled to treat the component members as possessing a several authority.'"

"The hundred was as much, according to Palgrave, the organic germ of the Anglo-Saxon commonwealth, as the hærad was of the Scandinavian."—*Middle Ages*, vol ii, p. 381, 377-8.

As regards national unity, the Anglo-Saxon scheme had, from the beginning, two defects: one of organisation, the other of power. First, the alderman of the borough appears not to have sat in the national council; second, the suffrage was not universal. The first defect has widened into the gulf which separates the People from the House of Lords. The second has enabled the Lords to govern the People, and can never be remedied till development and the suffrage become universal.

"Very few," says Hallam ("Middle Ages," v. ii, pp. 276-7-9, 367) "at present imagine that there was any representative system in that age, much less that the ceorls or inferior freemen had the smallest share in the deliberations of the national assembly. In simple life, judicial power is always of more consequence than the legislative. The liberties of these Anglo-Saxon Thanes were chiefly secured, next to their swords and their free spirits, by the inestimable right of deciding civil and criminal suits in their own county courts, held twice in the year. The theory that the Anglo-Saxon constitution was built on universal suffrage, could not stand the first glimmerings of historical knowledge in a mind tolerably sound."

Respecting the position of the borough alderman, and as to the Saxon witenagemot, Hallam (p. 376, v. ii, and 230, v. iii) continues :—

"Sir F. Palgrave contends for aldermen elected by the People in boroughs, sitting and assenting among the King's witan (Edinb. Rev., xxvi, 26). 'Their seats in the witenagemot were connected as inseparably with their office as their duties in the folkmote. Nor is there any reason for denying to the aldermen of the boroughs the rights and rank possessed by the aldermen of the hundreds; and they in all cases were equally elected by the commons.' The passage is worthy of consideration, but not satisfactory to my judgment. My position is, that inferior freemen had no share in that assembly. Later, Sir F. Palgrave adopts the notion that forty hydes of land were a necessary qualification."

"According to Sir F. Palgrave, we are not to look to feudal principles for our great councils of advice and consent. They were the aggregate of representatives from the courts leet of each shire and each borough, and elected by the juries to present the grievances of the People, and to suggest their remedies. The great council of the Norman Kings was, I believe, little else than a continuation of the witenagemot, the immemorial organ of the Anglo-Saxon aristocracy in their relation to the King. Of the representation of the courts leet, we may require better evidence. It is remarkable that aldermen, in the municipal sense, are never enumerated among the constituents of a witenagemot or a council."

The wants and virtues of manhood are of the body, mind, and character.

"The Church" may be so organised as that much of manhood will be outside of it. Then priestcraft will make broad and deep its hells, it will thunder excommunications, and burn heretics. Whilst "religion" is of force, or fraud, the manhood of the age will be organised without or against it, and *so* the manhood will be a failure, because the religion is a farce.

Education may be restricted to the few, and education being the multiple of mental power and material production, many will be the paupers and demagogues.

Material comforts may be rendered impossible to the multitude by bad legislation and indirect taxation, and there is a complicated evil result accordingly, of physical degeneration and discontent.

As the One only is developed in body, mind, and character, there is at once autocracy and good Government.

As the few only are so developed and organised, there is oligarchy a necessity and an advantage.

So also, in proportion, with the many and the all.

Material, political, and religious freedom is the crown of progress, and its proportions are the guage of nationality.

Feudality, Priestcraft, Despotism, Oligarchy, Villeinage, and Freedom,—all these jostle one another in our history, but from the time when the absoluteness of the Feudal system held in definite and positive relationship the whole of such manhood as then existed, there has not been, nor can be again, anything like finality, *until the whole manhood of the all* is developed and organised in a free and equal voting Democracy.

From the time when associated numbers forced a choice between despotism and representation, and when fixity of tenure replaced feudal oppression by industry,—to the time when representation shall be equal, and when opinions and religion shall be free,—is essentially but one epoch.

The more defined epochal divisions of English history are :—

1st. The Epoch of Force. The period of primitive Teutonic Associations, of Anglo-Saxon conflicts, and of German, Frank, and English Feudality, until services became fixed, and tenure, in the nature of rent.

2nd. The Epoch of chattel and corporate rule. The era of transition, and conflict of industrial manhood with the rough rudimentary Feudal manhood.

The gradual fixing and settlement of property, prior to the development of the complex and accomplished manhood of modern times, and its extrication from the influences of mere property.

3rd. The Epoch of Manhood. Its completion in equality. The triumph of industrial, mental, and moral manhood-development over chattel qualifications. Of Individuality over Corporations.

In each epoch the individual possesses just as much freedom as he can command, and no more.

The first epoch commences with the story of Tacitus, and can hardly be said to close until Charles II turned the tenure of chivalry into freehold.

The second and middle epoch is that which now draws towards a conclusion. The first was the era when force transgressed the rights of property; the second is that in which property assails the rights of manhood.

The third, upon which we hope soon to enter, is that in which manhood itself will hold the balance of power against both property and force. We have to develop such a national manhood as shall complete freedom in equality, and discard for ever the idea of force or property as applied to the religion or the franchise of others.

It was the necessary condition of this transition period, that the rough aggressive individuality of the middle ages should yield to the conservative influences of property. For ages the conflict raged between the idea of right as attached to fixed ownership, and the ideas of force and military service. The higher industrial manhood gradually overcame the lower and more elementary manhood, but that done, it had to extricate itself from the forces and influences concentred upon fixed property, and *there* the powers and traditions of Feudality linger to this day.

The history and the Acts of Parliament of these eras of germinating manhood represent :—

1st. The struggle of the primitive institutions of England against Feudality.

2nd. The struggle of the Feudal head for command of the purse and the sword.

3rd. The struggle between King and Church for command of the religious element, and for the creation of a factitious religious unity.

4th. The general contest of King, Church, Barons, Urban Oligarchies and Free Burghs, Families, and People, in different combinations.

5th. The gradual growth of the national manhood and its gradual appropriation of all those elements of power. A multiplication of material comforts elevating the man. Equality, or political manhood, governing itself at home and abroad in finance and intervention. A religious manhood superseding the Church. It is "the whole and the all" advancing.

Much learning has been expended in the attempt to fortify right with tradition. The fact is that no more "freedom" ever exists, than, from the actual state and elements of Society, *must* exist, and there is never a revolution without a reformation. Each state of Society has its constitution, written or unwritten. The organisation always *follows* the power. Feudality only became evil when its simple relationships existed no longer, and when a more complex civilisation required not so much an intenser, as a *completer* Individuality.

The utmost that can be truthfully conceded to the idea of universal suffrage appears to have taken place at the period of transition from the feudal, to what we will call the modern industrial system, when the severity of the feudal system had become relaxed, and the advantage of a true representation had commended itself to the Sovereign by subsidies much exceeding the ancient tallages. The theory of military service had declined, men easily became freeholders, and entitled as such to the suffrage. The new system was not organised; wealth, luxury, and centralisation had not discovered the advantages which distance, numbers, and influence would confer on a Government. The machinery of corruption had to be created. Parliaments were annual, and if members were willing to be sold, they could not be bought. Representation based upon local and minor associations had united with barons and clergy to conquer freedom. But those bodies not being constituted of, or based upon, an adequate individual manhood, "representative Government" became at last a vast centralised corporation, touching the People but once in seven years, and often overpowering the minor corporate and individual influences.

The very necessity of "representation," arises from the fact that numbers render impossible the *direct* participation of the Individual in the Executive or Legislative. From that period history tends to the action of corporate bodies on corporate bodies, of feudal and sub-feudal heads, of oligarchies against oligarchies, privilege against prerogative. Standing armies, standing Churches, and indirect taxation gradually become normal, *and organised bodies act on the defenceless inorganic remnant of the People.* Notwithstanding many brilliant rallies, Individuality is always liable to be overpowered by Centralisation, until Development has guaranteed Individuality by Equality, —that completer and intenser freedom, without which civilisations cannot be healthy, and centralisation itself must be incomplete or unbalanced and despotic.

The student who looks at *life* instead of being bewildered by systems, knows that in a wandering warlike life, courage, energy, and loyalty *must be* ordinary *individual* qualifications. He who has these *must be* free; he who has them not *must* become a slave or villein.

When property becomes fixed, nomads are a nuisance. Property is the object of legislation. Land tends to become fixed as numbers increase. Numbers associated compel representation. Industry is then the basis of the new manhood, and the prolonged struggle of Industry, aided by its first-born, capital, against surviving forms of feudality, and against corporate and privileged power,

—*that* is the political history of every State, from the hour when fixity of tenure supersedes the wandering "companion"-ship of war and the chase. As Industry is manifolded by steam power, capital, and education, we reach all the sooner that Manhood-Development and Equality, which will be inevitable, universal, and final.

That is of necessity the epitome of the history of all franchises, representations, and progress.

§

Marshalling thus the facts of the organisation of each age, according to the essential spirit and power that created it, we find, in the beginning, that the primitive Teutonic era of association for armed assault or colonisation possessed unrivalled excellencies.

When, as Cæsar discourses, the princes of our German ancestors "each had a multitude of men, and allotted what portion of land they pleased to individuals, and obliged them the year following to remove to some other part;" when, as Tacitus relates, "in battle it is infamy in the Prince to be surpassed in courage, it is infamy in the companions not to follow the brave example of their prince,—it is an eternal disgrace to survive him;" and when in council, those who approved the leader *and* the enterprise, stood up and offered their assistance;—there, we say, the organisation expressed the power because it *must*. Between that simple and direct relationship of Prince and companion, there *could* get no hostile corporate influence or interest.

Fixed property did not exist. Representation had no *raison d'être*, and *manhood was itself a franchise and a Parliament.*

From Feudality to Equality is a long span, but the best organisation can never again express the individual power of the commonalty, till Individuality is developed and organised equally and universally, and the evils necessary to the old world are swept from the path of the new.

Religion enforced or favored by the State, and manhood disenfranchised, are the shapes which aggression now takes, and the Barbarism which the age permits. The latter is a barbarism which barbarism could not perpetrate, and which civilisation cannot afford to continue.

Completeness of nations must come from completeness of individuals, and complete individual manhood therefore includes and necessitates political manhood. We find the rudiments of Democracy in Christianity, and its earliest history in the Bible.

Cæsar and Tacitus who come next, deal not with the universal rudiments of manhood, but with the particular working of a certain barbarous type. They show how in German woods were formed those associations which destroyed Rome, and laid the foundations of such freedom as Europe since enjoyed in the military feudal system.

That freedom, however, must pass away with the system. Of all freedoms, the German had only that oi "assembly." The Individual was not complete. The organisation could be neither complete, final, nor universal.

The freedom of the Germans was that of the fraternity and enthusiasm of a common enterprise. Tacitus says that, "the men, attached to the service of a prince, followed him wherever he went." They were called comites, or companions, Leudes, faithful and loyal. "The dignity and power of the princes consists in being constantly surrounded with a multitude of young and chosen people. *The companions refuse to acquire by sweat what they can purchase with blood.* The Germans knew only two capital crimes; they hanged traitors, and drowned cowards. These were the only public crimes among them."

Cæsar says "when any of the princes declared to the assembly that he intended to set out upon an expedition, and asked them to follow him, those who did not fulfil their engagements to assist, lost the public esteem, and were looked upon as traitors."

This, says Montesquieu, "is the substance of the history of the Gallic princes of the first race."

When the German nations invaded Gaul, the Visigoths subdued almost all the South, the Burgundians the East, and the Franks nearly all the rest. Of the Germans Tacitus says, they chose their king for noble extraction, and their leader for valour. "Reges ex nobilitate, duces ex virtute sumunt." Montesquieu says that *the fiefs of the Franks were not derived from that institution of the Romans* (p. 375, v. ii), that villeinage was not generally established in all parts of the monarchy of the Franks, and that military service was soon substituted for taxation. A capitulary of the year 864 says that it was the ancient custom for freemen to perform military service. It was a fundamental principle of the monarchy that whosoever was subject to the military power of another, was subject also to his civil jurisdiction. Thus the capitulary of Lewis the Débonnaire, of 815, makes the military power of the count, and his civil jurisdiction over the freemen, keep always an equal pace. Thus we see (from glossary of English laws, &c.), that at all times the duty of a vassal towards his lord, was to bear arms, and to try his peers in his court (p. 392, *ibid.*). The king did not long raise taxes on the lands belonging to the Franks.

Thus was constituted the free military system (at first of vassalage without fiefs) that had resisted Rome, and was to conquer England.

The County Court was not Anglo-Saxon, but old Teutonic. It subsisted, says Hallam, in this and other countries before feudal institutions had taken root. Also that great safeguard, "judgment by Peers," is aboriginal Teutonic.

In the next stage when property in land has become fixed, it must be protected against predatories and common thieves, and against desertion by its vassal cultivators. And we find (Montesquieu, v. ii, p. 378-9), that according to a capitulary of A.D. 864, freemen were required to do military service, and to find horses and carriages for the King's commissaries and ambassadors, and that the Franks soon changed the imposts of the Emperors into defence of frontiers, and marching against the enemy. We also find ("Middle Ages," v. ii, p. 292) all the freehold lands of England, except some of the Church, subject to three great public burthens of military service, and repairs of bridges, and royal fortresses. With regard to cultivation of land and to protection from thieves, Hallam (v. ii, p. 368) remarks :—

"Perhaps we are a little too much struck by the obligation of ceorls to reside on the lands they cultivated. We are to remember that he who deserted his land, and consequently, his lord, did so to become a thief. Hlafordles men, of whom we read so much, were invariably of this character. What else indeed could he become? Children have an idle play to count buttons and say: Gentleman, apothecary, ploughman, thief. Now this, if we consider the second as burgesses in towns, is actually a distributive enumeration, setting aside the clergy, of the Anglo-Saxon population; a thane, a burgess, a ceorl, a hlafordles man; that is a man without land, lord, or law. For the sake of *protecting the ceorl* from such men, and the *lord in his rights* to services, it was necessary to restrain the cultivator from quitting his land."

This period includes two great processes. The reduction of the free Ceorls into villeinage by the Normans, and their re-enfranchisement by the operation of mutual interest and natural causes. Also the narrowing of the representative basis from the Conqueror to H. II, and then the broadening of it by means of the money necessities of the Kings, and the general spirit of freedom.

"The Anglo-Saxon peasantry of England," says Hallam, "were not villeins, but the original Britons were extirpated, absorbed, or enslaved. The Thanes were very numerous.

"It is an improbable and even extravagant supposition, that all these hereditary estates of the Anglo-Saxon freeholders were originally parcels of the royal demesne. Whatever partitions were made upon the conquest of a British province, we may be sure that the shares of the army were coeval with those of the general. English Lords had their courts and suitors, with much of the intrinsic character of the feudal relation, though in a less mature and systematic shape than after the Norman Conquest. Even the Ceorls were considered lawworthy for a century after, and their lives were valued at 200 shillings. Thanes were valued at 1200 or 600 shillings. The Editor of King Alfred's Will, says 'all Ceorls by the Saxon constitution might choose such man for their landlord as they would.' Up to H. II, their lot was not one of mere servitude. At the time of H. II, and after, the Ceorl was absolutely dependent, but not to any but his Lord, who was, however, indictable only for murder, rape, or mutilation of the Ceorl. 'A genuine Saxon could only become a slave in not paying a weregild, or by some legal offence.'"

Gradually, domains became reduced by sales, demises, and sub-infeudations. Land, the cheapest of articles, was often the price of labour. The lord wanted less labour, and there was more of it. Services became less onerous and uncertain. After unmolested residence for a year and a day within a walled town or borough the villein became free.

"The greater part," says Hallam, "enfranchised themselves by running away, and by the middle of the fourteenth century a large proportion were free." Chancellor Fortescue (temp. H. VI and E. IV) remarked: "There is scarce a small village in which you may not find a knight, an esquire, or some substantial householder, commonly called a frankleyn, possessed of considerable estate; besides others who are called freeholders, and many yeomen of estates, sufficient to make a substantial jury."

"Two subjects," says Hallam, "tend in a very material degree to illustrate the progress of society, with which civil liberty and regular Government are closely connected,—first, the servitude or villeinage of the peasantry, and their gradual emancipation; secondly, the continual increase of commercial intercourse with foreign countries."

The narrowing, and then the broadening of the representative basis, we recur to in a subsequent chapter. Hallam tells us that "the rule and intention of our old constitution was that each county, city, or borough should elect deputies out of its own body, resident among themselves, and consequently acquainted with their grievances and necessities. The representation of towns in Parliament was founded upon two principles,—of consent to public burthens, and of advice in public measures. To grant money was the main object of their meeting; and if the exigencies of the administration could have been relieved without subsidies, the citizens and burgesses might still have sat at home and obeyed the laws which a council of prelates and barons enacted. The lord sat for his vassals, the abbot for the monks. Spiritual peers sat by general custom of Europe and the common law of England." "This land standeth," said Chancellor Stillington, "by three states, and above that, one principal; that is to wit, lords spiritual, lords temporal, and commons, and over that, state royal."

Macaulay traces our institutions back to three fountains. *Imperial Rome, Papal Rome, and Feudal Germany*, and shows us the character of those limited monarchies of the middle ages, of which the English became the freest and best.

But German feudality, the conqueror of Rome and of England, presents in its barbarous and *powerful individuality* and simple organisation, such a contrast, and such a lesson, when compared with the colossal centralisation and weak individuality of Rome, that we must pause for a moment, and see the stand point of Imperial degradation from which the historian of our fathers wrote.

"In this respect (says Mr. Torrens M'Cullagh, in his Lectures on History) I am inclined to look upon this work of Tacitus as one of the most stupendous efforts of truly moral greatness that we know of. I allude especially to the triumph of self-sustaining energy it manifests. In most other biographies of nations, there are magnificent materials to work upon; Tacitus had worse than none. In all of them there is likewise the great ingredient of antagonistic powers in action to be depicted; but resistance was dead in his time. Heredotus is the chronicler of Grecian chivalry—the narrative of the most brilliant struggle that the world has seen, of moral discipline and daring, with gigantic brutal force. Thucydides is an antithesis from end to end. Livy tells us how the bloodhound cub was born and how it grew, amid every sort of danger, from its suckling time in the wolf's den till its matured ferocity, when every leaf in the forests of Asia and of Gaul had learned to tremble at its imperial howl. Polybius, too, had the same canvas to tint, though his colouring is more uniform.

"But Tacitus had a civilized desert for his landscape—a moral grave-yard for his scene. *The conflict of political principles and powers was over and past.* The cataract had worn itself down. No man dreamed any more of a Democracy; no man imagined the restoration of an aristocratic commonwealth was possible. The provinces had ceased to revolt; Numidia was become a domestic cornfield; and the Greeks had learned to dance gracefully in their chains.

"As far as the circumspective eye could reach, there was nothing to be seen but *the rotting superincumbent weight of Rome.* In the Babel chatter of the thronging of the forum, or in the dim silence of the night watch, no man any longer whispered—change. Had it been otherwise—had the sodden sense of helpless unresistance to imperial despotism, been less thoroughly felt as universal and inevitable,—Tacitus dared not have publicly let fall those scalding tears which form the current of his history."

Imperial Rome and Papal Rome, the inevitable embodiment of order and religion in an era when ignorance disabled, and force controlled the individual, disappear as inevitably as they came.

Feudality conquered Rome by means of the best leadership, and the best and freest vassalage of that age. It was individuality conquering organisation. But as a new civilisation multiplied wants, and required more Government, and as religion forced its claims upon the nation, these more complex arrangements demanded a completer individual competency, and that being wanting, the interests and selfishness of Church, King, and Family prevailed for centuries in England.

Papal Rome remains upon us as a State-paid priesthood, and in a prayer book that is an album of fine old masses bound together by Act of Parliament.

Macaulay (vol. i, p. 2, "History of England"), complains that Ireland is "cursed by the domination of religion over religion," and (p. 181), dilates on "the most instructive fact that the years during which the political power of the Anglican hierarchy was in its zenith, were precisely the years during which national virtue was at the lowest point."

And the judicial Hallam (vol. ii, p. 600, "History of England") concurs :—

> "That the severe remark of Clarendon, that of all mankind none form so bad an estimate of human affairs as Churchmen, is abundantly confirmed by experience; that the clergy have an influence which *no other corporation* enjoy over the bulk of a nation, and are apt to abuse it for undue ascendancy, unjust restraint, or factious ambition; that *the hope of any real good in reformation of the Church by its own assemblies, to whatever sort of reform we may look, is utterly chimerical.*"

Adam Smith thus deduces the power of freedom of towns, and explains the cessation of villenage :—

> "In countries such as France or England, where the authority of the Sovereign, though frequently very low, never was destroyed altogether, the cities had no opportunity of becoming entirely independent. They became, however, so considerable that the Sovereign could impose no tax upon them, besides the stated farm-rent of the town, without their own consent. They were, therefore, called upon to send deputies to the General Assembly of the States of the kingdom, where they might join with the clergy and the barons in granting, upon urgent occasions, some extraordinary aid to the King. Being generally, too, more favourable to his power, their deputies seem, sometimes, to have been employed by him as a counterbalance in those assemblies to the authority of the great lords. *Hence the origin of the representation of burghs* in the States General of all the great monarchies in Europe.

"At first, the farm of the town was probably let to the burghers, in the same manner as it had been to other farmers, for a term of years only. In process of time, however, it seems to have become the general practice to grant it to them in fee, that is, for ever, reserving a rent certain never afterwards to be augmented. The payment having thus become perpetual, *the exemptions*, in return for which it was made, naturally *became perpetual too*. Those exemptions, therefore, *ceased to be personal*, and could not afterwards be considered *as belonging to individuals* as individuals, *but as burghers of a particular burgh*, which, upon this account, was called a Free-burgh, for the same reason that they had been called Free-burghers or Free-traders.

"The principal attributes of villenage and slavery being thus taken away from them, they now, at least, became really free in our present sense of the word Freedom.

"Nor was this all. They were generally at the same time erected into *a commonality or corporation*, with the privilege of having magistrates and a town-council of their own, of making bye-laws for their own Government, of building walls for their own defence, and of reducing all their inhabitants under a sort of military discipline by obliging them to watch and ward; that is, as antiently understood, to guard and defend those walls against all attacks and surprises by night as well as by day. In England they were generally exempted from suit to the hundred and county courts; and all such pleas as should arise among them, the pleas of the Crown excepted, were left to the decision of their own magistrates."—*Smith's* "Wealth of Nations," pp. 103-4-8, v. ii.

Macaulay thus speaks (History of England, v. i, pp. 19, 22, 25, 27, 29, 31, 35, 40) of our liberties and their consolidation:—

"For the century and a half which followed the Conquest there is, to speak strictly, no English history. The subject race still made its sting felt. Assassination was of daily occurrence. The whole nation was in a conspiracy to screen the murderers.

"The first pledge of *their* (Normans and English) *reconciliation* was the great charter won by their united exertions. *Here commences the history of the English nation.* The history of the preceding events is the history of wrongs inflicted and sustained by various *tribes*.

"Then first appeared with distinctness that Constitution, &c., and the House of Commons held its first sittings.

"The greatest victories of the middle ages were gained at

this time against great odds by the English armies. They are to be attributed to the moral superiority of the victors, *a superiority which was most striking in the lowest ranks.* The French had no infantry that dared to face the English bows and bills. *Every yeoman*, from Kent to Northumberland, *valued himself as of a race born to victory.*

"The great lords, unable to gratify their tastes by plundering the French, were eager to plunder each other. 'The realm would not,' in the phrase of Comines, the most judicious observer of that time, 'suffice for them all.' Two factions engaged in a long and fierce struggle for supremacy. The adherents of Lancaster rallied round him a line of bastards, and the adherents of York set up a succession of impostors.

"Meanwhile a change was proceeding, infinitely more momentous. *Slavery was fast disappearing.* Some faint traces of the institution of villenage were detected by the curious so late as the days of the Stuarts.

"When these two great revolutions (mixture of races and elevation of peasantry) had been effected, *our forefathers were by far the best governed people in Europe.* Between the aristocracy and the working people had sprung up a middle class, agricultural and commercial.

He then goes on to trace the character of the Old English monarchy :—

"It was one of a class of limited monarchies which sprang up in Western Europe during the middle ages, and which, notwithstanding many diversities, bore to one another a strong family likeness. They had institutions partly derived from *imperial Rome*, partly from *papal Rome*, partly from the *old Germany.* In all the King's office became by degrees strictly hereditary. *All had municipal corporations enjoying large franchises*, and senates, whose consent was necessary to the validity of some public acts. *Of these kindred constitutions the English was, from an early period, justly reputed the best.* The King alone was entitled to convoke the estates of the realm, and dismiss them. His assent was necessary to all legislative acts. His hereditary revenues, economically administered, sufficed to meet the ordinary charges of Government. He was also feudal lord paramount of the whole soil.

"But his power was limited by three great constitutional principles, *so ancient that none can say when they begun to exist*, so potent that their natural development has produced the order of things under which we live.

"First, the King could *not legislate without the consent of his Parliament.* Second, he could impose *no taxes without their consent.* Third, he was *bound to conduct the executive administra-*

tion according to the laws of the land, and if he broke those laws, his advisers and agents were responsible.

"No English King has ever claimed the general legislative power.

"That the King could not impose taxes without the consent of Parliament is admitted to have been from time immemorial a fundamental law of England.

"That he was bound to conduct the administration according to law was established at a very early period.

"No candid Tory will deny that these principles had, five hundred years ago, acquired the authority of fundamental rules."

Also the instant physical force guarantees which maintained the freedom of those days:—

"If, not content with occasionally oppressing individuals, he dared to oppress great masses, his subjects promptly appealed to the laws, and that appeal failing, appealed as promptly to the God of battles. They had in reserve a check which soon brought the fiercest and proudest King to reason.

"The effect of wealth has been to make insurrection far more terrible than maladministration.

"*In the middle ages, resistance was an ordinary remedy.* If a popular chief raised his standard in a popular cause, an irregular army could be assembled in a day. Regular army there was none.

"Any comparison between our ancient and modern polity must lead to most erroneous conclusions, unless large allowance be made for the effect of that restraint which resistance and the fear of resistance constantly imposed on the Plantagenets. As we cannot employ physical force, it is our wisdom to keep all the constitutional checks in the highest state of efficiency. A nation of hardy archers and spearmen might, with small risks, connive at some illegal acts.

"Comines pronounced our Constitution a just and holy thing.

"After the wars of York and Lancaster the links which connected the nobility and commonalty became closer and more numerous than ever. The knight of the shire was the connecting link between the baron and the shopkeeper.

"Our democracy was from an early period the most aristocratic, and our aristocracy the most democratic in the world.

"The palace was guarded by a few domestics whom the array of a single shire, or of a single ward of London, could with ease have overpowered."

And Montesquieu's argument (p. 364, v. ii) against the existence of a *general state of villainage* in Gaul applies to England also :—

"That there was a general regulation for establishing in all parts the state of villainage is *as false as the principle from which it is derived.* If at a time when the fiefs were precarious, all the lands of the kingdom had been fiefs or dependencies of fiefs, and all the men in the kingdom vassals or bondmen, subordinate to vassals; as the person that has property is ever possessed of power, the king who continually disposed of the fiefs, that is of the only property then existing, *would have been as arbitrary a monarch as the Grand Seignior; which is absolutely contradictory to all history.*"

And here is the rationale of this formally absolute power :—

"As Duke of the Duchy of France and Count of Paris, Hugues Capet assumed the title of king. He had received, by the acclamations of his army, a crown in which the other feudatories saw, or thought they saw, the keystone of the arch of their own baronial power. For their dominion over their vassals resting on *a theory of tenures and dependencies which supposed the existence of some ultimate suzerain,* from whom their own fiefs were holden, and in whom the whole feudal hierarchy had their common head, and stay, and centre. They were not aware of the mighty force of names and titles, of fictions and of forms, and especially of their force when shadowing out any of the real substrata of the peace, and order, and social prosperity of mankind. They knelt down with closed hands, and reciting solemn vows before a titular sovereign, and did not perceive, or foresee, that they were thus gradually elevating that empty pageant of royalty into an effective sovereign, destined at no remote period to attain prerogatives by which their own states would be subjugated and their own prosperity reduced to insignificance and want."—*Sir J. Stephens*' "Lectures on the History of France," vol. i, p. 142, 143.

These remarks must suffice to establish the sort of Freedom that existed, *and that could not but exist,* under the Feudal system. And these authorities prepare the mind to believe and to understand the more exact details of our ancient local freedom and self-Government.

How this sort of freedom, founded upon force and necessity, differs, and must differ from that equality which comes to a nation *prepared for it* by Free School, Press, Church, and Assembly, is the problem of a later, and of the present age. Industry involves, doubtless, a higher manhood than war.

During the reign of Ed. III, three great principles were established. The illegality of the King's raising money without consent. That the two houses must concur to alter laws. The right of the Commons to enquire into abuses, and to impeach ministers.

From Ed. III to the civil wars of York and Lancaster, Parliament established the following concessions. Its exclusive right to tax, and to direct and check expenditure. That supply depends upon redress. Security against illegal ordinances. Control of the royal administration. The punishment of bad ministers. The establishment of their own privileges.

In the 9th Hen. IV is the earliest authority for two eminent maxims of Parliamentary law; the Commons' exclusive right to originate money bills, and that the King shall not take notice of matters pending before Parliament.

"Prerogative," says Hallam, "with the Norman Government, rather resembled a scramble of wild beasts when the strongest takes the best share." At first this Norman prerogative modified the principles of resistance inherent in feudality, but want of money, continental ambition, feudal insubordination, emancipation of villeins, and the opening up of commerce, prepared the nation for the new era.

§

The national intellect and soul of England first began to organise itself somewhat "for the whole and for the all," in the era of Cromwell, and a consideration of the Acts of Parliament made and repealed within thirty years of that epoch, is a most instructive admonition for our own age.

English history here divides into two branches. The one part of the nation emigrated and established in the West a complete Democracy, which, after the struggles and reactions of eighty years, has conquered the oligarchic sections, and is assimilating the American nation; the other remained, and, after a struggle of one hundred and seventy years with prerogative and privilege throughout the country, is now following its brethren fast on the road to political equality.

Of America, it was said by Jefferson, "The Republicans are the nation."

Of England, the same may be said of Puritans; they always definitively gain the last victory, and Republicans and Puritans are one breed.

The forces that repudiated the despotism of Charles the First, constituted the entire material, political, and religious freedom of the country. The first acts of Charles the Second were devoted with much skill and entire unscrupulousness to their destruction, and their reinstatement has been the progressive work of the English nation since. That work is not even yet accomplished.

The powers that overthrew the Stuart were the Puritans, the Press, and the Republican army.

The powers that restored his son were the Church, and a great portion of the landed gentry, aided by the multitude unprepared for a Republic.

Charles the Second undertook to turn the whole force of the law and of the State against the first. He undertook to reinstate and to recompense the second against and at the expense of the People.

Let us take first the *Army*.

The 12 Car. II, c. 20, was an Act for completely disbanding the whole of it.

The 13 Car. II, stat. 1, c. 26, was an Act for declaring the sole right of disposing of the militia in the King, reciting that the contrary had almost ruined and destroyed the kingdom, and that evil and rebellious principles had been thereby instilled.

Take now the *Press*.

The 13 and 14 Car. II, c. 33, recites, "the general licentiousness, and many schismatical, heretical, and seditious books, for prevention whereof no surer means can be advised than *reducing the number of printing presses, and ordering and settling the art and mystery of printing*, by Act of Parliament."

Then the *Quakers*.

13 Car. II, c. 1. "Quakers refuse oaths, and assemble under pretence of worship endangering public safety to the terror of the People, maintaining secret correspondence, &c." It was enacted, that for printing against the taking of oaths, or refusing to take them, or assembling more than five persons over sixteen years of age, they should forfeit to the King,—first offence, £5; second, £10; third, transportation.

Next against *Puritans* generally.

The "Act for uniformity of prayers and sacraments," 13 Car. II, c. 4. Whereas a "great number of People were following their own sensuality, and without fear of God, to the hazard of souls;" the King had approved certain alterations for allaying present distempers and settling the peace of the nation. Then follows form of assent to book of prayer, and declaration that it is not in any case lawful to take arms against the King.

Nonconformists were next attacked by the 17 Car. II, c. 2 (A.D. 1664), "restraining Nonconformists from inhabiting corporations." "Whereas divers persons, &c., have not assented to the prayer book, and some of them have preached and distilled poisonous principles of schism and rebellion."

Then follows form of oath against taking arms against the King, or attempting alterations in Church or State. Penalty for preaching or coming within five miles of town without having taken the oath, £40 or six months imprisonment without bail.

See now how the King recompensed his friends at the expense of the People.

And first the *Church.*

An Act, 1 Eliz., cap. 1, had restored to the crown the ancient jurisdiction over the state ecclesiastical and spiritual, and given the crown power to appoint commissioners to reform, amend, &c., all errors which could be, &c., by ecclesiastical power. This power had been abused by the King, and was abolished by the 16 Car. I, c. 11. Also the powers next mentioned were taken from archbishops, &c.

The 13 Car. II, c. 12, "explained" the last Act. It enacted, that "archbishops, &c., may exercise all manner of ecclesiastical jurisdiction, censures, and coercions, &c."

So much for reinstating his ecclesiastical allies in power ecclesiastical. He also clothed them with secular jurisdiction by the 13 Car. II, c. 2, "an Act to repeal an Act for disenabling all persons in Holy Orders to exercise any temporal jurisdiction or authority as *Justices of the Peace or Members of Parliament.*"

The Act thus repealed, the 16 Car. I, c. 27, recited that "whereas bishops, &c., ought not to be entangled with secular jurisdiction (the office of the ministry being of such great importance that it will take up the whole man), and it is found by long experience that their intermeddling hath occasioned great mischiefs and scandal both in

Church and State, out of care of the Church and Souls, &c."

Next we see the *landed interest* rewarded at the expense of the nation for ever.

The 12 Car. II, c. 24, in "an Act for taking away tenures in capite and by knight's service and purveyance, and for settling a revenue upon his Majesty in lieu thereof." From the 24th February, 1645, all tenures are to be turned into free and common socage.

As "a full and ample recompense to the King, rates of excise on beer, ale, cider, perry, mead, strong waters, coffee, chocolate, sherbet, and tea were granted to the King, his heirs and successors."

Well might this King's Parliament join in reciting (12 Car. II, c. 14) the "power miraculously demonstrated in this wonderful and glorious restoration to kingdoms new born and raised from the dead, on this the day which the Lord hath made, &c.," and enact that "every subject shall annually resort to Church" to give thanks!

§

During this momentous epoch, from the great settlement and fixing of the rights of person and property of Englishmen, by the two Charters of the 9 H. III, A.D. 1224, down to the approaching recognition of the rights of opinion and of equality, various great landmarks stand out from the mass of legislation, and there is also a strange mosaic of passion, brutality, and fierce extremes. Thus we have the declaration that "no man shall henceforth lose life or member for our venison," and the Act 2 H. IV, c. 15, and others, for the burning of heretics.

We have Acts against Quakers, preaching, and the printing press; and Acts of excommunication against breakers of the Charter, and for compelling bishops to pronounce it. And the Archbishop of Canterbury (4 H. IV, c. 3) "promises that benefit of clergy shall not be extended to any clerk, secular or religious, convicted of treason or being a notorious thief."

Acts for preventing clergymen from being justices and members of Parliament, and Acts reinstating them; Acts for restraining,—and for enabling ecclesiastical tyranny.

Till the Reform Bill the great national landmarks of Parliamentary history were only seven.

1st. The Magna Carta and De Foresta won freedom for Church, Barons, and Freemen, by the combined forces of those three estates.

The necessity for the latter Act may be seen from the clause that "a freeman may make in his own wood a mill, fish pond, pool, &c., and may have hawks, herons, &c., and also the honey which may be found there, &c."

2nd. The Act 25 Ed. I* (A.D. 1297). The "Confirmation of Charters" as the common law. It declares judgments against the charters void, and

* The statute 34 Ed. I, st. 4, commonly called "de Tallagio non concedendo," is mutilated, and questionable history.

undertakes that "we will never draw such aids, tasks, and prises into a custom for any thing that hath been done or that may be founden by roll, or in any other manner ; and we have granted for us and our heirs, and to all the communalty, that never for any business will we take aids, tasks, nor prises of our realm, *but by the common assent of the realm,* and for the common profit of the said realm, saving the ancient aids and prises due and accustomed."

3rd. The Act 26 H. VIII, c. 1 (1534), whereby the King became the supreme head of the English Church, and freeing us from Papal supremacy, chained religion like a dead body to the State.

4th. The Act 16 Car. II, already detailed, which turned feudal tenure into freehold to repay the chivalry for restoring Charles II, and mulcted the nation for ever by shifting the charges from the chivalry upon the excise.

5th. The Act 1 W. and M., s. 2, c. 2 (A.D. 1688), commonly called the Bill of Rights, "declaring the rights and liberties of the subject, and settling the succession," declares :—1st. That dispensing power in the King is illegal. 2nd. That the dispensing power lately exercised was illegal. 3rd. That Ecclesiastical Courts are illegal. 4th. That levying money for the Crown without grant of Parliament is illegal. 5th. Confirms right of petition. 6th. That raising or keeping a standing army in state of peace, unless with consent of Parliament, is illegal. 7th. That Protestant subjects may have arms for defence. 8th. That elections shall be free. 9th.

Confirms freedom of speech and of debates in Parliament. 10th. That excessive bail shall not be demanded. 11th. That jurors shall be duly returned. 12th. That grants of fines of persons before they are convicted, is illegal. 13th. That Parliaments ought to be held frequently. 14th. That these are the true, ancient, and indubitable rights of Englishmen.

6th. The Act 1 G. I, c. 38, which made Parliaments septennial.

7th. The accepting of the value of 1692 (see Macaulay, v. iv, p. 315), little more than one-fiftieth of the present value, as the basis of the land-tax. This was the second great land swindle at the expense of the nation. Nevertheless, the 38 G. III, cap. 60, declares that it "conduces to strengthening the public credit, and augmenting the national resources, that the duty now payable for one year on land shall be made perpetual, and that the sums be raised yearly."

§

These acts represent the ebb and flow of legislation, and through them all the general advance of the nation.

Nevertheless, it was well nigh said in history of England that she died in childbirth,—that she brought forth the man-child America, and perished of the strain upon her system.

The revolution and the reformation that came at once upon us kindled in our manhood at that epoch a *quality* such as the world has seldom known, but it was not broadly based enough on an universality of Freedom in School, Press, Church, and Assembly,—its *quantity* was not enough to maintain freedom, much less to carry it on to Equality, and so, as Democracy could not prevail to conduct the future of England, it went forth to create and to inspire another nation.

What has England done since? She has done a great deal of shopkeeping and shoplifting the world over. She has tried to murder or maim her progeny in the West. She assailed the Republic of France, and when it brought forth Napoleon, who hewed in pieces the feudal system, she mortgaged her industries and passed her children through the fire to uphold it, and took on tick all the infamies of Europe for twenty years.

She has founded Colonies, that have immediately reversed her system of Government. She has founded empires, but has denied and misunderstood the main elements of their administration,—justice, land tenure, and religion. She is the greatest Mahommedan and Christian power, and is mighty in opium sales and in missionaries.

And what is it that England wants? *Is it enough of manhood* and its rudiments at our base,—in our political foundations, that, as Milton said, "those who choose shall be fittest to choose the best, and England shall at last be organised not only for and by 'the all,' but for *the whole of the all*,—the educated manhood of England?"

Surely nothing but this can secure for us the

rule of the true nation and make us free within and honorable without.

Having nearly neutralised if not mastered the party amongst us, whether in Church or in State, who would oppose this, we are at last getting over our parenthesis in history,—this abyss of two hundred years, and are going on to that Equality which Stuarts and Legitimists, Priestcraft and Ignorance have so long looked for and feared, as coming beforehand to torment them.

We must cease to believe that, in affairs international, the converse of wrong is right,—that because we erred in intervening, therefore non-intervention is always policy and Christianity. That we must *either* keep or slay our brethren, and that the protest of Cain is the teaching of Christ.

Doubtless this completion of our manhood, *wholly and thoroughly, in quantity and quality,* is the process which re-commenced in 1830, and which has yet to be urged on, through, or over all opponents.

For the science of politics, which but manifests the laws of God, is absolute.

We must have the revolutionary energies of our common men to match and neutralise in permanence the conservative instincts of wealth, prerogative, privileges, and caste. This we must have, lest revolution itself should rise from the abyss.

From education to association, from association to equality, is the law, based in nature and necessity.

Stop education and you stop the rest, *but it must be stopped at the beginning or not at all.*

Give to man education, and he will, *he must* associate, and take the rest that is his right.

Therefore of three things one :—

Oppose Education, and go back to Barbarism ; grant Education, and deny manhood, and necessitate revolution ; or go on freely, fairly, and fully, to complete recognition of the national manhood.

The first course is murder. The second suicide. The third is Life, Conservatism, Democracy, and Statesmanship.

The Puritans were, are, and will be the nation ; and we have been but little indeed of a nation till we began to return to Puritanism.*

To confess manhood and deny it not, is the only course for those who intend to rule in England. Labour and capital will go on to unite their energies and interests, and to subdue their opponents. The true aristocrats of trade, birth, and intellect, will help on the work. Wealth will not subdue the spirit of commerce, for manhood will rise with it. We shall continue and enlarge the age of Cromwell and the Puritans, and shall never be above praying, thinking, and fighting for the right.

Thus England is not of those nations, over

* Is it too much to say that it was the principle of Puritanism (and chiefly, if not only, that part of it which is a strong religious life, independent of endowed systems), which, under the teaching and leadership of such men as Bunyan, Wesley, Whitfield, &c., kept the better part of the English nation alive until the great outward and visible reaction of 1832.

whose carcasses the chariot wheels of history and civilisation jolt as they pass on in their career.

For this world is *organised.* Order rules, and not disorder. Human nature has certain requirements which must be met, if not in a perfect way, in the best way possible, if not by one nation, then by another which will sweep over it to empire.

Where there are not enough complete men in a State to understand their material, mental, and spiritual interests, and to organise for material, mental, and spiritual freedom, those interests will be arranged for them according to the general worth or worthlessness of the actual manhood.

The Church will be farmed. The State will be farmed,—for the profit of the farmers. The national manhood will fare somewhat as an Irish estate with an absentee landlord and a rapacious middle-man. The words of Volney will perhaps better fit the situation:—

> "They sold the favour of the Prince to the Visier, and the Visier sold the Empire. They sold the law to the Cadi, and the Cadi sold justice. They sold the altar to the Priest, and the Priest sold Heaven. Men will never cease to be tormented till they shall become intelligent and wise,—till they shall practise the art of justice, founded on a knowledge of the various relations in which they stand, and the laws of their own organisation."

When a State possesses an adequate number of men completely enough developed, the man will govern himself, and these creatures of chaos and old night will be scattered, as chased the legions of light the hordes of the abyss.

Till "the whole of the all" are prepared and

organised for equality, the State and the Individual must suffer, for that is the sum of political questions, their only *final and universal* solution.

Up to 1832, the national manhood was transfixed and petrified by oligarchic influences. The Reform Bill was the guarantee of its mobilisation, and the recommencement of its life.

Macaulay says, that the revolution of 1688 "finally decided the great question, whether the popular element should be suffered to develop itself freely, and to become dominant." This were surely said with greater propriety of the Reform Bill of 1832. That transferred the "right divine," from the families who farmed the revolution of 1688, to the middle classes. The coming Bill will establish the principle of the political competency of the People, if it does not enfranchise them. The most profound researches into the past can only show that those possessed the franchise who were free, and that those who were free possessed the franchise or its accepted equivalent of power.

The suffrage must evermore advance or recede with the power of the developed associated manhood of the age and nation. The all will be enfranchised when the all (or a great majority of the all) possess in their own souls the *elements* of freedom, and can combine and assert the everlasting twofold truth of conservatism and progress.

THE PROBLEM.

Can Democracy Organise?

"The British Government is one of the wisest in Europe, because there is a body which examines it perpetually, and is perpetually examining itself."—*Montesquieu*, v. iii, p. 60.

"If the constitution of England and America were compared with regard to their forms and substance, that of America would be found to approach the more nearly to a popular elective monarchy, and that of England to an aristocratic republic."—*Goldwin Smith*, 22nd January, 1866.

"Laws ought to be no less relative to the principle or passion, than to the nature or organisation of each Government; this is the key to an infinite number of laws.

"It is the nature of a republican Government that either the collective body of the People, or particular families, should be possessed of the supreme power."—*Montesquieu.*

T 2

"The question now is, whether, and how, shall England pass from an aristocratic to a Democratic Republic."

"Every conceivable law must properly originate in one of these three points of view; but none should be made and enacted without regard to all three; and the one-sided view in which they have originated is an essential defect in too many laws. Now from this threefold aspect we have three preliminary essentials for every system of legislation: 1. A complete *general theory of right;* 2. A perfect exposition of *the end which the State should propose itself*, or what is, in fact, the same thing, an accurate definition of the limits within which it is to restrict its activity, or a representation of the especial ends which are actually pursued by this or that State union; 3. A theory of the *means necessary for the existence of a State*; and as these means are necessary partly for the sake of internal cohesion, and partly in order to assure the possibility of action, —a theory of political and financial science. The first-mentioned alone is eternal and immutable as human nature, while the others allow of modifications."—*Baron W. von Humboldt*, p. 183, "Sphere and Duties of Government."

Chapter II.

THE PROBLEM.

"The whole art of the legislator is correctly to discern beforehand the natural inclinations of communities of men, in order to know whether they should be assisted, or whether it may not be necessary to check them."—*De Tocqueville.*

"We must vindicate,—what? new things? No! Our ancient legal and vital liberties, reinforcing the laws enacted by our ancestors, by setting such a stamp upon them that no licentious spirit shall dare henceforth to violate them."—*Sir Thomas Wentworth,* "Parl. Hist.," 11.

"Bitter jest, that the most civilised portion of the globe should be considered incapable of self-Government."—*D'Israeli.*

"How long shall *principals* continue bound by chains of iron, *trustees* by nothing but cobwebs."—*Bentham.*

"I say that it is demonstrated that genuine representation alone can give solid power, and that in order to make the Government strong, *the People must make the Government.* . . . According to the original principles of your system . . . you do no more than restore the genuine edifice designed and framed by our ancestors."—*Charles Fox,* 1797.

"Not laws, but tyrannous ordinances, if imposed on him without his suffrage given in person or by deputation."—*Sir William Jones,* 1782.

"Some doubts might be cast on the penetration of men who, whilst they complain of the pressure of taxation, send to Parliament hordes of military and naval officers, who have an interest in making that taxation still greater."—*Herbert Spencer.*

We have seen that good Government exists where power is rightly distributed and completely organised.

Also that it is an axiom that all Governments consist of a Principle, a Passion, or a motive power, and of an Organisation, and that every Government that has not a single preponderating power tends either towards its establishment, or to anarchy.

It is therefore essential to enquire respecting any given nation, whether the actual preponderating power is in harmony with the actual Constitution; or whether it has warped or is warping the original or actual Constitution; or whether it tends to reconstruction and return, or to some new principle and organisation.

Because if the preponderating power be *enough* a power to gradually overcome resistance, *then progress can be conservative*; if not, it must be revolutionary.

And to judge of the progress or decline of a nation, this enquiry must be conducted by the light of the fact, so oft repeated, that all real progress is from the rule of the one, to that of the few, the many, and the all. In Democratic Governments the preponderating power is the power of the whole,—the all rule the all, and therefore there is the minimum chance of corruption, displacement, or decline.

There are therefore two necessary phases of enquiry,—*relative and positive*. Relative,—"Is the organisation in harmony with the power; and are either of these changed or changing?" Positive,—"Is the nation advancing towards the rule of the all, halting with the rule of the few or the many, or going back to the rule of the one?"

Obviously the only case in which there can be at the same time *a single preponderating power*, a power *rightly* and *definitively* distributed, is the case where that power is in the People, and where a universal political equality levels all sectional and sinister ascendencies. In fact, Democracy is the highest degree of organisation *springing from* the highest degree of freedom.

These principles of enquiry suggest three questions which the practical politicians of England should be prepared to answer.

First. What are the *principles* of our politics? and what is the preponderating power in the State?

Second. What is the ruling *tendency* of our politics?

Third. What are the results? Is our progress in the right direction, and at the right pace?

Does it lead away from our ancient Constitution, or back to it? Does it lead to the rule of the all, or to the rule of the few,—to Democracy, stagnation, or destruction?

But to get the right political perspective of events, to estimate their relative importance, and to realise our progress or decline, it is necessary to observe where we were in the former times—say a thousand years ago,—what then was our Constitution, and what the preponderating power.

And as it will appear that the tendency of our national organisation has been from local self-

Government to centralisation, and that the tendency of our national principles now is from family rule to national rule, or Democracy, the great question is, whether the spirit and power of Democracy is strong enough to organise the forms of centralisation, or whether the two have got to fight it out.

In answer to the question what are now the principles and preponderating power of our politics? we say,—the British Government is an oligarchy tempered by monarchy, middle-class promotions, capital, strikes, trades' unions, a half free Church, free assembly, and the fourth estate.

In other words we have got as far on the political road as the rule of the few, with the many helped, thirty years ago, to a foothold on power by the all, and the all kicked down as a ladder no longer useful.

The preponderating power of the families has broken the balances of the constitution, and the most that monarchy is allowed to do, is to choose for us and for itself, the reigning oligarchy.

Our theory is that of mixed Government. Our preponderating power is oligarchy. The fact is, that we are ruled by a Premier-President, chosen about (on an average) every four years, and by a Democracy gradually encroaching on the oligarchic usurpation, *and already able, in crises, to assert its sovereignty.*

The Politics of England are not moulded either

on the principle of Manhood, of Property (or Thinghood), or, entirely, of Feudality. We are ruled neither by labor, capital, nor land, but by a compromise of the last two. Labor cannot be said to be represented by the ten pound franchise, and we have amongst us a depopulated Ireland and a million of paupers.

Our Politics in Foreign affairs are neither Intervention or non-Intervention. But we have just left off murdering our brethren by the first, and are now intent on the "great principle" of *only* seeing them murdered, which is safer, cheaper, and just as moral. This is clearly not a policy of "*Manhood*," it is the safe and timorous policy of capitalists, who have got a certain victory over the policy of tradition and of the families, which has always sought to maintain the vermin of legitimacy in Europe at the charges of the British nation. *Now*, the shopkeepers and the chivalry rule, and of the two, the former are rather the more jealous of the People.

As to the shopkeepers, the Chancellor, on April 7th, 1864, informed us that the total import and export trade of England, had grown in 1863, to nearly £444,000,000, about three times the amount of 1843. We were further told that whereas "from 1842 to 1852, the taxable income of the country increased by 6 per cent. ; in the eight years from 1853 to 1861 it has increased from the basis taken in 1853, 20 per cent. This intoxicating augmentation of wealth and power is entirely confined to classes of property."

Three thousand persons, according to the Income and Property tax returns of July 20th, 1864, possess an income of about £25,000,000, rather more than the total revenue of the whole mass of agricultural laborers in England and Wales.

As to the landowners, the census of 1861 shows that the number of male landed proprietors of England and Wales decreased from 16,934 in 1851, to 15,066 in 1861, so that *the concentration of land had grown* 11 *per cent. in ten years.* At this rate we should soon repeat the state of things under Nero, when half the province of Africa was owned by six gentlemen.

Thus (as it would be quoted on change), *manhood,* already five hundred per cent. below par, decreases relatively to property, year by year; and, in another view, it is the one "unknown quantity," that increases day by day in power.

To the second question we answer, The ruling tendency of English politics is nevertheless undoubtedly to Democracy,—the Power and Rule of the All. This tendency is vouched since 1832, by a series of Popular Victories. All things tend to the preponderance of numbers and intelligence. It is a running fight. Democracy is let loose upon privilege, and notwithstanding the concentration of property and land power, flanks every political position to which privilege successively retires.

To the third question,—" What are the results

of the principles that rule in English politics; is our progress in the right direction and at the right pace?"—we answer, there are two tests of those results.

The ideal best Government produces, as we have seen, a general diffusion of advantages amongst individuals. It encourages the growth of individual genius and of the highest class of excellence; and it contributes to an intense and invincible feeling of nationality. We have seen that this ideal best Government is Democracy.

And the ideal best Government also gives Material, Political, and Religious Freedom.

How near, then, is the British nation to these results and this ideal?

The British nation has certainly not got material, political, or religious freedom. There is consequently not a proper diffusion of advantages amongst individuals. And whilst there is much free development of individual genius and excellence, and an intense feeling of nationality, greater freedom would develop more numerous instances of the first, and would certainly elevate as well as intensify the last. The chief freedom of Englishmen may be described,—and it is a great deal,—as the freedom to try to get freedom by any means short of rebellion.

The "results," then, point wholly to the necessity of increasing and complementing our freedom.

The fact of thirty years unequalled advance under a modified Democracy is an argument for an increased Democracy.

1832 not only gave us a new start in political freedom, followed by conquests since of material freedom, and of intellectual freedom, and by efforts after religious freedom.

It turned back the reaction of one hundred and eighty years. It was the second great victory in our historical development of Feudality to Democracy. It gave the signal for that advance which will be the destruction of our mixed Government, and which will ultimately secure to us a peaceful instead of a violent revolution, and save us from the horrors of national dissolution and decay.

This follows from the principle or the truism proclaimed by De Tocqueville, and before alluded to, "that a Government equally divided between two adverse principles must either pass through a revolution or fall into complete dissolution."

In discussing, therefore, the *results* of the ruling forces of our Government, we find them as varied as the mixture of forces and principles. They are good as far as public opinion, the final court of appeal, inclines towards a virtuous Democracy, and the future will be well, as the incline, whilst irresistible, is sufficiently gradual and peaceable.

It is this mixture and conflict of principles and social forces that makes an analysis of the situation so difficult.

As a question of finality as to the political sovereignty, we shall probably go on with three processes.

We shall probably go on to make public opinion more and more absolute by making its constituent forces more and more equal and homogeneous. A true Democratic equality will reign in all but form.

The People's instruments, their Representatives, will become more and more delegates, but delegation will become more and more honorable, for there will be a completer unity of opinion and a greater equality of information.

The People's instruments, the Executive, will become, by shortened Parliaments, and by greater freedom and equality every way, more dependent on the People, while the Premier's power becomes, possibly, even more concentrated and complete.

What is the nominal head of the republic is not a matter of essence, but of form. Kinghood, as now, will reign, whilst the People, instead of the families, govern; and if triennial Parliaments are adopted, our Premier-President will be assimilated to the American,—he will be more powerful and more dependent.

As the national manhood approaches maturity and universality, we shall, and of course must, become more self-Governing, Equal, or Democratic.

Meanwhile, *the nature or organisation* of our Government is the "mixture,"—of King, Lords, and Commons. *The Principle* of our Government, or *the animating and directing passion*, tends now to be evermore more Democratic.

Hence, our necessary policy.

"Laws," says Montesquieu (in that celebrated passage so often quoted, in which he expounds 'the very important distinction from which he draws many consequences, for it is the key of an infinite number of laws'), "laws ought to be no less relative to the principle or passion, than to the nature or organisation of each Government."

Hence, as Disraeli once said profoundly, but in another connection, "our true policy is to carry out the new principles by means of existing forms." Hence, again, to accept Democracy is conservative, to oppose it is revolutionary.

§

Having ascertained in "Principle, Tendency, and Results," how far England is a Democracy, the great question remains, what are the next steps which England is prepared to take in that direction?

Democracy, the rule of the all, is Society mobilised. Oligarchy is Society petrified. England is half petrified, and half mobilised.

A Democratic nation may exist whenever the national manhood is sufficiently developed to associate for self-Government, Democracy being the measure of the admitted rights and values of manhood.

We therefore put aside for the next score of ages all theories of plural voting and protection of minorities, for were they right in theory anywhere, they would be superfluous here.

The theory of all progress is that of an advance towards Democracy, and the theory of conservatism is that that advance be graduated.

If the advance be barred,— there is revolution.

Progress in England *cannot* be barred. Free

Press, Speech, and Assembly, Commerce, Education, Labour, Capital, Political Economy, and Christianity, forbid that. They guarantee industrial, political, and religious freedom,—with revolution, or without it.

Monopolies, Caste, and Priestcraft have got, here as everywhere, to surrender or to be destroyed.

The question for *conservative* England is, "How best to graduate the next realisation of Democracy?" The question for *Democratic* England is, "*How large a measure of privilege can be next attacked and destroyed, and how soon?*"

The question presses. England, politically, is not yet where she was officially in Cromwell's time, though in average education and productiveness much better. The Lords absorb all three estates. The Executive absorbs the Legislative. Scottish and Irish Parliaments are destroyed. Centralisation is intense. To give new *organic advantages* to minorities were to increase that which is already in excess,—to do that which must speedily be undone,—to do that which, till undone, would perpetuate a war of interests, classes, and sections.

Conventionally phrased, the question now is, *not* shall England pass from an hereditary Monarchy to a Republic. She really elects her ruler already by a species of double or treble election, for a constituency returns him, the House of Commons and public opinion accept him as chief, and then the Sovereign sends for him. The question now is, "Whether and how shall England pass from an aristocratic to a democratic Republic?"

"It is (says Montesquieu) the nature of a Republican Government, that *either the collective body of the People, or particular families,* should be possessed of the supreme power."

THE PREPONDERATING POWER OF THE PAST, AND ITS ORGANISATION;

OR,

DEMOCRACY AND LOCAL SELF-GOVERNMENT.

"After this manner, oh mighty prince, are none other realms of the world disposed and inhabited. For though there be in them men of great power, of great riches and possessions, yet they dwell not nigh to another, *neither so many inheritors and possessors of land are elsewhere as in England.*"—*Chancellor Fortescue*, in 15th Century.

"It is not only evident that small freeholders were always numerous, but we are perhaps greatly deceived in fancying, that the occupiers of villein tenements were usually villeins." —*Hallam's Middle Ages*, vol. iii, p. 262.

"Estates for a term of years were not uncommon in Ed. I, yet far outnumbered, as I should conceive, by those of a freehold nature."—*Hallam's England*, vol. iii, p. 42.

"The great council of the Norman Kings was, I believe, little less than a continuation of the witenagemot, the immemorial organ of the Anglo-Saxon aristocracy in their relation to the King."—*Hallam's Middle Ages*, v. ii, p. 230.

"The real presumption as to the municipal Government of Anglo-Saxon boroughs, has been acutely indicated by Sir F. Palgrave, arising from the universal institution of the court-leet, which gave to an alderman chosen by the suitors a jurisdiction in conjunction with themselves, as a jury over the greater part of civil disputes and criminal accusations, as well as general police, that might arise within the hundred."—*Ibid*. v. iii, p. 219.

"Until a comparatively late period no authoritative local representative bodies existed for legislative purposes. The inhabitants themselves were summoned in primary folk-motes." —*Toulmin Smith.*

"Magna Carta. 'To all archbishops, &c., and to all bailiffs and faithful subjects' are granted, &c., and to all our realm these liberties for evermore."

"2 Ed. III, cap. 8: 'Also it is accorded that it shall not be commanded by the great seal or the little seal to disturb or delay common right, that though such commandments come, the justices shall not therefore leave to do right in any point.'"

"34 Ed. I, s. 4, c. 4: 'All clerks and laymen shall have all their liberties and free customs as freely as at any time they had them best and most fully, and any statutes contrary to them shall be void for evermore.'"

"It is common to assert that our liberties were bought with blood. It is far more generally accurate to say, that they (even Magna Carta) were purchased by money."—*Hallam's Middle Ages*, v. 3, p. 161.

"The distribution of *landed property* in England by the Anglo-Saxons, appears to have been regulated on the same principles that directed their brethren on the continent. Part was converted into estates of inheritance for individuals; part remained the property of the public, at the disposal of the State. The former was called *Bocland;* the latter *Folcland.*

"Folcland was the land of the folk, and might be occupied in common, or in severalty. In the latter case, it was probably parcelled out in the *folcgemot*, or court of the district, and the grant attested by the freemen present, but could not be alienated, and on expiration of the term, reverted to the community. It must have been apportioned by the nation in its solemn meeting; earlier by the shire or other collection of freemen.

"Bocland was held by book or charter, and had been severed by an Act of Government from the Folkland, and converted into an estate of perpetual inheritance. Folkland was subject to many burthens from which Bocland was exempt. Bockland was subject only to the trinoda necessitas, contribution to military expeditions, and repairs of castles and bridges. The natural origin of Folcland is the superabundance of good land above that at once appropriated by the tribes, families, or gentes, and on it depends the definition of the march and the 'gau,' with their boundaries. Over the Folcland at first, the king alone had no control."—*Hallam*, pp. 404-5-6-7, v. ii, "Middle Ages."—Quoting Allen's "Inquiry," Sir F. Palgrave, and Kemble's "Codex Diplomaticus."

Chapter III.

THE PREPONDERATING POWER OF THE PAST, AND ITS ORGANISATION;

OR,

Democracy and Local Self-Government.

"From Tacitus to 1688 there is no real break in the chain. The English Constitution has been the result of the maintenance through ages,—by men free when roaming the forests of Germany, and no less free when landing on the shores of England,—of the active sympathies and aspirations of free men."—*Toulmin Smith.*

"When the German and Scythian nations overran the Western provinces of the Roman Empire, the confusion which followed lasted for several centuries. The chiefs usurped the greater part of the lands of those countries.

"The law of primogeniture hindered them from being divided by succession: the introduction of entails prevented their being broke into small parcels by alienation.

"The natural law of succession took place among the Romans, who made no more distinction in the inheritance of lands than we do in moveables. But primogeniture came to take place not immediately, but in process of time, that the power might not be weakened by division. Entails are founded upon the most absurd of all suppositions,—the supposition that every successive generation have not an equal right to the earth, and to all that it possesses."—*Adam Smith*, "Wealth of Nations," v. ii, pp. 81-2-3-4-5.

"The personal expense of the great proprietors having gradually increased, their retainers and unnecessary tenants were dismissed. Tenants could agree to rise of rents only upon condition of a term of years; and having in this manner become independent, the great proprietors were no longer capable of interrupting justice or disturbing peace."—*Ibid.*, pp. 127-8-9.

We believe that our spirit and our forms can be reconciled, and that that fact demonstrates our vigorous life, and constitutes our safety. And following the simple and profound distinction already alluded to, we shall now shortly consider, both what was of old the "Principle, or Passion," or motive power of affairs in England, and also the Organisation that expressed that principle and power, that in fact grew out of it.

It is obvious that *the real* guarantee of popular freedom, and of motive power and organisation, then existed and was generally present throughout the country. Nay, that in circumstances where the People were a set of independent centres of action, instead of one united homogeneous whole, the very preservation of the principle of freedom depended upon the constant use and assertion of *local self-Government.*

For as organisation can only exist by living agents, and as the natural and inevitable tendency of officials is to magnify their offices, enlarge their sphere, and strengthen their position, so, everywhere and always, when organisation is removed from the constant living pressure of the People, it tends to mere bureaucracy, centralisation, and despotism.*

And, in times when religion was farmed by Church or King, and there was for the People neither press nor general intercommunication of any kind, the only means whereby they could control the organisation, was the representative system, based upon local self-Government.

* Thus "*statute law*, which is made by a body existing and acting by virtue of a derived authority only, will be always tending to encroach on *common law*, which springs immediately from the folk and people."

Centralisation, then, meant despotism, or at least the power to be despotic. Centralisation, now, means the perfect administration of the governing will, whether of the one, the few, the many, or the all.

The question now is, how universality of suffrage and power can use centralisation for the People, "the People,"—that grand modern phase—"the People, one and indivisible," that never existed until now, whose soul is public opinion, and whose will creates or crushes cabinets.

Thus the problem changes with the hour. Local self-Government was stolen from the People. Centralisation was substituted against the People, but may become their perfect weapon. Public opinion anticipates the franchise, and commands votes, voters, representatives, and Governments.

This being the case, universal suffrage is not the *question*. That, or practically that is sure to follow, although universal education must precede it. The question is, whether *centralisation and universal suffrage*,—an intense concentration of means, and an intenser development of the universal will, are not the fated characteristics of the politics of the future,—De Tocqueville has said it, —"*the organisation of Democracy.*"

The Germans, England, America, France, and the Napoleons begun it. America is completing it, and the rest follow.

"Centralisation (said Landor) is the grasp of despotism; municipalities are the commons and promenades of a free People. By the contraction of the one, and the enclosure of the other, we are losing our strength and freshness every day." Landor had not read the latest lesson of statesmanship,—that intensest unity and universal will are not contradictory phrases, but postulates of the same conclusion.

Thus, organisation, which ought to be the mere creature and vehicle of the sacred passion and will of a true People, has, in all ages and countries, save one, magnified itself against it, and in many has overbalanced and crushed it. The machine, Government, destroys its proprietor the People. We must advance yet another step before we shall have learnt of our foes to conquer them.

Twice already in our history has the democratic element preponderated (over the spirit of clanship); in the wandering warring companionship of primitive Germany; and when freeholders were very numerous in England, and all freeholders, if not all men present at "the county," had the suffrage.

Twice has centralisation got the better of Democracy. At first feudality conquered it, but had in its turn to yield to Norman prerogative and popular power. Then came the union of the families, the Tudors, opulence and administrative centralisation, and increased foreign intercourse. But numbers increased at a greater ratio than capital, and the people went down once more, to rally twice in four hundred years,—under Cromwell and for the Reform Bill,—against that family and oligarchic influence which has mainly ruled this country since the end of the fifteenth century.

§

One of the chief elements, and perhaps the preponderating motive power of the later Anglo-Norman times, was embodied, during one of the best known and freest portions of our history, in the general mass of the freeholders, a situation, perhaps, best according with Aristotle's definition of the excellence of middle-class Government, and combining the conservative influences of a stake in the land, with the progressive instincts of a Democracy.

We have seen what was the great council of the Anglo-Saxon, and then of the Norman Kings.

Shires were divided into tithings or hundreds; the cities and boroughs into wards. All the wards and hundreds formerly met together in full shire and borough folk-mote at certain times. Individuals were often chosen to act for the whole in common council.

As town councils represent, as to local affairs, the wants and wishes of the majority of the burgesses, ascertained by means of the several ward-motes,—so Parliament is composed of the assembled representatives of all the several local associated groups (shires, cities, and boroughs) throughout the land, and when local self-Government is healthy, represents the wants and wishes of the majority of the realm in national affairs.

"It may be here remarked (says Toulmin Smith) that the House of Peers is, constitutionally speaking, a remarkable and very interesting illustration of the ancient *combined folk-mote and representative assembly.* It has been already stated that, on certain mutual relations being entered into, of a reciprocal and not servile nature, one person attended the folk-motes of freemen on behalf of several others;—responsible for them and their deeds there, as well as for himself; and watchful of their interests. *The Lords appeared thus*,—just as a jury does,—in a double capacity, as freemen in their own behalf, and also, but expressly and importantly, as representing a body of others.

"As this point of the representative quality of the House of Lords will be new to many, it may be useful to give a single illustration, out of many that might be quoted. In the 14th Edward III, an aid was very importunately asked by the Crown. But the Lords and Commons were not easily made to forget their duties and true functions. So "the Prelates, Counts, and Barons," says the record, "*for themselves and for all their tenants*, and the Knights of Shires, *for themselves and for the Commons of the land*," answered, &c. The Lords represented themselves, and those who stood in the voluntary relation of homage to them: the Knights of Shires, &c., represented, also, themselves (this is not unimportant), and those *freemen, who being in homage with no man*, would otherwise have no voice in the Common Council of the realm. This is a subject very pregnant with matter for the reflection of every thoughtful man.

"In another respect the House of Lords reminds us of the ancient composition of the Common Council. *Every title in that House* is one which was *anciently elective* and represented special local communities and interests."*—*Toulmin Smith's* "Local Self-Government," p. 84.]

§

The Ministerial functions were those of the tything-man, hundred-man, mayor, sheriff, and king. The same idea and character of functions belong to each, varying according to extent. In

* "The title of 'marquis' was conferred upon those who held the command of the *Marches*, as the boundaries between England and Wales, and England and Scotland, were called when those countries were hostile to this nation.

"The title of 'earl,' is derived from the Saxon word *eorl*, noble. The earl formerly had the government of a *shire*. After the Conquest, earls were called counts, and from them their shires have taken the names of *counties*.

"The viscount, *vice-comes*, was the deputy of the earl."

each the functions are, constitutionally speaking, and apart from usurpation and encroachment, strictly and simply ministerial.

Hallam concurs with the other authorities as to the very large and democratical foundation of the county and borough franchise, and as to the "material guarantees" the People had for their freedom :—

"Whoever may have been the original voters for county representatives, the first statute that regulates their election, so far from limiting the privilege to tenants in capite, appears to place it upon a very large and democratical foundation. For (as I rather conceive, though not without much hesitation), not only all freeholders, but all persons whatever present at the county-court, were declared, or rendered, capable of voting for the knight of their shire. Such at least seems to be the inference from the expressions of 7 H. IV, c. 15, 'all who are there present, as well suitors duly summoned for that cause as others.' And this acquires some degree of confirmation from the later statute, 8 H. VI, c. 7, which, reciting that 'elections of knights of shires have now of late been made by very great, outrageous, and excessive number of people dwelling within the same counties, of the which most part was people of small substance and of no value,' confines the elective franchise to freeholders of lands or tenements to the value of forty shillings.

"The representation of towns in Parliament was founded upon two principles; of consent to public burthens, and of advice in public measures, especially such as related to trade and shipping. Upon both these accounts it was natural for the kings who first summoned them to Parliament, little foreseeing that such half-emancipated burghers would ever clip the loftiest plumes of their prerogative, to make these assemblies numerous, and summon members from every town of consideration in the kingdom. Thus the writ of 23 E. I, directs the sheriffs to cause deputies to be elected to a general council from every city, borough, and trading town.'

"The Great Charter of John was secured by the election of twenty-five barons, as conservators of the compact. If the king, or the justiciary in his absence, should transgress any article, any four might demand reparation, and on denial carry their complaint to the rest of their body. 'And those barons, with all the commons of the land, shall distrain and annoy us by every means in their power; that is, by seizing our castles, lands, and possessions, and every other mode, till the wrong shall be repaired to their satisfaction; saving our person, and our queen and children. And when it shall be repaired they shall obey us as before.' It is amusing to see the common law of distress introduced upon this gigantic scale; and the capture of the king's castles treated as analogous to impounding a neighbour's horse for breaking fences."—*Hallam's* "Middle Ages," v. iii, pp. 111, 163.

As to the details of the ancient origin and nature of Parliament; the right of suffrage; conference of members with constituents before voting the taxes; penalties for absence from Parliament; the prompt *answering of all petitions*, and other safeguards of the Constitution, the work of *J. Toulmin Smith*, on "Local Self-Government and Centralisation (John Chapman, 1851)" is a valuable treatise.

Take the following as to the origin and antiquity of our Constitution:—

"The student of our Constitution must take up the records of his race from the earliest times, even from the page of Tacitus, and follow them down, unbroken, till the Revolution of 1688, if he would faithfully fulfil his task. *There is no real break in the chain.* The same great principles will be found to run through the whole, and to assert and re-assert themselves vigorously, from time to time, as encroachments and attempts at oppression made it necessary. The Historian, dazzled by externals, may dwell chiefly on the troubles and deeds of those in high places, but these external marks do not reach so far below the surface as the space and manner of their telling would seem to import. The inner political and social life of the nation has remained, through all these centuries, extraordinarily little changed in character and spirit.

"It suffices, as to the latter (our constitutional system), to say, that it must not be implied that, at any one past period of our history, any one man arose, so farseeing and so gifted that he was able to map out a system of Institutions which has endured through ages, and embodied perfection. The English Constitution has a truer origin than that. *It has been the result of the maintenance, through ages, by men free when roaming the forests of Germany, and no less free when landing on the shores of England, of the active sympathies and aspirations of free men;* which they succeeded, through their strong practical good sense, in preserving in full activity, when in a more settled state, by falling, probably almost insensibly, into courses of habitual action and intercourse among each other, which, as we look back upon them now, it is impossible not to feel to surpass, in practical wisdom and efficiency, what the highest human presight could have chalked out as a system."—Pp. 17-18.

With respect to the democratic basis :—

"It is demonstrable that the principles of the English Constitution are, that the will of the folk and the people is the only foundation for the authority of any in whose hands any public functions may, for any time being, be lodged; that some definite means must always be had recourse to of truly ascertaining that will; that all in authority are to be at all times, directly responsible, for every act, to that will; that no new step can be taken, new law made, nor new office created, but after express appeal to that will; that all Local affairs shall be managed and controlled by the Local bodies only,—general affairs, affecting the common good of the community, being those only the management of which it is proper for the general Government to control."—Pp. 17, 18, 19.

This is indeed the same principle of local sovereignty, which has lately been contended for in America, under an exaggerated form as "State rights."

That Representative Assemblies frequently met and were alone able to make general Laws, in the time of the Anglo-Saxon Kings, is clear from the express letter, as well as internal evidence, of many of those bodies of Laws still extant. A learned writer on that subject has given a list, which he declares to be an imperfect one, of *more than* 120 *English Parliaments under Anglo-Saxon Kings.* Others have reckoned a much greater number.

When William summoned Harold to abide by the oath he had made to support the former in his claim to the crown of

England, the answer he received was, that "it would have been the height of presumption on his (Harold's) part to have entered into any compact concerning the kingdom without the general consent and statute of the Common Council and People." The Historian who records these remarkable words lived himself in the reign of William I's son, Henry I.

"The reign of William I not only furnishes instances of the meeting of the national assembly, but highly interesting information as to the composition of that assembly.

"The forms of the writs issued by John, in the 15th year of his reign, to all cities and boroughs of the realm, as well as to the Peers, in reference to a Parliament, are still extant.

"Magna Charta is demonstrable to have been made and assented to, in and by a Common Council of the whole realm. The edition of it of the 9th Henry III, expressly states that an aid was granted to the King by the earls, barons, knights, free tenants, *and all others of the kingdom.*

"To add but one more to authorities which may be accumulated to almost any extent, the express and most significant words of the ancient and constitutional Coronation Oath (at least as old as Edward I's time), which the Kings of England had to swear, were, that the King should "keep and guard the Laws and Customs which the folk and people shall have chosen (quas *vulgus* elegerit)."—P. 76.

As to Parliamentary representation and various *modern* attempts to narrow its basis from that of the whole body of the freemen, Mr. Toulmin Smith proceeds :—

"As to counties, it is clear from Stat. 8 Henry VI, c. 7,—*the first open successful attempt to narrow, for oligarchic purposes, the parliamentary franchise,*—as well as from earlier statutes and records, that every man, of whatever "substance and value," had, before the passing of that Act, a voice in the election. But, as to towns, *the same narrowing of the franchise was never accomplished until the passing of the* (so-called) *Reform Act.* Whatever some individual places were pusillanimous enough to submit to, the rule of the Common Law was, and is, clear and unmistakeable. A celebrated election committee of the 23rd James I,—a committee composed of the ablest body of lawyers that England ever produced,—after the fullest consideration, declared what was "the common law, that is the common right," on this subject. It affirmed that "of common right, *all the inhabitants,*—householders,—and residents within the borough,—ought to have voice in the election, and not the freeholders there only."

§

The Magna Carta, 9 H. III (A.D. 1224), and the Carta de Foresta, secure the rights of the Peasants, the Barons, and the Church. "First, that the Church of England shall be free, and shall have her whole rights and her liberties inviolable. And to all the freemen of our realm all the liberties underwritten." And the Magna Carta is directed "To all archbishops, &c., and *to all bailiffs and faithful subjects*," are granted, &c., "and *to all our realm* these liberties for evermore."

The Statute 52 H. III, cap. 1 and 2 (A.D. 1267) says, "whereas many great men refused to be justified by the King and his Court like as they were wont in the time of the King's noble progenitors, the more discreet men of the said realm being called together as well of the higher as of the lower estate, the said King hath made, &c., which he willeth to be observed for ever of all his subjects, as well high as low. All persons as well of high as of low estate shall have and receive justice in the King's Court. Moreover, none shall distrain any to his Court who is not of his fee, or upon whom he hath no jurisdiction by reason of hundred or bailiwick."

This Act is important as showing that the question of franchise was one of *habitation*, not of property.

The 2 Ed. III, c. 8, A.D. 1328, says, "also it is accorded and established that it shall not be commanded by the great seal or the little seal to disturb or delay common right; that *though such commandments come, the justices shall not therefore leave to do right in any point.*"

25 Ed. I, c. 3 and 4 (A.D. 1297). The Charter to be sent to Cathedral Churches and read before the People twice a year. Excommunication against breakers of the Charter to be pronounced twice a year. *If Bishops neglect this,—to be compelled.*

28 Ed. I, c. 1 (A.D. 1300). Charter had not been observed, because no punishment had been enacted against offenders.

"Be it known that the great Charter of the liberties of England *granted to all the commonalty* of the realm shall be kept in every point, and shall be read *four* times in the year before the People in full county. *Three good men shall be chosen in every shire court by the commonalty of the same shire to enforce penalty,*—imprisonment or fine.

And cap. 8 enacts that *the People shall have election of their sheriff in every shire,* where the shrievalty is not of fee, if they list.

And 34 Ed. I, s. 4, c. 4, even enacts that *all clerks and laymen* of our realm shall have all their liberties and free customs as freely as at any time they had them best and most fully, *and any statutes contrary to them shall be void for evermore.*

1 H. V, c. 1, mentions that representatives shall be "citizens and burgesses of the cities and boroughs," and shall be chosen by men, "*citizens and burgesses resiant dwelling and free in the same.*"

In the year 1297, five hundred and sixty-nine years ago, in the statute by which Edward the First confirmed the Magna Charta, he bound himself and his heirs not only to the dignitaries of the State, but to "all the commonalty," not to take "aids, mises, or prises," but by the common assent of "all the realm."

In 1306, in the same reign, it was further enacted by the "Statutum de Tallagio non concedendo," 34 Ed. 1, stat. 4, c. 1, that no tallage or aid,—that is, no tax—should be imposed or levied without the assent of the archbishops, bishops, earls, barons, knights, burgesses, and "other the freemen of the commonalty."

Moreover, the limiting Act of H. VI, 1429, was passed in the infancy of the King (literally so,—he was seven years old), and at a very disturbed period.

It is also notable that elections have been, and now are, decided in the first instance, and according to the writ, by the "view," or persons present, without distinction or enquiry, and that that is final unless a poll be demanded.

§

Bentham elaborates very forcibly the point that the franchise was possessed even by so-called *Villeins* :—

"Behold now the words of the statute, 7 H. IV, c. 15. After reciting the grievous complaint of the Commons (in the French original Communalté) of the undue election of the Knights of Counties . . . . sometime made of affection of the Sheriffs, and otherwise against the form of the writs, to the great slander of the counties, and hindrance (retardation) of the business of the Commonalty in (of) the said county,—it enacts that, at the County Court, after proclamation, '*all they that be there present, as well suitors* duly summoned, AS OTHERS, shall attend to the election of the Knights for the Parliament, and then in the full county' (court) they shall proceed to the election, freely and indifferently, notwithstanding any request or commandment to the contrary."

"EVEN AS TO VILLEINS,—were they, after all, really excluded? Look to the *words*, clearly not: who were the persons by whom the elections were to be made? Suitors summoned as such, and they alone? No: but '*all they that be there present.*' Well, but (says somebody) in the state of villeinage, no will of his own could any person be said to have. So much for *surmise*; and, but for particular inquiry, not an unnatural one. Well now as to the *fact*. Eight and twenty years before the time in question, viz., anno 1377, was passed the statute 1 R. II, of which c. 6,—a chapter of considerable length—is in the old French, and in the *vulgate* edition, not translated. From this statute it appears that already, even at that time, villeinage was a condition very different from slavery. *Rent* did they pay; and though, instead of money, it was in the shape of *services*, yet these services were certain. In this statute what is assumed as a general fact, is—that they were able to pay *a fine* to the *King*, besides making *satisfaction* to their *Lords*. The main offence imputed to them is—obtaining liberation from those services by forged deeds.

"The existing *copyholders* are the posterity of the ancient villeins. *Tenants*—the villeins were—the copyholders are—so were they and are they styled—*by copy of Court Roll.* Deriving from the Records of the Court the title to the lands they occupied, what can be more natural than that to *that* same Court they should be under an *obligation*,—under which is included the *liberty*,—of access and resort to it. But supposing any of them *present* at any such Court, how is it possible that they should not have been included in the assemblage designated as above by the word 'others'?"—*Bentham*, "Plan of Reform," pp. 82-3-4.

And, continues Bentham, on the pretences which led to a narrowing of the suffrage:—

"So much for the strong and prosperous reign of H. IV, in which virtually universal suffrage was then established. Comes now the weak and disastrous reign of his *idiot* grandson, under which, under the *sort of pretences* that will be seen, it was curtailed."

"Statute 8, H. VI, c. 7: 'What sort of men shall be chosen, and who shall be chosen knights of the Parliament."

"Item: Whereas the election of knights to come to the Parliaments of our Lord the King, in many counties of the realm of England, have now of late been made by *very great, outrageous, and excessive numbers of people, dwelling within the same counties* of the realm of England, of the which, most part was of people of *small substance*, and '(or)' of no value (*i. e.*, worth), whereof every one (of them) pretending a voice *equivalent*, as to such elections to be made, *with the most worthy* knights and esquires dwelling within the same counties, whereby manslaughters, riots, batteries, and divisions among the gentlemen and other people of the same counties, shall *very likely* rise and be, unless convenient and due remedy be provided in this behalf. (2). Our Lord the King, considering the premises, hath provided, ordained, and established, by authority of this present Parliament, that the knights of the shires, to be chosen within the said realm of England, by *people dwelling* and resident *in the same counties*, whereof every one of them shall have *free land or tenement* to the value of forty shillings by the year at least, above all charges."—P. 85, "Bentham's Plan."

§

As to the complete and literal character of our self-Government of old, Mr. Toulmin Smith contends that:—

"It is quite clear, from the ancient records, that *until a comparatively late period*, the size of all towns and cities being much smaller than at present, and the population of counties much less, *no authoritative local representative bodies existed for legislative purposes*. The inhabitants themselves were summoned in primary folk-motes, to decide every question. The general folk-motes were thus very different things from a modern town's-meeting, where the question in hand has not been *sifted by the many sections separately*."

"The election must *always be in full folk-mote*. This is a most important point, and special attention will have to be called to it hereafter. As in all other proceedings of institutions of local self-Government, this affair is to be done *openly and in sight of all*. A statute relating to the election of members of Parliament was passed in the 7th Henry IV, c. 15, which, being precisely declaratory, on all its points, of the common law of the land, may be usefully quoted.

"At the next shire-mote to be holden after the delivery of the writ of Parliament, proclamation shall be made in the full shire-mote, of the day and place of the Parliament, and that ALL THEY *that be there present* (as already quoted), and this also 'without any commandment of the King, by writ or otherwise, or of any others.'"

"There was no delayed polling. The entire election had to be got over between the hours of eight and eleven in the forenoon."

"The importance of frequent meetings of the Common Council of the realm was always felt. *The universal term of election* TO ALL OFFICES *except the Crown itself was, and is, constitutionally speaking, annual at the utmost.* The choice of representatives to Parliament followed the rule. A new Parliament met at least once a year."—Pp. 79, 80, 81.

The revolutionary energies and ideas of feudality, the broad basis of our national self-Government, and the preponderance of custom over king, are well shown by Hallam in the following :—

"At length (10th year of Rich. 2) the Duke of Gloucester, and Arundel, Bishop of Ely, were commissioned to speak the sense of Parliament; and they delivered it, if we may still believe what we read, in very extraordinary language, asserting that there was an ancient statute, according to which, if the King absented himself from Parliament without just cause during forty days, which he had now exceeded, every man might return without permission to his own country; and moreover, there was another statute, and (as they might more truly say) a precedent of no remote date, that if a King, by bad counsel, or his own folly and obstinacy, alienate himself from his People, and would not govern according to the laws of the land and the advice of the peers, but madly and wantonly followed his own single will, it should be lawful for them, with the common assent of the People, to expel him from his throne, and elevate to it some near kinsman of the royal blood. By this discourse the King was induced to meet his Parliament, when Suffolk was removed from his office, and the impeachment against him commenced."

"If the King newly incorporate an ancient borough which before sent burgesses to Parliament, and granteth that certain selected burgesses shall make election where all the burgesses elected before, this charter taketh not away the election of the other burgesses. By original grant or by custom a selected number of burgesses may elect or bind the residue."—*Coke*, Fourth Institute.

"There seems on the whole great reason to be of opinion that where a borough is so ancient as to have sent members to Parliament before any charter of incorporation proved or reasonably presumed to have been granted, or where the word burgesses is used without anything to restrict its meaning in an ancient charter, the right of election ought to have been acknowledged either in the resident householders paying general and local taxes, or in such of them as possessed an estate of freehold within the borough."—*Hallam's England*, pp. 68, 45, vol. iii.

It has been well urged that "local self-Government puts an end to Demagogism. When men have the constant consciousness of their own rights and responsibilities, and discuss and control for themselves, specious pretexts can no longer be artfully used."

We believe, however, that this complete Government from local centres is incompatible with a complete nationality; and that as centralisation gains upon a country, it can only be met and matched by a universality of vote-power and education.

The combinations will be vaster, the unity more intense, and the individual units more completely equipped.—*Local self-Government will be supplemented or complemented* by an intense centralisation founded upon a universal individual self-Government—by a universally based and organised public opinion, which in truly democratic countries, will course like lightning through the body politic.

There are individual interests, municipal interests, and national interests. Where the relations of the individual are stronger, to the intermediate corporations or institutions, than to the nation (as they will be at a certain stage), there nationality suffers. National affairs can safely be left to local decisions, only where the spirit of nationality is strong enough to override local sovereignty. There can be no complete adjustment of the three interests, save in an advanced Democracy. "Nation" becomes a living organism only by a union of individuality with centralisation.

Multiplicity has altered the form of primitive arrangements, and organisations are national and international. We have gone from Local Republics, or Oligarchies, to the People one and indivisible.

Local work is done by municipalities. General work, by the Senate. The two departments cannot now come together before rudimentary assemblies of the People.

And yet the People is in theory rightly sovereign.

What is the remedy?

The enabling, and restraining, and levelling, and elevating, and unifying power of a fourfold manhood-development, by free school, press, church, and assembly. The People must avail themselves of this new necessity and principle of organisation, to carry into effect the true meaning of the representative system.

Nationality is now too intense and infinite to be mated otherwise. Unity can alone return to Governments and People, by securing thus the guarantees of a universal knowledge, interest, and power.

The material factors of national unity,—railways, canals, telegraphs, banks, postal services, &c., did not then exist. As to the People, intelligence lay in patches throughout the country, unable to communicate. And we know that without education, and consequent powers of association, official centralisation must always get the better of the People. That appears to be the inevitable history of nations from the era of feudality to the era of equality. Individuals are not completely enough prepared by education to associate for political and social purposes, and so corporate interests and sectional organisations subvert their freedom.

From the organisation of feudality to the organisation of Democracy, there neither has been, nor could have been, anything definitive in politics.

All other forms and powers,—like those which conferred such intense Individuality upon the few under the feudal system,—have to yield to that universal individual development which can alone make centralisations at once permanent and complete. And De Tocqueville tells us that the principal security of American freedom is not so much popular suffrage, as the administration of nearly all the business of society *by the People themselves.*

USURPATIONS AND INNOVATIONS.

How they came and what they will lead to.

The Dynasty of the Families.

"From the accession of the house of Tudor (and union of the Families, H. VII, A.D. 1485) a new period is to be dated in our history,—far more prosperous in the diffusion of opulence and the preservation of general order than the preceding, but less distinguished by the spirit of freedom and jealousy of tyrannical power."—*Hallam.*

"Any comparison between our ancient and modern polity must lead to most erroneous conclusions, unless large allowance be made for the effect of that restraint, which resistance and the fear of resistance constantly imposed on the Plantagenets. As we cannot employ physical force, it is our wisdom to keep all the constitutional checks in the highest state of efficiency. A nation of hardy archers and spearmen might, with small risks, connive at some illegal acts. The effect of wealth has been to make insurrection far more terrible than maladministration."—*Macaulay.*

"For who sees not that while such assemblies are permitted to have a longer duration (than annual), there grows up a commerce of corruption between the ministry and the deputies."—*Swift,* A.D. 1720.

"The (septennial) Act 1 Geo. I, c. 38, poisoned the Constitution."—*Bentham.*

"In eighty-six years, nine families alone obtained eighty-three consulships."—*Napoleon's* Cæsar.

"The aristocracies of modern Europe are aristocracies neither of arms nor of law, but of social and political privilege alone."—*Goldwin Smith.*

"The most natural intermediate and *subordinate* power in a monarchy is the nobility."—*Montesquieu.*

"The debates in the English Commons serve to point out to the aristocracy those men that should be chosen for its agents."—*Napoleon III.*

"The reduction of the free ceorls into villenage is one of the most remarkable innovations of the Anglo-Norman period. Observations have been made on it by Mr. Wright in the Archæologia, he says, 'these feelings of hatred and contempt for the peasantry were brought into our island by the Norman barons in the latter half of the eleventh century. The Saxon laws and customs continued, but the Normans acted as the Franks had done to the Roman Coloni; they enforced with harshness the laws which were in their own favor, and gradually threw aside, or broke through, those which were in favor of the serf."—*Hallam's* "England," v. iii, p. 261.

"The introduction of the feudal régime occasioned one such change, of which the importance cannot be overlooked. Social preponderance and political power passed from the towns to the country; private property and private life assumed pre-eminence over public. This first effect of the triumph of the feudal principle, appears more fruitful in consequences, the longer we consider it."—*Guizot.*

"The advantage which the landlord has derived from the invariable constancy of the valuation of the Land Tax, has been principally owing to some circumstances altogether extraneous to the nature of the tax. In the state of things which has taken place since the revolution, the constancy of the valuation has been advantageous to the landlord, and hurtful to the Sovereign."—*Adam Smith,* "Wealth of Nations," v. iii. p. 261.

"*That aristocratic law of inheritance* which is fast accumulating the land of England in a few hands, and disinheriting the English People of the English soil."—*Goldwin Smith.*

"If you are a standing menace to aristocracies, you are equally *a standing menace to State Churches.* A State Church rests upon the assumption that religion would fall if it were not supported by the State. On this ground it is that the European nations endure the startling anomalies of their State Churches, the interference of irreligious politicians with religion, the worldliness of ambitious ecclesiastics, the denial of liberty of conscience, the denial of truth. Shall I believe that Christianity, deprived of State support, must fall, *when I see it without State support not only standing, but advancing with the settler into the remotest West?* Will the laity of Europe long remain under their illusion in face of this great fact?"—*Ibid.*

Chapter IV.

USURPATIONS AND INNOVATIONS:

How they came, and what they will lead to.

"A very droll spectacle it was, in the last century, to behold the impotent efforts of the English towards the establishment of democracy. As they who had a share in the direction of public affairs were void of virtue; as their ambition was inflamed by the success of the most daring of their members, &c., the people annoyed at so many revolutions, in vain attempted to erect a commonwealth."—*Montesquieu*, v. i, p. 26.

"The offices and emoluments of Government are not sufficient for the whole aristocratic party at the same time. They have therefore divided themselves into two sections, in order to enjoy power turn about."—*James Aytoun.*

"The influence of Roman notions never prevailed very much here, and though, after the close alliance between the Church and State established by the reformation, the whole weight of the former was thrown into the scale of the crown, the mediæval clergy were anything rather than upholders of despotic power."—*Hallam.*

"When the ministers of religion, who of all men should be men of an independent character of mind, are the salaried servants of the State, they generally become the useful instruments of the State, and they are of high value to corrupt and tyrannical Governments."—*Disraeli*, 14th July, 1865.

"The time may come when the working classes may clamour with earnestness and some approach to unanimity for a share of electoral power. If their demand takes the form which is given to it now by those who assume to speak in their name, there is no choice but to resist. No evils of resistance can outweigh the evils of concession. Discontent, insurrection, civil war itself, will in the long run produce no worse dangers than absolute and unrestrained Democracy. Resistance, therefore, even to the uttermost, to such claims as these, may be contemplated without misgiving as to the result."—Pp. 570, 571, *Quarterly Review.*

When the preponderating power is an aristocracy chiefly of privilege, although not, as Napoleon phrased it, "an aristocracy without nobility," when the influence of property, superseding that of force and feudality, has not yet yielded to Manhood-Development and Equality,—there is then a period of usurpation and transition, when the shadows and names of the past rule, because the power of the future is unprepared.

Throughout all history, especially from the time when "voluntaryism" yielded to Feudality, and the Individual arm ceased to be a power in the State, to that other time when the individual will regain equality in a higher form and more complex civilisation,—during our own history, from Teutonic associations on the one hand, until we shall reach the era of equality on the other, we see through all action and re-action, *two simple processes*—First the immaturity of the national manhood, and the organisation of sectional interests; and second, the gradual development and organisation of the national manhood to supersede those interests.

The necessity of order develops the organising power of our race. As our whole manhood is not prepared by material, political, and religious freedom for power, the various interests of man organise themselves outwardly in sections and corporations. Whilst man prepares himself for the completer individuality required by a higher civilisation, the forces of superstition, monopoly, privelege, and prerogative, perfect the machinery of tyranny. Then is the progress of manhood more real than apparent: the progress of corporate and sectional interests more apparent than secure.

Whilst the outward show of the one boasts itself, the real motive power is being developed and organised against it. Where a State does not possess a sufficient number of men prepared to conquer industrial, political, and religious freedom, parasitical growths will gather upon the industries, the institutions, and the religion of that State. The first act of Manhood-Development is to cleanse itself from these parasites.

Man cannot command religious freedom, and the Church organises herself as a separate corporate interest outside the man, contending with the King, the State, and the Families for supremacy.

Man cannot command political freedom, and there is organised a kind of family dynasty, which contends with King and Church for the chattel, the People.

Man cannot command material freedom, and interests of primogeniture and direct taxation, of military, naval, and class monopolies, are organised to profit by his weakness.

And all these factious sectional organisations, are in fact, but tenants by sufferance to that organisation of the whole as to manhood, and the all as to numbers, which surely advances.

Centralisation has been organised against and without the People, and Democracy now proceeds to take possession of it in the name of the People.

The period of great organic changes in the development of modern English tyranny can hardly be divided into distinct epochs, though broadly speaking, the year 1429, when the suffrage was limited; the year 1534, when Henry prepared to repeat the policy of Constantine, and *to* assume the headship of the Church; the year 1660, when the Families struck their land-bargain for themselves and against the People with the Stuart, were signs of the preponderance of various partial and sinister powers. The suppression of the Scotch and Irish nationalities and Parliaments, the tampering by the landlords (suspiciously near the revolution of 1688,) with national sources of revenue, fixing the land-tax at the valuation of 1692, and the unconstitutional extension of annual into septennial Parliaments, make up the list of attempts at enforced concentration; and between Church and State of an unhealthy Unity.

During the period now in question, centralisation was the necessary consequence of events. Education, which is the universalising principle, being neglected, centralisation went on alone without the People.

But all such attempts at preparing the organisation for the use of one power, whilst it ought to be and will have to be adjusted to and harmonised with another, can but end in collapse or destruction, or in tedious and doubtful recovery.

And so this great and splendid palace, built up by infinite pains, for the use of the one or the few, will at last be claimed and inhabited by the People.

The relative position of Democracy and its opposites,—prerogative and privilege, is in every age and country the real position of the nation.

"Here then," says Montesquieu, v. ii, p. 209—v. i, p. 212, "is the fundamental constitution of the Government (the English,) we are treating of. The Legislative Body, being composed of two parts, they check one another by the mutual privilege of rejecting. They are both restrained by the executive as the executive by the legislative."

"England will perish when the legislative power shall be more corrupt than the executive."

We are thus furnished with a test of agreement with the *fundamental constitution of our Government.* "The Lords and Commons check one another, they constitute the legislature, and check, and are checked by the Executive."

And we shall find as the chief characteristics of Government during the last two hundred years :—

1st. That certain families generally, and a certain class always, supply the Premiers.

2nd. That certain families, or a certain class, farm the Executive.

3rd. That certain families unite and control Lords and Commons,—the Legislature.

4th. That such checks as exist are due to the jealousies of rival families, to the press, and public opinion, to the few real representatives of the People, to the Crown and constitution.

5th. That such results have followed, as might have been expected in State and in Church,—as to Land-laws, Poor-laws, lengthening of Parliaments, corruption, waste, standing armies, &c., &c.

6th. That a certain example of absorption of power has been set which the People will follow without confusion of function as to Executive and Legislative, and in such a way as to constitute the latter a fountain of life, health, and unity.

Democracy in England, after a conservative reaction of ages, has, since 1832, rapidly seized upon certain elemental powers, of the press, of economics, and of the franchise, which enable it to fight the fight of the People with ever increasing advantage.

Yet Democracy and Privilege are still so nearly balanced, that though the People's tribunes (and the People's elect, as Gladstone) carry their measures, they are liable to be enacted by opponents, not by those who have fought the fight and who wear the laurels. *This* is one of the guages of Democracy. A man is more a man where he who wins the battle wears the crown, not only of opinion, but of official recognition and power.

The principle of delegation is, however, so far accepted, that if mere party chiefs obstruct till their party is dissolving, they often then become delegates of the People, as before they were delegates of *faction*, and take the places belonging of right to the true *representatives.*

Thus, on the one hand, our People sometimes govern without reigning. On the other, the families always reign, whether they govern or no.

The Premiership was not very long since as was the Consulship in the worst ages of Rome. The analogy is startling:—

"We see how far are carried the jealousy and animosity

which *the virtue and activity of the new men* light up in the heart of certain nobles. The nobility transmitted from hand to hand this supreme dignity (the consulship), of which they were in exclusive possession. Every new man, whatever his renown and the glory of his deeds, appeared unworthy of this honour. *The consulship would have been considered profaned*, if, even with superior merit, a new man had obtained it. This eminent post in which the nobility were in a manner entrenched, and to which they had closed all the avenues." (*Napoleon's* Cæsar, v. i, pp. 324-64.)

Thus have our own prime ministers,—however hostile to the preponderating *tendency* of politics, —often remained fixed upon the country they held back for the term of their natural lives. And if individual premiers cannot always come back to power, the class remains.

Dante met, in the Inferno, a soul whose body was at the same period of time pretending to be alive and active in Italy, and so have we met in England, disastrously active, and apparently in their natural state, certain Statesmen whose reputations have long since expired, but who continue to prove their existence on the solvitur ambulando principle, and to defy the will of the People in the People's House!

Thus the most tremendous political lampoon ever penned, aptly describes what has been our own situation.

At present the English *People* rule by paroxysms of public opinion, and their power is shown by turning the *representatives* of the few into the *delegates* of the all.

Public opinion, well led, wins the day, but as for the man who won the People's victory, he may be congratulated on the fact by some one else who has ratted rather than be shelved, or he may, after a desperate and life-long battle, become, or refuse to become, in his turn, one of the privileged.

The extent to which our unprivileged Statesmanship is rewarded with official recognition, is a measure of our advance, and this advance, far enough from the right and the ideal, seems almost infinite since the epoch when Pitt and the People were mastered by a lunatic and his keepers, whose policy was made national only by making ignorance national, or by involving the nation in war.

And what an abyss of class abuses has not the last century bridged over! We see it in perusing such passages as the following, from one of the most distinguished of Americans:—

> "I have often," wrote the great Jefferson, "amused myself with contemplating the characters of the reigning sovereigns of Europe.
>
> "Louis XVI was a fool. The King of Spain was a fool, and of Naples the same. The King of Sardinia was a fool. All these were Bourbons. The Queen of Portugal was an idiot by nature, and so was the King of Denmark. The King of Prussia was a mere hog in body as well as in mind. Gustavus of Sweden, and Joseph of Austria were really crazy, and George of England was in a strait waistcoat. There remained, then, none but old Catherine of Russia, who had been too lately picked up to have lost her common sense. And so endeth the book of kings, from all of whom the Lord deliver us, and have you, my friend, and all such good men and true, in his holy keeping."

§

Mixed blood, public arenas, the realised advance towards Democracy, and the position of England, replenish our aristocracy, and produce some of the foremost of the world's Statesmen. Yet the position of Rome, sketched by a master hand, in relation to the questions of equality, offices, land, rural depopulation, a money aristocracy, and want of general high political culture, is, whether in contrast or warning, most instructive and suggestive:—

"From A.D. 535 to 621,—eighty-six years,—nine families alone obtained eighty-three consulships.

"Cineas, sent by Pyrrhus to Rome in 474, finds nobody open to corruption, and compares the Senate to an assembly of kings. Jugurtha, in 643, finds his resources quickly exhausted in buying everybody's conscience, and exclaims, 'Venal town, which would soon perish if it could find a purchaser.'

"Society was placed in new conditions, for the populace of the towns had increased, while the agricultural population had diminished.

"*The great landed properties had absorbed the little*, slaves had taken the place of free labour, &c. And, lastly, the allies were weary of contributing to the greatness of the empire *without participating in the rights* of Roman citizens. It was natural that they should aspire to be treated as *equals*.

"The richest citizens, in sharing among them the public domain, had finished *by getting nearly the whole into their own hands*, either by purchase from small proprietors, or by forcibly expelling them. Not only did the vast domains,—*latifundia*,—appertain to a small number, but the knights had monopolised all the elements of riches of the country. Formed over the whole face of the empire into *financial companies*, they worked the provinces and formed a veritable *money aristocracy*.

"Thus not only was the wealth of the country in the hands of the patrician and plebeian nobility, but the free men diminished incessantly in numbers in the rural districts.

"The principal families in possession of *the soil and of the power* desired to preserve this double advantage, without being obliged to show themselves worthy of it; they seemed to *disdain the severe education* which had made them capable of filling all offices, so that it might be said that there existed then at Rome an aristocracy without nobility, and a democracy without the People."—*Napoleon's* "Life of Cæsar," pp. 238-43.

The absorption of land by the few, the denial of equality, the powerful plutocracy distrusting the

People, the increase of rural population without increase of rural dwellings, the monopoly of soil and power, the disabilities of large and powerful minorities, secular and religious, are all reproduced in English politics, with the added infamy of the Irish Church, and of subscriptions which the clergy writhe under, but which the Church will not or cannot remove.

Professor Goldwin Smith also thus refers to the innovations of privileges and aristocracy :—

"The Roman aristocracy was an aristocracy of *arms and law*. The feudal aristocracy of the middle ages was an aristocracy of arms, and, in some measure, of law; it served the cause of political progress in its hour and after its kind; it confronted tyrannical kings when the People were as yet too weak; it conquered at Runnymede as well as at Hastings.

"But the *aristocracies of modern Europe* are aristocracies *neither of arms nor of law*, but of *social and political privilege alone*. They owe, and are half conscious that they owe, their present existence only to factitious weaknesses of human nature and to the antiquated terrors of communities long kept in leading strings and afraid to walk alone.

"If there were nothing but reason to dispel them, these fears might long retain their sway over European society. But *the example of a great commonwealth flourishing without a privileged class*, and of a popular sovereignty, combining order with progress, tends, however remotely, to break the spell."

From autocracy to middle-class Government is an advance. From the one to the many is an advance. From intervention for Bourbons to non-intervention for Freedom is an advance,—just as it is better to see your brother killed than to kill him yourself. From a twenty years' fight against republics to four years of falsehood against a republic is an advance. We are advanced in education in a cheap and able press, and in the possession of vast appliances, wrung from the despotism of the past, with which to attach at a greater vantage the despotism of the present.

§

It is a period of wonderful transition. Land is absorbed, but there are land societies. Equality is denied, but by those who contend for plural voting, which will never be allowed, as its only alternative. Plutocracy is powerful, but capital may unite with labour, and labour will acquire and wield capital. The Church transmits her formularies, but nobody knows what they mean. The Church (endowed) survives with other relics, but the People demand free patronage and choice.

On every side we see the weakness and the strength peculiar to the middle and oligarchic class reign, and we look for the advent of the entire educated national *manhood* upon the scene.

Without the all, the many cannot complete the victory of opinion over caste and privilege.

Self-Government is not only a means, but an end, and one of the greatest recommendations and best tests of good Government is that it educates the all for empire. For all manhood is imperial. Every man with a soul and a conscience in him is of the blood royal of the Universe. To withhold power from true manhood is not only treason against manhood, but treachery to the State.

That bad or indifferent statesmanship can be soon exploded, and bad or indifferent Statesmen speedily, politically destroyed, is one of the most conspicuous signs of a healthy political life and a competent national manhood. The contrary signifies a community where thinghood, property, and tradition has overcome manhood, and rules over it. Englishmen are Free. Man here is not a chattel. *He is only ruled by chattels.*

Whatever may be thought of America, where "old men" lie on political death-beds while yet in early youth and vigorous bodily health, and where "Families" do not overshadow the nation,—it is surely a sign of a state in no wise commendable, that in England the national opinion has supported names against Principles and Truths, and does allow, to the most venerable political sinners, not only a space meet for repentance, but an opportunity—nay, an incentive to sin on without hope for the nation or fear for themselves. It might lately have been said that the more a "Statesman" has sinned, and the longer he has been about it, the better the English like him.

In a word, we have "the Ins and the Outs, and the Outs and the Ins," and it is, as yet, not in the power or the will of the nation to cast both off and away together, and entrust the destinies to any outside a certain magic circle. We approach, however, a time when manhood will assert itself, explode this English fetish, the "Families," and rule in concert with them or against them.

It is characteristic of Democracy,—the fact affects all the postulates of good Government, that a man must *remain* worthy, to remain in power. On Sunday, he may be President presumptive, on

Monday, as the phrase goes, "a dead cock in the pit."

Throughout American history there have been, except in the era of oligarchic ascendency, no governors who did not govern, or rulers who did not rule on behalf of the People. The only period when tainted men could rule, was the era of conservatism and oligarchy.

But the first crisis has miserably destroyed those men, and the nation has destroyed the very institutions for which they compromised republicanism and enfeebled the nation.

England, too, is following on the inevitable road, and industrial progress, the American stimulus, and the state of the labour market, will help on the political and social change from family or oligarchic rule.

It is not our intention here to attempt to depict the England of this period with its minority class sovereignty; its class land-laws favoring the rich, and its unwise settlement laws for the poor. Let the *Times* and the author of "the Scarlet Letter," describe the old familiar face, and tell from opposite standpoints the same story:—

> "The English (says the *Times* of 19th October, 1864), live under squires, territorial potentates, extensive employers, and local oligarchs, and under this régime, they endure an amount of positive tyranny or negative neglect, that they would *not find surpassed under the most despotic system of the continent.*"

If this had not been the *Times,* it would have been Mr. Bright.

And Nathaniel Hawthorne, writing of a specimen village in Warwickshire, observes :—

"Life is there fossilised in its greenest leaf. The man who died yesterday, or ever so long ago, walks the village street to-day, and chooses the same wife that he married a hundred years since, and must be buried again to-morrow under the same kindred dust that has already covered him half-a-score of times. The stone threshold of his cottage is worn away with his hob-nailed foot-steps, shuffling over it from the reign of the first Plantagenet to that of Victoria. Better than this is the lot of our restless countrymen, whose modern instinct bids them tend always towards "fresh woods and pastures new." Rather than such monotony of sluggish ages, loitering on a village-green, toiling in hereditary fields, listening to the parson's drone, lengthened through centuries in the grey Norman church, let us welcome whatever change may come—change of place, social customs, political institutions, modes of worship—trusting that, if all present things shall vanish, they will but make room for better systems, and for a higher type of man, to clothe his life in them, and to fling them off in turn."

§

Other enabling causes of this general monopoly of office and power, are innovations affecting the representative system in its various branches of the franchise, the distribution of seats, and the parliamentary term. The first, depriving the People of power; the last, removing representatives from the influence of their principals, the People, and submitting them to the influences of those who ought to be the People's servants.

The Reform Act partly gave to feudality in the counties, what it took from it in the boroughs, but it also unconstitutionally swept away various rights of voting for towns and boroughs,—of householders, without regard to the amount of rent, rates, or taxes paid by them (as Aylesbury, Cirencester, &c.);

of householders, paying scot and lot, that is assessed to the poor rate (as Bridport, Westminster, &c.); of burgage tenants at a very low rent (as in Clithero, 1*s.* 4*d.*, Westbury, 4*d.* or 2*d.*, Berealston, 3*d.*); inhabitants paying scot and lot (as Abingdon, Great Marlow, Southwark, &c.); inhabitants generally (as Hertford, Preston, &c.); and Potwallers, or persons furnishing their own diet (as Honiton, Taunton, &c.).

These various rights of voting were *recognized* in 1786 by the 26 Geo. III, c. 100, an Act passed to *prevent occasional* inhabitants from voting:—

"To the great prejudice of the real inhabitants, who bear the burthens of such cities and boroughs, and to whom the right of sending members to Parliament belongs, and that no person shall be admitted to vote, as an inhabitant paying scot and lot, or as an inhabitant householder, housekeeper, and potwaller, or as an inhabitant householder resiant, or as an inhabitant of such city or borough, unless he has been actually and *bonâ fide* such, *six calendar* months previous to the day of election."

As to Parliaments, the 1st Ed. II (A.D. 1311), shows that they were annual. The 4 Ed. III, c. 14 (A.D. 1330), is simply this:— "Ensement est accorde qe parlement soit tenu chescun an une foitz ou plus si mestier soit." Before this the 3rd Edward I, c. 5, declares (A.D. 1275), "and because elections ought to be free, the King commandeth upon great forfeiture, that no great man or other by force of arms nor by malice or menacing shall disturb any to make free election."

The statute of Rich. II, c. 12, is concerning "levying expenses of Knights of Parliament," and the 23 H. VI, c. 10, is "the order for levying their wages." Cap. 14 in the same year mentions the writ "quod in pleno comitatu."

The 16 Car. I, c. 1, "whereas by the laws and statutes of this realm, Parliaments ought to be holden at least once every year, said laws, &c., shall from henceforth be duly kept and observed," and if Parliament be not summoned under the great seal then in all times hereafter it shall be assembled as declared therein. 16 Car. II, repealed such part of this as was in derogation of prerogative. The 1 W. and M. puts it as a matter of true, ancient, and indubitable right that Parliaments be held frequently.

The 6 W. and M., c. 1, enacts that Parliament shall be held every three years, and not to last more.

The 1 G. I, st. 2, c. 38, makes Parliament seven times the length it was in the days of English freedom.

Swift, writing to Pope (A.D. 1720-1), thus denounces long Parliaments :—

"I adored the wisdom of that Gothic institution which makes them annual; and I was confident, our Liberty could never be placed upon a firm foundation until that ancient Law were restored among us. For, who sees not, that, while such assemblies are permitted to have a longer duration, *there grows up a commerce of corruption between the Ministry and the Deputies*, wherein they both find their accounts, to the manifest danger of Liberty, which traffic would neither answer the design nor expense if Parliaments met once a-year."

And the Hon. T. Brand confessed that through not enforcing the calls of the House by taking members into custody who did not attend, the control which the independent members ought to have over the conduct of the ministers is entirely lost. And he further stated (May 21, 1810, Cobbett's Debates), that :—

> "He found the question one of enormous difficulty and of extreme importance. *Septennial Parliaments* had a tendency from the length of their term to weaken the relation between the elector and the representative. . . . The one term was too long to please the People, and the other (annual), too short to satisfy the members."

Bentham thus refers to the shortening of the Parliamentary term :—

"Towards the close of the reign of Charles the First (16 C. I, c. 1), at the opening of the Long Parliament—the annual holding of fresh Parliaments having been so long violated (none from 1627 to 1640), *triennality* was for the *first* time established instead. Why? Because Parliament did not feel itself strong enough to exact more.

"In Charles the Second's time (16 C. II, c. 1), the provisions extorted from the father, and found too efficient, were repealed, and inefficient ones substituted.

"In William's time (6 W. and M., cap. 1), their inefficiency having been proved, others were substituted. The duration was made triennial. Why? Because by this time the value of a seat to the occupant was pretty fully understood.

"The Act 1 G. I, c. 38 *poisoned the constitution.* Most probably the scheme was that of his advisers, the benefit to them being manifest; as to the monarch it was problematical. Their constituents had seated them for three years ; they seated themselves for four more. The monarch was no usurper, he was fairly seated. Not so Honorable Gentlemen."—*Plan*, pp. 296-7-8.

§

We have said that the concentration of power will continue, that the Legislative and Executive, though separate in function, will only represent one preponderating power, and that power the equal voting People.

The reasons for a separation of the Legislative and Executive are, that they thus secure a division of function, and prevent tyranny.

The first reason always remains, and will prevail.

The second is always subject to invalidation by the actual preponderating power.

But with this broad and grand distinction,—that when this separation of functions and powers is assailed by the One, the Few, or the Many, it is assailed by partial, sectional, or sinister interests. That when it is assailed by the All, it is assailed by that interest which is universal, and by that power which tends to equality of interest and right.

When the educated equal voting All achieve a union of *power*, they do it for concentration, not for tyranny, and the only question about it is, whether the People are truly prepared wisely to wield so powerful a weapon.

Thus the question started by the Lords has been taken up by the People—(whether the former will not regret the starting of it, time will show). The question—" Is this separation of estates a good thing? Is it not, on the whole, better for one estate, ourselves, to swamp Commons and King, and to reign alone?"

That a similar question is always being worked out by living nations, is a matter of fact, as shown by De Tocqueville, respecting "mixed Government." Elizabeth was the last of the Kings. "The Families" came in definitively with the second Charles, and their "Dynasty" has ruled us since. The first year of his return was occupied by Parliament in voting his expenses, in looking after regicides, and in loosing land from burdens, and fixing the loyal landlords in power. The People had come in and gone out with Cromwell. The King neither could nor would appeal to the People against the families, and so the real power transferred by Cromwell from the hands of the One into those of the Many, went back again, not to the One or to the Many, but to the Few.

The Knights, says Earl Russell, gave great stability and dignity to the popular House, even from the olden time with us. Nevertheless, for centuries until 1832, the mixture of the "Commons" with King and Lords, was the "chimera" and pretence of our Constitution.

No doubt it was the operation of a great natural law,—the gradual spread of intelligence and self-restraint, and consequent powers of organisation, that enabled the Few to check the power of the One, but it is the operation of that self-same law of progress that now has carried power from the Few to the Many, and that threatens to carry it from the Many to the All, till the whole educated manhood of the nation will be the one homogeneous ruling power.

It is now feared, lest a new league between Capital and Labour should answer the old one between Prerogative and Privilege; lest the lower middle classes and labouring classes—the many and the all, should combine against the one and the few, and a new and strange class despotism should arise to trouble "the balances of the Constitution."

This is the phantasm that softens the brain of politicians, and appals the heart of autocracy everywhere. THE PEOPLE CAN NO LONGER BE "BALANCED,"—neither by their crimes, nor their credulity, nor their gratitude, nor their ignorance, nor their fear. They are getting *knowledge, self-restraint* (a large proportion of their most active politicians are total abstainers), and consequently power of *organisation, or unity.* "The State, it is the People," and what if manhood can balance itself!

"Too late! Too late!" is the cry. And as Mill declares that plural voting for the few is the *sauve qui peut*, and will soon be the only alternative to universal suffrage and popular class legislation, behold the People organise,—again, Gladstone and Bright uprear the standard which fell from the hands of Chatham, virtual representation is again declared a farce, and the "Bedford Protest" is repeated,—not *this time,* declaring that because American principles might logically be extended to England, therefore they cannot be right, but that because they are logical they are right, and that because they are right they shall become law.

"Minorities must be represented."—Good, Mr. Mill, and they always will be. But let us now first see to it that *majorities* shall be represented, and let the one, the few, and the many give the all a turn.

Nevertheless, it is not without much misgiving that many will see the true national royalty going to the national manhood. The division of functions must always be maintained, although the power will become one and indivisible. All we can reply is, "if the balance of constitutional power is gone, *thank the Lords for it,* for they have been the sappers and miners of the constitution."

§

Mixed Government exists only where change or dissolution impends.

The one, the King, ruled, and he pretended to take "the mixture" into partnership when he wanted supplies. Presently, the Families got possession of "the mixture," and kept it till 1832. At each change there has been a revolution, the first with war, the second peacefully.

Thus "functions" have been kept "separate," but not with the result of a "balance." There has been a "mixture," but it has been intelligently extolled only by the one ingredient that has been the strongest, and has ruled.

Be it, however, ever remembered, that up to quite recent times, *no nation had ever been ruled but by its sections.* "The man, the assembly, or the class," had ruled, but a national self-governing entity, never. Nor will it ever be contended by sane men that legislation and executive should be confounded; the only question is, whether it be not *right, as well as inevitable,* that as the People advance, "individualities," both of persons and classes, should recede, and that as the all become more and more accomplished, and individually completed, their representatives should not, nay, must not, become *rather delegations than powers.* When the majority are Statesmen, can the minority monopolise Statesmanship?

As the all become educated, the difference between delegates and representatives lessens, for both People and representatives draw nearer to a common standard of truth and right. There are three kinds of representation, corresponding with three stages of national character. In an evil State, there is no representation strictly so called, but men are ruled by force, fraud, or corruption. In the middling stage, there is representation proper; intelligence chooses, and the representatives are too much above their constituents to be delegates, and not enough above them to tyrannise. In the advanced stage, advanced minds can only lead by expressing,—perhaps by eliciting,—the will of the People.

It is, in fact, obvious, that as national manhood advances,—acquires the real governing qualities,—the national will becomes more uniform, pressing, and absolute. As Statesmanship becomes universal, artificial precautions, and forms of all sorts, yield to the substance of universal Statesmanship.

"It was," says that great master of men and ideas, Louis Napoleon (p. 309, v. ii, 'Life and Works'), "it was the division and independence *of powers* which Montesquieu designates as the vital principle of liberty. And that if in any Society whatever, the man, the assembly, or the class which makes the law, has also the power of executing it, there must be disorder and anarchy." The Constitution also of 1848 declared: "The separation of Powers is the first condition of free Government." It is a necessity arising out of the very necessity and nature of aggregate action.

"When," says Montesquieu, "the legislative and executive powers are united, in the same person, or in the same body of magistrates, there can be no liberty, because apprehensions may arise lest the same monarch or senate should enact tyrannical laws, to execute them in a tyrannical manner.

"Again, there is no liberty if the judiciary power be not separated from the legislative and executive. Were it joined with the legislative, the life and liberty of the subject would be exposed to arbitrary control; for the judge would be then the legislator. Were it joined to the executive power, the judge might behave with violence and oppression.

"There would be an end of everything, were the same man, or the same body, whether of the nobles or of the People, to exercise those three powers, that of enacting laws, that of executing the public resolutions, and of trying the causes of individuals."—*Montesquieu*, vol. i, p. 199.

§

"Perfect Government," speaking relatively, is

that which combines unity or order with as much freedom as the character of the given People can admit. Perfect Government, absolutely speaking, is Democracy, where alone freedom and order can meet in full proportions and in indissoluble unity. Where the all govern, there can be no separation of power, though there may be of functions. By "powers" understand "functions."

Separation of *Powers* is the first maxim of free Government;" separation of *Power* is rather the necessary maxim of a People not yet ripe for freedom, and therefore jealous, and, in fact, incapable of a perfect unity.

Executive and Legislative, as functions, must not clash, but as powers, the outcome of a living nation, and as wielded by men who partake of, or oppose the general national tendency, they must agree or disagree with that tendency. If they disagree, then one must rule, or the other impede. In the last case there is obstruction or anarchy, in the first there is that "one preponderating power" which all living countries possess, or to which they tend.

Wherever there is life there will be Sovereignty one and indivisible, whether it be the muddled Sovereignty and abject organism of so-called "mixed Governments;" the more highly developed Sovereignty, where one man rules by the public opinion of a half educated race, or where he has first to develop the public opinion he rules by; or where the public opinion of an instructed People rules both in form and in substance.

In all cases as the organism is high, not the functions, but the power will be practically one. Where it is low, the confusion of the many, or the tyranny of the one have to be provided against, and weakness, divisions, "balances," "mixtures," and neutralisations, ensue.

In France, true Democracy is not yet possible; there, says Napoleon truly, "the legislative power should examine, discuss, control, and moderate, but never rule." Nor in England, where, according to the same authority, "the debates *in the Commons serve to point out to the aristocracy those men that should be chosen for its agents.*"

In America, the People virtually legislate and rule; they have swallowed up "debates, debaters, and oligarchy" together, and the eyes of all nations are turned towards the example.

We may regret the change, but can it be avoided? Give a share of power to the People, and they will, they must, take it to fight you for the rest. It is Destiny, not Constitutions, that acts here, and that controls events. Deny the People power,—there is revolution. Grant it, and responsibility elevates and educates, education multiplies labour, labour becomes capital, and capital, labour, and education universalised, are Democracy, "tempered" only by itself.

If the middle class regret the threatened concentration of power they must blame the Families, and the Families must blame the Kings, for both thought that the Constitution should be balanced without *the People.*

Rather conclude with De Tocqueville, that only evil or pusillanimous men or nations need fear the People, that the balance of social and political interests, and the natural conservation of the whole educated manhood of a nation, will in due time replace with advantage artificial make-weights and compromises, and that "to attempt to check Democracy is to withstand the will of God!"

In free countries powers will always be separated in function, but the sovereignty of the all tends always more completely to develop and assert itself.

Hallam defines the modern situation,—its strength and weakness, and shows more than ever the need of constant parliamentary contact with, and dependence upon the People "who can never be corrupted."

"The reign of Charles II, though displaying some stretches of arbitrary power, and threatening a great deal more, was, in fact, the transitional state between the ancient and modern schemes of the English constitution; between that course of government where the executive power, so far as executive, was very little bounded except by the laws, and that where it can only be carried on, even within its own province, by the consent and co-operation, in a general measure, of the Parliament."—*Hallam's* "England," p. 355, v. ii.

"The real vice of this Parliament was not intemperance, but corruption. Clifford, and still more Danby, were masters in an art practised by ministers from the time of James I (and which indeed can never be unknown where there exists a court and a popular assembly), that of turning to their use the weapons of mercenary eloquence by office, or blunting their edge by bribery."—*Ibid.*, p. 395.

De Lolme shows in the strongest light the advantages of the British Constitution in the following respects:—The advantage of having fixed the executive in the crown as in a sacred and inexpugnable depositary, constituting a check on those inordinate ambitions which in all Republics ever brought on the ruin of liberty. The unity of the executive also gives greater facility in restraining it. Its indivisibility has constantly kept the views and efforts of the People to one and the same object. Tyranny often mocks the efforts of the People, not because it is invincible, but because it is unknown. Executive unity induces the greatest men in the State to unite in common cause with the People in restraining it. The propounding of the business of legislation by the representatives, prevents the undermining of laws by precedents and artful practices of the Executive. Pp. 196, 215-16-18, 431, 478.

De Lolme clearly explains the necessity of restraining both Executive and Legislative, the former by keeping it undivided, the latter by dividing it, and thus tempering and giving time, caution, and prudence to its decisions. He says :—

"In order, therefore, to ensure stability to the constitution of a State, it is indispensably necessary to restrain the legislative authority. But here we must observe a difference between the legislative and the executive powers. The latter may be confined, and even is the more easily so when undivided: the legislative, on the contrary, in order to its being restrained, should absolutely be divided.

"In a word, the result of a division of the executive power is either a more or less speedy establishment *of the right of the strongest*, or a continued state of war:—that of a division of the legislative power, is either truth, or general tranquillity."—*De Lolme on the Constitution*, pp. 219, 222.

What becomes of all these carefully planned and balanced results of the Constitution, if the families absorb the executive, and propound and settle the business of legislation for the representatives? We answer that by giving to the House of Commons, *the peer's house,* so preponderating a power, the peers have really put it in the power of the People to absorb the power by altering the representation.

This will be the use and the end of the "usurpations and innovations" of the family dynasty.

Oligarchy has overpowered the influence of King and Commons, but Equality has got to destroy Oligarchy in the name of a completer nationality.

In overshadowing the power of the Sovereign, *the Families* have pronounced their own approaching neutralisation.

Montesquieu tells us ("Spirit of Laws," p. 20, v. i) that "the most natural intermediate *and subordinate* power in a monarchy is the nobility, which in some measure seems to be essential to a monarchy, whose fundamental maxim is, no monarchy, no nobility; no nobility, no monarch."

Mill throws them a crumb of comfort, when he says ("Representative Government"), "An aristocratic House is only powerful in an aristocratic state of Society. The really moderating power in a democratic constitution must act in and through the democratic House."

But Mill elsewhere confesses that the only alternative to universal suffrage, which must elect this people's House, is plural voting.

According to him, therefore, the families must go for plural voting, or must devote themselves to that general preparation and education of the People for power, which will "moderate" and energise all things.

THE PREPONDERATING POWER OF THE FUTURE, AND ITS REQUIREMENTS.

INDUSTRIAL FREEDOM;
POLITICAL FREEDOM;
RELIGIOUS FREEDOM.

"Every tax must finally be paid from rent, profit, or wages, or from all of them. Every tax which falls finally upon one only of these three sorts of revenue is unequal; every tax ought to be equal, certain, and not arbitrary, convenient in time and manner, and as little burthensome as possible in expense of levying, in obstruction of industry, in forfeitures, or in visits, &c., of tax gatherers.

"Land and capital stock are the two original sources of all revenue. When by taxes upon the necessaries and conveniences of life, the owners of capital stock find that it will not purchase the same as it would in another country, they will be disposed to remove to some other. The industry of the country must fall with the removal of capital."—*Adam Smith*, vol. iii, pp. 255-6-7-8, 429-30.

"I should be sorry to see the dangers of universal suffrage and of unlimited Democracy averted, or sought to be averted, by such invidious schemes as granting to the rich, a *plurality of votes*, or by contrivances altogether unknown to our habits, such as the plan of Mr. Hare, although sanctioned by the high authority of so profound a thinker as Mr. Mill. The subject is full of unknown pitfalls."—*Earl Russell* on the English Constitution.

"I am bound to express my opinion that the doctrine to which the hon. gentleman appears to incline, that the Protestants of Ireland or the *members of the State Church in any one of the three kingdoms are a sort of privileged people*, for whose wants the State is to make provision, caring little what may become of the wants of others—*I do not believe that it is founded* on reason, on the constitution, or on history."—*Gladstone*, 28th March, 1865.

"When the sacredness of property is talked of, it should always be remembered that any such sacredness does not belong in the same degree to landed property. No man made the land. It is the original inheritance of the whole species. Its appropriation is wholly a matter of general expediency. When private property in land is not expedient, it is unjust." —*Mill*, "Political Economy."

"The influence of religion proceeds from its being believed; that of human laws from their being feared."—*Montesquieu.*

"None of the brethren shall suffer so much barbarism in their families as not to teach their children and apprentices so much learning as may enable them perfectly to read the English tongue."—*Bancroft's* "Colonisation of the United States."

"All which concerns religion lies beyond the sphere of the State's activity."—*Baron Alexander Von Humboldt*, p. 96, "Sphere and Duties of Government."

"Yet of persons whose interest in the foundation is entirely subsidiary and subordinate, the whole of whose rights exist solely as the necessary means to enable them to perform certain duties—it is currently asserted, and in the tone in which men affirm a self-evident moral truth, that the endowments of the Church and of the Universities are *their* property.

"*Their* property! In what system of legislative ethics, or even of positive law, is an estate in the hands of trustees the property of the trustees? It is the property of the *cestui que trust:* for whose benefit the trust is created. This, in the case of a national endowment, is the entire People.

"'*Qui trompe-t-on ici?*' asks Figaro—'Qui vole-t-on ici?' may well be asked. What man, woman, or child, is the victim of this robbery? Who suffers by the robbery when everybody robs nobody? But though no man, woman, or child is robbed, the Church it seems is robbed. What follows? That the Church may be robbed, and no man, woman, or child be the worse for it. If so, why not, in Heaven's name?

"The laws of property were made for the protection of human beings, and not of phrases. As long as the bread is not taken from any of our fellow creatures, we care not, though the whole dictionary had to beg in the streets.

"Let those who think it a robbery for the nation to resume what we say is its own, tell us whose it is; let them inform us, what human creatures it belongs to; not what letters and syllables."—Pp. 12-17-18, v. i, *Mill's* "Dissertations," "Jurist," February, 1833.

Chapter V.

THE PREPONDERATING POWER OF THE FUTURE, AND ITS REQUIREMENTS.

"I warn the aristocracy not to force the People to look into the subject of taxation,—not to force them to see how they have been robbed, plundered, and bamboozled for ages by them."—*Cobden*, A.D. 1846.

"The practice of funding has gradually enfeebled every State which has adopted it. Is it likely that in Great Britain alone, a practice, which has brought either weakness or desolation into every other country, should prove altogether innocent?"—*Adam Smith*, v. iii, p. 432.

"The one thing necessary is that the power of the purse should be actually and effectively in the hands of the real representatives."—*Bentham.*

"The thirty tyrants of Athens ordered the suffrages of the Areopagites to be public, in order to manage them."—*Montesquieu.*

"The Ballot is a moral engine, which, once established in any constituency, will spread like wildfire throughout the country."—*Cobden.*

"The right of primogeniture was established, *and the reason of the feudal law was superior to that of the political and civil institution.* It is an excellent law in a trading republic to make an equal division of the paternal estate."—*Montesquieu.*

"An ecclesiastical organisation allying itself with political power, can never now be the source of any good."—*Draper.*

"The ecclesiastical power is extremely proper in a monarchy, especially of the absolute kind, a barrier (against tyranny) ever useful where there is no other."

"The ancient Romans fortified their empire by indulging all sorts of religious worship, but their posterity destroyed it by rooting out the various sects. An unacquaintedness with the true limits of ecclesiastical and secular power, was the most pernicious source of all the calamities that befel the Greeks."—*Montesquieu.*

We have shown that manhood, not only the preponderating, but also the only power of the future, has to be developed upon a fourfold basis, of freedom in School, Press, Church, and Assembly, and in its three forms, material, political, and religious. It has to inaugurate the true reign of opinion, and vindicate its supremacy against the rule of brute force, and of mere chattel proprietorship.

In England, however, two of the *bases* of Manhood-Development, Free School, and Free Church, are wanting, and all of its *forms* are incomplete.

Past conflicts between the many, and the few, or the one, between rival endowed Churches, beween the Families and the Sovereign, and between Families and Families, had resulted in one short victory of Popular Sovereignty; in a formal assertion of constitutional right by the Families; in a virtual coalition between King, Families, and Church against People; in a centralisation of Power in the Families; and finally, in "Constitutional" Government by an Executive Committee called the Cabinet Council, uniting Executive and Legislative, and concentrating all power (subject to popular outbursts in lieu of the old self-Government) in the hands of a Premier-President, who rules for an average four years, is usually chosen by the Sovereign out of a small circle of Families, and who, as popular election and the approval of the Commons are also necessary, is the subject of the principle of treble election.

The decimation of the Families by the wars of

the Roses was a work of necessity and mercy. The vices of Henry VIII were doubtful national blessings, for although they led to the loosening of the despotism of Rome, they identified the State with formalism. The victory of Nobles over Kingship was a victory for the People over both, for it was an advance towards Democracy. The battles of Cromwell vindicated the principle of national Sovereignty.

All other causes, however, were comparatively of slight effect, until, in the fulness of time, the steam engine lifted the labourer from the earth, and re-created commerce.

The effect of this was threefold.

1st. Capital has increased faster than population, and the great problem which Mr. James Mill and others seemed to consider insoluble, has been solved in the interests of the People.

2nd. Commerce unites in interest and action two of the most powerful forces of States. Labour created capital, capital is recognised as power, and power produces equality or revolution.

3rd. This union of labour and capital, of the many and the all, is destined to match and overcome that other alliance between the new aristocracy of wealth and the old aristocracy of birth, which has been the mainstay of oligarchy in England. This new union draws nearer and closer year by year. It must promote a more equal distribution of material advantages and of power, and will avoid on the one hand poverty, and on the other that spirit of extreme luxury, the antagonist of the real spirit of commerce.

This new power must really favour Democracy not only in politics but in religion. For a true Protestantism (endowed or enforced Protestantism is a contradiction in terms) is the religion of individual freedom and responsibility, as opposed to a religion of form, force, favour or proxy.

The Power thus created has closed the era of reaction, which began with the return of the Stuart and ended with the Reform Bill. It has gained two great victories,—free press and free assembly. It has partly gained four others,—Parliamentary Reform, Free Trade, Free Schools, and Direct Taxation.

Thus the Power that was held by the One, the Few, and then by the Many, is now passing to the All. The franchise is justly recognised as an end as well as a means. The chimera of "mixed Government" is visibly dissolving, the hydra head of Popular Sovereignty glares into the sanctum of Mill, affrights the respectable soul of the "Spectator," and shakes the dilettanti radicalism of Grey. "The actual predominating force" is already, in crises, in the People, and yet there is no national "dissolution," but instead thereof a peaceful revolution, which immensely strengthens the national unity, and assures international peace, by multiplying ad infinitum the independence and interrelations of the People,—and of the Peoples.

In fact, *our* "inevitable (white) nigger" has

come to the fore, and all parties will compete for him.

The mutual wants and interests of mankind are the fulcrum. Labour (or Capital) the lever. Between them they have moved the world.

This is the new spirit and power. What, in England, are the old forms which it has got to use or to burst ?

§

"The Feudal system bastardised,"—its spirit and power gone, its former perversions and obstructions remaining,—this is the situation. Commerce has got to win Liberty for itself, and to confer it upon land, or Land will stifle and expatriate commerce, and with commerce, labour and capital.

This situation is met, on the one hand, by a proposal to create a new and unheard-of Feudality by a "protection" or multiplication of the beaten minorities. It is met, on the other, by a plain and frank acknowledgment that the People now *must* reign, and that the occupation of Conservatism is not to obstruct right, but to graduate progress.

The Material, Political, and Religious aspects of Democracy in England, claim each their place and notice. They combine to create the coming preponderating power and royalty of the nation's manhood.

Commerce, we say, has got to win complete freedom, and to convert and to save the Exchequer.

Politics have got to win it and enfranchise the People. Religion must win it and free the Church.

And the spirit of Freedom is the motive power in all. In commerce it springs from the love of material good. In politics, from the love of power and of freedom, and a sense of responsibility in every human breast. In religion, it scorns compulsion, it defies tradition, it bows to no earthly master, and will seek no mastery save over the willing souls of men.

Ten per cent. is appreciated, even by celestial minds, and limited liability tempts to unlimited operations. Commerce is no respecter of persons. Credit associations ransack Europe for money, and the universe for investments. There is no noble in the land who has not a share in a shop; and material development will help moral development and political propagandism.

Socially, two processes are going on. Labour and capital threaten to unite their forces against privilege, and the Peerage, as it assimilates capital, would make of it another "bulwark of the Constitution." The result is inevitable. The middle classes will buy privilege of the upper, but the lower classes will buy power of both.

And as the result of the whole is to extend the operations of labour, and to cause wealth to increase *in a greater ratio than population,* the inevitable end will be that *labour rises in the market and in the social scale,* it will have a larger share in the results of capital, and in social life there will be greater homogeneity, equality, and unity, and in political life an advancing Democracy.

Thus steam power has been the great agent in multiplying labour, in creating capital, and in preparing the conditions of their co-operation.

It is steam power and Democracy that will have done it all. Royalty will descend to the People, and we also shall count our kings by the million.

INDUSTRIAL FREEDOM.

The principle of industrial or material freedom has to do with the three great desiderata in Governments,—Safety, Power, and Honesty. For it has to do with individual and national *Development;* with *Economy* of Power; with *Honesty* in the raising, and in the application of taxes.

The main test and chief factor of the material well-being of the all, is the increase of the proportion between labour or capital, and population.

Material freedom means also equality. It means *freedom to get, to spend, and to save wealth.* In other words :—

Freedom of trade,

Direct taxation, and

Economical and honest Government.

All three are inextricably bound up together as a free system.

It is unnecessary to dilate on the meaning or merits of free trade, or on the desirability of giving it full and consistent effect.

Direct taxation involves the knowledge of and the control of national expenditure. It means equality of payments, or rather, proportional payments.

Where the majority have attained political manhood, they will both know and control. Where the majority are political minors, they do not want to know and they cannot control. It is eminently just that in a Democracy a slight capitation tax should pay for personal protection, and a graduated property tax for protection to property.

Economical Government means simply that the nation shall neither be cheated nor used by its servants. That what it does it shall do with the best economy of power. That it shall not be committed to projects it disapproves. It means that what it does it shall do with the will, the power, the splendour, and the persistence of a great and free People, but that it be just to itself while it is generous to the world.

In fact, "that those who *pay* shall be also those who *govern*," is of the essence of the rights of the People, and of all true freedom, national honour, and just economy.

Oligarchy not only pits families against the nation, but it divides the nation into hostile classes and interests, and gives to one class the power to govern and to tax all the others, while exempting itself. The history of the great reactionary period from Cromwell to the Reform Bill were sufficient proof of this. The great fighting and family interest involved the nation in a series of bloody wars with which the nation had no concern whatsoever, and that same interest all the while industriously lightened its own burdens and heaped them up upon the People.

The wars "to maintain the Balance of power in Europe," and against the American and French Republics, were wars of the "families" against the Peoples,—paid for by the People of England, and which postponed their political enfranchisement, and pledged and pawned their industry and lives.

Contrary to all common sense and right, these wars by our oligarchy against Peoples now weigh, not upon the hereditary property of these hereditary rulers, but *chiefly upon labourers' and trade incomes.* The few undertook them. The all fought them and pay for them, and the national debt rose from 100,000,000 under Geo. III, in 1760, to 830,000,000 under Geo. IV, in 1820; in 1863, the interest of that debt was twenty-six millions, and the revenue from Customs and Excise forty-one millions.

Who chiefly pays this is but too obvious. The professional, mercantile, farming, and *every other class* is burdened to relieve land.

§

And the Act 12 Carol. II, was in fact the corrupt consideration passing by the King to his supporters. It relieved land from the conditions of feudal tenure, and in fact made ownership absolute, and "in recompense and compensation," (for what?) it enacted duties on all "beer, ale, cider, perry, and strong waters for ever." It robbed the poor man of his beer, and relieved rich men of taxation whilst it made them the more able to pay.

Macaulay thus notices the concessions of Charles II to the landed interest:—

> "Every landed proprietor, who held by knight service, had to pay a *large fine* on coming into his property, and could not alienate one acre without *purchasing a licence.* The Sovereign was guardian to infants, and not only entitled to a *great part of the rents* during minority, but could require a ward *under heavy penalties* to marry any person of suitable rank. A royal letter to an heiress was the chief bait to needy sycophants. That these abuses should not revive was the wish of every landed gentleman in the kingdom. They were therefore solemnly abolished by statute. This concession was easily obtained from the restored king."—V. i, p. 153.

So much for this part of the bargain between Feudality and the King. *Feudal tenure was changed into fee simple.* The King got his crown. The nation paid for it by excise duties then granted.

Macaulay further says, that in 1798, the land-tax was made permanent at four shillings in the pound. In peace, before Geo. III, sometimes only two and three shillings were needed. After the American war never less than four shillings. "*The lords claimed no right to alter the amount,* but demanded special commissioners."—V. iv, pp. 315–16.

During 106 years, including the time of the Stuarts, the Commonwealth, and William III, Parliament annually passed a land-tax Bill, during war of four shillings, during peace of two or three. "At one shilling in the pound it brought in half a million," in 1692. Land rental was therefore about ten millions, and was the most productive of all

State resources. The rental now cannot be less than 170 millions, on which a reasonable rate would relieve industry and minimise the pauperism, vice and crime now created by law.

Almost immediately after the revolution of 1688, came *another land-jugglery,* but for which the land-tax would now produce more than all the burdens that oppress trade. *This of course was the era of the next "act of settlement"* at the restoration. As Macaulay mildly says, "the value of 1692 has remained unaltered down to our time." Landowners have been wise in their generation.

§

It appears that landowners pay not eight and a half millions out of seventy millions taxation, although their income must be more than a fourth of the £600,000,000, of which Mr. Gladstone says the working classes earn under £250,000,000, and those above them £350,000,000.

The following is an approximate calculation lately published, and founded upon the revenue for the year ending March 31st, 1864 :—

1st. Taxes from which landed property is entirely exempt; Fire Insurance, Probate duty, Cart-horse duty, £3,367,380.

2nd. Taxes so arranged that land shall escape its due proportion ; Legacy and Succession duties, £2,251,580, Income tax £9,101,994. Of the latter, landowners under schedule A probably pay about one-third, or say £2,730,000. Of the former, also one-third, or £750,000.

3rd. Taxes falling chiefly upon the wealthy

upper, and wealthy middle classes, £4,928,741, of which land probably pays half, or £2,500,000. These taxes are such as stamps, wine duty, game certificates, &c.

4th and 5th. Taxes injuring trade and falling upon the smallest middle classes and the working classes,—tea, sugar, malt, tobacco, licences, &c., £29,480,036. Spirits, £12,685,401. Supposing there to be six millions of families in the country, it may be assumed that the landowning class would not contribute more than the average rate of corn, malt, tobacco, licences, and spirits.—or £4 10*s.* per family. On tea, sugar, and all the other items of this class, the average is £2 10*s.* The landowner's family may consume five times the average, or £12 10*s.* each. Multiply £17 by thirty thousand landowning families, the result is £510,000.

6th, 7th, and 8th. Post-office, £3,937,308, of which landowners pay but a fraction, say £300,000. Hereditary revenue,—land-tax, crown lands, &c., £1,660,416. Miscellaneous, £3,309,035, such as contributions from Indian revenue, old stores, &c.

Hence it appears that of a total revenue of £70,721,891, landowners contribute about £8,450,416.

In connection with this subject, various points are admirably put in the "Financial Reformer" of July, 1865. It says that indirect taxation realises annually to the State the forty millions, "*at a cost vastly exceeding that amount, in actual payments* connected with the *collection, and in the expenses attendant upon fiscally created pauperism, disease, and criminality.* If Government officers were stationed at the doors of every shop to demand the duties, and the extra charges of the collectors upon the duties, not all the regular troops in England, backed by pensioners, militia, yeomanry, and volunteers, would suffice to enforce this system for a month."

Farmers exemption from fire insurance, probate, and cart-horse duty; their payment on half the rental only, as income tax; the valuation of real estate by the Succession Act of 1853, as a life annuity only, other property paying on the full value, and paying at once; the present corn law protection to the extent of four millions per annum (on eighty millions of quarters)—all these are but slight immunities accorded to land, in comparison with the main national grievance. The "Financial Reformer" puts the state of facts with truth and force.

"After the Conquest, William's chief leaders and their retainers, held their grants of land subject to onerous feudal obligations, personal and pecuniary, all strictly in the nature of RENT; and they were liable to forfeiture for non-fulfilment of those obligations. Lands were so held down to the time of the Restoration. Whatever else beyond this *Rent* was required for State purposes was levied by direct taxation—a fifteenth, a tenth, sometimes even a seventh of all property or income being taken for the occasion.

"During this period of 594 years, the country was governed and defended at home, and carried on great wars abroad, without incurring a farthing of debt; but, on the 21st of November, 1660, all this was changed, and a complete fiscal revolution effected. On that day the Convention Parliament of Charles II—probably by previous compact with the profligate Sovereign, who afterwards gave away an unexplored continent, sold a city, and became a pensioner of France—*by a bare majority of* 151 *votes to* 149, and in defiance of indignant protests from many of its most eminent members against this infamous spoliation of Crown, State, and People, abolished all these feudal obligations—*converted themselves and their landholding brethren from tenants of the State into owners in fee;* and, in lieu of their own rents, granted to the Crown excise duties for ever, in 'full compensation,' as they had the impudence to allege, for the repudiation of their own just debts to the State! Whilst they thus *threw their own proper burdens upon those who had no land,* and no property but their labour, *they were careful to preserve intact exactly similar obligations incumbent upon sub-tenants to themselves,* as lords of manors, asserting with matchless effrontery, that to abolish them also, '*might be very prejudicial,*' as it undoubtedly would have been, but only to these robbers of the State.

"That this tax was originally intended to be assessed, year by year, on the full actual value, and to increase in produce as the value increased, is abundantly manifest from the fact that the Act of Parliament imposing it provided for the appointment of commissioners to assess the value annually; but, by another trick of landholding legislation, perpetrated in 1697, and quite in keeping with its predecessor of Charles the Second's time, it was enacted that, for the purposes of this tax, *the value should be taken only as it stood in* 1692, and should ever afterwards so remain. Hence it is that, whilst in some stagnant parts of the country the tax is now really four shillings in the pound of the present value, in places which have thriven greatly since 1692, it is only the fraction of a farthing."

Adam Smith also explains that "by the land-tax it was intended that stock should be taxed in the same proportion as land. When the tax upon the land was four shillings in the pound, or at one-fifth of the supposed rent, it was intended that stock should be taxed at one-fifth the supposed interest (per cent. of money value).

Of the entire expenditure during the fourteen years of William III (seventy-two millions), forty-nine millions were raised by taxes, and *more than a third* of this was paid by land tax, whilst to the expenditure of 1863-4, it contributed a *sixty-fourth part,* and is assessed in many instances not on land but on dwelling houses. According to the original intent, it would now produce fifty millions annually.

Naturally, this system of legislating in person, and paying by proxy,—this "feudal system modernised," which retains power to the land, and casts the responsibilities and conditions of its tenure on the People who don't hold it, created the "national debt" and raised it in one hundred and sixty years, to eight hundred millions in 1815, whereas five hundred and ninety-four years of real feudality, kept the burdens in the land, and paid expenditure out of income.

The extent to which the British Constitution is violated,—the People misrepresented, and those class interests favored, is shown by an analysis of the two Houses, prepared from the description in Dod. The Lords are mainly in the fighting and aristocratic interest. The Commons have about 215 members for the fighting interest; 218 peers, or connections of peers; 106 in the legal interest; 11 for railways; whilst for the whole mercantile, manufacturing, and shipowning interests, there are only about 84 representatives. And all this is in addition to the vast power of courtly and parasitical influences.

Thus true is it that Government *by* is always and everywhere Government *for*.

The present system of taxation is as void of true conservatism as of justice.

Wages are wealth. Wages are nearly half the income of the country. They are more injured by bad

Government or revolution than any other incomes, and consequently those who earn them have a greater stake in the country, although the property of each individual be so small.

Also it is certain that the contributors to one half of our revenue, exercise no influence on its *imposition, incidence,* or *distribution.* The *largest* aggregate contributors of the other half, who do share the right of deciding these things, are altogether overpowered by the influence of the *smaller* aggregate contributors.

§

The incidence of taxation, its amount, and the connection between it and liberty, is thus put by Montesquieu :—

"The public revenues are a portion that each subject gives of his property, in order to secure or enjoy the remainder.

"To fix these revenues in a proper manner, regard should be had both to the necessities of the State and to those of the subject. The real wants of the People ought never to give way to the imaginary wants of the State. Often have ministers of a restless disposition imagined *that the wants of their own mean and ignoble souls were those of the State.*

"In free States, taxes may be laid either on person, lands, or merchandise, on two of these, or on all three.

"In the taxing of persons, it would be an unjust proportion to conform exactly to that of property. At Athens it was judged that every man had an equal share of what was *necessary for nature;* that whatsoever was necessary for nature *ought not to be taxed*; that to this succeeded the *useful,* which ought to be taxed, but less than the *superfluous* ; and that the largeness of the taxes on what was superfluous prevented superfluity.

"Taxes ought to be very light in despotic countries.

"It is a general rule that taxes may be *heavier in proportion to the liberty of the subject.* This has always been and always will be the case. It is a rule derived from nature that never varies.

"*Taxes may be increased in most republics,* because the citizen who thinks he is paying himself cheerfully submits to them.

"This (a free) nation is passionately fond of liberty, because it is real; and it is possible for it, in its defence, to sacrifice its wealth, ease, interest, and to support the burthen of *the most heavy taxes*, even such as the most despotic prince durst not lay upon his subjects."—V. i, pp. 274-7, 244, 283-4, 412.

This is not the place in which to discuss the necessary details of a change from fiscal laws to direct taxation. The principle is admitted, so far that the whole drift of modern finance has been the use of direct taxation, even of the income tax, to reduce indirect taxation, and to "lighten the springs of industry."

The following nine reasons against indirect taxation, may, however, be here summarised with advantage:—1st. It does not tend to excite interest in politics. 2nd. Consequently, the *national resources are wasted* in protecting and collecting, wasted in use, and also misapplied. 3rd. *Trade is obstructed*, and artificial pauperism created; the consuming power of the People is reduced, and the general demand also lessened. 4th. The charges for interest, profits, and risk of capital advanced in payment of the duties by wholesale dealers and retailers (varying from 25 to 200 per cent.), constitute an *extra burden* on the People beyond the amount received by the State, of at least *twenty millions sterling* per annum. 5th. It thus costs the People a large proportion *of their entire wages* in prices enhanced by taxes and extra charges occasioned by them. This is proved by returns from the leading co-operative stores. 6th. *It constitutes a blockade* of our coasts, rivers, and harbours, and so promotes the perpetuation of jealousies and prejudices which are the frequent cause of war. 7th. It robs the country of the enormous increase of comforts and wealth, now proved to result from the repeal of customs and excise duties, by the experience of the past twenty years, and the increase in trade and improvement of the People consequent thereupon. 8th. The increase of trade and intercourse tends to prevent war, and the decrease of them encourages it.

The following calculation of the cost of excessive preserving of game is important, if only an approximation :—

"Calculating the acreage of England at 32,500,000 and 16,000,000 acres on which one hare or rabbit is kept, and supposing that one hare to every four acres is a fair quantity for sporting purposes, there is an excess of hares and rabbits of twelve millions. Taking these in equal quantities, the hares represent £900,000, the rabbits £300,000, or a total of £1,200,000. But two hares and two rabbits eat as much as one sheep, and destroy as much as they eat. This would keep three millions more sheep than are kept at present. At forty shillings per sheep, twelve months old, we ought to get £6,000,000 worth of food. The difference between that and £1,200,000 is an indirect tax of £4,800,000 on the People's food, and would pay for all the cattle and sheep imported for more than a year."

Toulmin Smith thus speaks of the mystification and profligacy of the present system :—

"The results of the *alteration from a system of direct taxation*, based on local self-Government, to an indirect one, based on centralisation, have been, and are truly startling. The National Debt is no mean instalment of such results. But every constitutional principle has become habitually violated. Parliamentary assent to any money votes has become almost a mere form. *Expenditure* is made *without the least reference to the assent and consent of the folk and people first had* and obtained; as the common law and the Constitution require. And if any man would,—in order to awaken attention to a subject so importantly affecting the power of each man to use, to the best advantage, the opportunities and faculties he has, —show to his neighbours the part and amount of the burthen which, through their apathy, has been stealthily fastened upon them, he is stopped, at the outset, by that craftily-devised scheme of centralisation, by which *each place* is no longer separately assessed, and its share separately and cheaply collected, under responsible officers, but its share *is undistinguishably merged in a great and mystified whole*, and that whole is collected, wastefully and extravagantly, under a centralised and altogether irresponsible machinery.

"Men may, peradventure, be startled when called upon to pay, in a *direct* form, *twenty-five per cent.*, or more, of the income of each (this being a low estimate of the proportion now, 1851, *actually paid by most in the middle classes of life*) towards the national taxation."—*Toulmin Smith*, on "Local Self-Government," p. 385.

And Bentham ("Plan," pp. 40-43) insists on the controlling power of the purse :—

"The one thing needful is,—that the *power of the purse* should be actually and effectively in the hands of the real representatives, *that* being the power by the exercise of which, for the defence of the People against Stuart tyranny, all other needful powers were acquired.

"At various periods in the history of this country, *this all-productive power* was actually in the hands of the People; witness statute after statute.

"*If in those days*,—when the press was unknown—when scarce any man but a priest could read—when there was nothing worth the reading—no, not so much as the Bible to be read,—if *the People could without danger*, in those days of ignorance and barbarism, *possess and exercise the power of the purse*,—in these days shall cowardice or tyranny find in pretended universal ignorance a pretext for scaring universal suffrage?

"What we want is, *under the existing forms of subjection*, the ascendancy of the democratic interest. Less than this cannot save us.

"What ground for any apprehension of danger in a *partial* Democracy, with monarchy and aristocracy by the side, and at the head of it, and for keeping it in order, a standing army?

"The thing required is,—leaving the executive where it is, —*that the controlling part of the Government shall be in the hands of those whose interest it is that good Government shall take the place of misrule*, in every shape, particularly in the two most intimately connected—*waste and corruption, corruption and waste*."

POLITICAL FREEDOM.

Political freedom means the franchise. It means free trade in land; a just settlement law for the poor; and *equality*, the essence, as we have seen, of Democracy, *in the distribution* of seats, and of electoral power. It means the rule of a majority of the whole educated People. It means that large, religious, and powerful minorities shall no longer be outraged by the rule of the *sections*. It means that the large and living towns shall no longer be reduced to *negations* by dead and dirty acres, and by old and foolish squires.

It involves both free acquisition and free use of political power. The possession of land is always a test of this.

PRIMOGENITURE is incompatible either with the free acquisition or use of power, for it tends to a perpetual concentration and monopoly, and so to unequal representation.

It makes land dear and concentrated, for under it owners may buy, but (such is the tendency) cannot sell.

It often encourages two spendthrifts at once. The father on the timber, the son on the chance of surviving the father. The father spends by despoiling the estate. The son spends at an unnatural rate of interest, and if the tenant for life would improve the estate, he is often prevented by the consideration that his improvements become parcel of the entail, and cannot, under whatever pressure be made available for his own needs. The system injures the estate as well as the tenant for life and in tail.

Primogeniture sacrifices the interests of the widow, and of all children but the eldest son, to the proud and lofty object of concentrating family power, and creating a family. It is an imitation of royalty, without its reasons. It is a remnant of feudality without *its* reasons for sudden and effectual military service. The Dowager wife descends, on the death of her husband, from her equal throne, and after a life maternal authority; the daughters are charged on a fraction of the estate; and the younger sons complete the sacrifice. Primogeniture may make "families," but it is evidently against the (modern) State. It studies the best advantages (of the pride, exclusiveness, and indolence) of the fewest number. If the State did not provide for cadets, cadets would revolt against primogeniture.

Montesquieu thus shows how Primogeniture was introduced, and its inexpediency, especially in a trading country like England:—

"As soon as the fiefs became hereditary, the right of seniority was established. The ancient law of partitions was no longer subsisting; the fiefs being charged with a service, the possessor must have been enabled to discharge it. The right of primogeniture was established, and the reason of the feudal law was superior to that of the political or civil institution."—V. ii, p. 486.

"It was a spirit of vanity that established among Europeans *the unjust law of primogeniture.* So unfavorable to propagation, is that it directs the attention of a father to only one of his children, and turns his eyes from all the others; is that it obliges him, in order to make a solid fortune for one only, to hinder the settlement of the rest; lastly, is that *it destroys the equality of citizens, which constitutes their wealth.*

"The propagation of mankind is vastly promoted by a mild Government. All republics are certain proofs of this. Nothing invites strangers more than liberty and wealth, which always follow the former: *The equality of citizens, which commonly produces an equality in their fortunes, brings plenty and life into every part of the body politic*, and extends them through the whole."—V. iii, pp. 405-10.

"It is an excellent law, *in a trading republic*, to make an *equal division of the paternal estate* among the children. The consequence of this is, that how great soever a fortune the father has made, his children, not being so rich as he, are induced to avoid luxury, and to work as he had done.

"As a great share of virtue is very rare where men's fortunes are so unequal, *the laws must* tend as much as possible to infuse a spirit of moderation; and *endeavour to re-establish that equality* which was necessarily removed by the (aristocratic) constitution. The spirit of moderation is what we call virtue in an aristocracy; it supplies the place of the spirit of equality in a popular State.

"It is the business of particular laws to level as it were, the inequalities, by the duties laid upon the rich, and by the ease afforded to the poor.

"As to men of over-grown estates, everything which does not contribute to advance their power and honour is considered by them as an injury."—V. i, pp. 54-8, and 64.

§

We have seen two great English champions of freedom treating this question of EQUALITY. The one advocates Democracy; the other a species of graduated manhood,—a "sliding scale" *which will enable the American to go on importing our manhood from us.* Mill says Equality is impossible, Gladstone advocates a fearless advance towards it:—

Mill declares that "whoever does not desire equal universal suffrage, cannot too soon begin to reconcile himself to plural voting," and when terms of capitulation are recommended by cool onlookers like Mr. Mill, victory cannot be far distant. But it is not in England that such terms will either be offered by a party, or accepted by the People.

In England, minorities have ruled from time immemorial. But they have ruled by power, not by sufferance. Since Kings ruled as despots, Families have ruled as communists. An age or two ago steam began to create the power called public opinion, which has since confronted Family Government. Between these two the conflict for power now rages. The Families constitute the whole Upper House. They own two-thirds of the county seats, and more than half the small boroughs. And the evil which Mr. Mill anticipates from popular Government is a class rule, a *popular* class rule, and the remedy he prescribes is that very *minority class rule,* which if defeated in one form, shall reappear in another! The great principle of the sliding scale is promoted from corn to manhood.

But this is not the way in England. The facts only unveil the real principle of this minority Government, and make it hateful. Englishmen may suffer awhile the rule of the old traditional minorities, but henceforth all new minorities that climb to power, must do so *by conquering a majority* by the natural process of reason and publicity.

Thus the contest is between the new England and the old. But the *essential principle* of this contest is "minorities and majorities," Families or Men, the People or the Sections. A balancing of class interests against the onward and majestic march of the whole nation, one and indivisible. They, therefore, but ill understand the temper or the metal of Englishmen, who imagine that, having gotten the victory by force, they will surrender its results to cajolery or indirection,—that having stormed the Malakoff of Oligarchy, they will set up over it the flag of the enemy,—the symbol of defeat and reaction.

The fight means just this :—"Is or is not the majority to rule?" To the victors will be the spoils. Not even Mr. Mill will get them for the vanquished.

With her comparatively narrow basis of men and land, old England can only survive by adopting the principles of the new; and the new England will conquer by using present forms whilst evoking the true and noble spirit of the British Constitution.

Without this, England would soon be an island in the sea,—an island, and nothing more. Of two things one, we must cast out *our* Oligarchy, or degrade our nationality against Democracies. *We must stand on Democracy or on nothing.* The strength and the truth of Commerce, of Politics, and Religion,—of the Body, Mind, and Spirit of the nation, must make us free, for we have now to run the world-race against Democracies, if we run that race at all. Walking in the paths of the Constitution, we should insist that its principles demand a much wider freedom than we now enjoy. We must recognise that freedom begins with the Few and ends with the All. That thus the base of a true nation widens from age to age, and that nationality and freedom together must broaden,—not downwards, but upwards, "from precedent to precedent" of glory.

Yielding to this truth, Mr. Gladstone thus enunciated the principle and stated the facts upon the strength of which he appeals to the country for an instalment of justice. He wants to lay his foundation on that which is catholic in truth, immutable in strength, and universal in numbers. None can flank his position, unless they go for a wider Democracy than his.

"What I would state is this:—Every man who is not presumably incapacitated by some consideration of personal unfitness or political danger, is morally entitled to come within the pale of the Constitution. . . . The present franchise may be said, upon the whole, to draw a line between the lower middle class and the upper working class. The lower middle class is generally admitted. The upper working class is generally excluded. Is that a state of things which is recommended to us by any clear or definite principle of reason? Are the upper portion of the working class really inferior to the lower portion of the middle class? I wish that question to be considered on both sides of the House. It appears to me that the negative of that assertion may be held with the greatest confidence."

And again as to the facts which we believe to be more reliable than the later hasty returns:—

"Somewhere between one-tenth and one-twentieth of the elements of the borough and county constituencies, taken together, is made up of the working classes themselves. I venture to maintain that if 49-50ths of the working classes are excluded, *it is on those who* MAINTAIN THAT EXCLUSION *to show on what it rests*."—Speech in the House, May 11th, 1864.

"I doubt whether, at the present moment, as large a proportion of the working classes holds the suffrage as held it in the month of December, 1832. Is that a proper or a right state of things?"

Surely here is either the wildest revolution or the soundest and safest conservatism.

And at Chester, on the 31st May, 1865 :—

> "I believe if we take the whole constituency of the country at about one million, the working men of that million, in the estimation of many, do not exceed 50,000, and hardly any one thinks they exceed 100,000. What do I mean by liberal principles? The principle of trusting the People, only relieved by prudence."

While Mill represents the conservatism of Democracy, Gladstone represents that equation between Conservatism and Democracy, which results in a safe progress. Others represent the timidity which does not rest absolutely on first principles, which fears to be too much in the right, and exerts enormous ingenuity to find a shorter road than the direct one; whilst Bright represents the living power and passion of Democracy incarnate, which is the motive force of all.

§

Mr. Cobden powerfully states the importance of the BALLOT, and if to be "one-sided" is to be strong, it is perhaps, after all, better *not* to have read "Thucydides." If one cannot be encyclopedic without being emasculated, it is best to be one-sided.

Mr. Cobden said :—"The Ballot is a moral engine which is not appreciated in England, because it is not sufficiently known. Let it once be established in any constituency, and it will spread like wildfire throughout the country."

Mr. Mill appears to us scarcely to make due

allowance for the position of the voter. He says, "slavish dependence" and "electoral intimidation" can be defied by the elector, although this is only true of few places and under certain particular circumstances.

He also argues against the Ballot, that voting is "a public and important act," whereas that is the very reason why the voter should be protected.

He argues from trade *combinations*, to the independence of the *isolated* voter.

The real ground of "ballot or no ballot" seems to be expounded by Montesquieu, the greatest of political writers. He says (vol. i, pp. 14-15, Trans., A.D. 1777) :—

> "The law which determines the manner of giving the suffrage is fundamental in a Democracy. It is a question of some importance whether the suffrages ought to be secret. The People's suffrages ought doubtless to be public (at Athens the People used to lift up their hands), and this should be considered a fundamental law in Democracy. *The lower class ought to be directed* by those of a higher rank. Hence by rendering the suffrages secret in the Roman Republic, all was lost. It was no longer possible *to direct* a populace that sought its own destruction. But when the body of the nobles are to vote in an aristocracy, *as the business is then only to prevent intrigues*, the suffrages *cannot be too secret*.
>
> "The thirty tyrants of Athens ordered the suffrages of the Areopagites *to be public in order to manage them*."

Distinguishing, then, between the dangers of want of direction, which are evidently those which Montesquieu provides against, and those of *intimidation*, which are what we have, to a great extent, to guard against, and allowing for the fact that our electors do not require "direction by those of higher rank," we get this conclusion,—that where ignorance, and consequent need of direction, are mostly to be feared, this great writer prescribes publicity, but that when intimidation is to be feared, then secrecy and the Ballot are necessary. The suffrages of the English are kept "public in order to manage them," and when the object is to "prevent intrigues," or to prevent the "tyrannical management of electors," then "suffrages *cannot be too secret.*"

The Ballot ought to be universal, or else to be granted to constituencies that demand it.

To make intimidation FELONY, is the only alternative, if, indeed, it be a practicable alternative. Without this, or the Ballot, there can be no political equality. The intimidator can *destroy the position* of his victim. Arm the latter with equal powers to strike, or enable him to defend himself. He can only defend himself in many cases, by secrecy, or by being enabled by law to *destroy the position* of his adversary.

RELIGIOUS FREEDOM.

Freedom demands also that Religion shall be without State-imposed political character and bias.

The fundamental objection to the much-discussed connection between Church and State is that *each is a Sovereignty, or nothing.*

Religion opposes every false sovereignty, and upholds all that are true. But if the nominal head of the Church be also the head of the

State, where the State is unjust the Church must either denounce its own head or be a party to wrong.

If *sovereignties* conflict, one of them must be destroyed. The actual results are seen in Roman Catholicism, where the Church is sovereign; in Protestant countries, where the State is sovereign; and in countries partly one and partly the other, where the sovereignties conflict.

The conflict tends to compromise and corruption. The State uses the Church for Statecraft; the Church uses the State for Priestcraft.

The spirit of Religion must rule, but it is hampered by the weight of secularity. The secular must also rule,—if not by opinion, then by force or by corruption.

Separation is the only peace that is not death. If Religion be only Religion, and its organisation, apart from the State, it will uphold the State, if it be right, and alter it if wrong. The Puritan principle has never been destroyed, and in America, where it is free, its ecclesiastical provisions are the most splendid and ample.

Common sense demands that no Church shall be "established" that is not infallible. If infallible, it cannot fail for want of establishment. If fallible, the sooner it fails the better. Whether fallible or infallible, bribery and force are no part of Religion.

Statesmanship demands, on the one hand, that Religion shall not be prostituted as an engine of Government, and, on the other hand, that favouritism shall not array section against section, and so weaken the State.

Purity demands that ideas of the market and the auction room shall not be inflicted on it by authority; that the People shall pay for and elect their own religious teachers; that Statesmen shall not buy the Church; that private individuals shall neither buy nor sell it; that it shall not become encrusted with abuses and traditions, irremoveable because they are established, and established in the sense of a settlement of the monies of the whole People upon the opinions and forms of a mere section, *a Malakoff of caste, corporate abuse, and hierarchical prerogative,* without, and against the People and their pre-ordained progress. The caste feeling resulting from the "establishment" of a sectional Church is one of the curses of middle-class society in England. Either the Church will become truly national by becoming Democratic, or it will cease to be national in any sense, and become more intensely sectional. If it be national, its funds (saving vested private interests) are national, and the nation may vote them. If it be not national, it ought to account for the use of the funds that are national, and of which it then has no ownership.

There is nothing in the ancient constitution of England savouring of such "establishments" of prelacy, sectarianism, wordly mindedness, priestcraft, and money changing.

They savour of Despotism, Centralisation, and Rome, of the notion that Religion is a matter of form, ceremony, and compulsion, and that His Majesty the People *can and ought* to be taken in and done for by his own creatures.

An established Church cannot be catholic without being licentious A Church cannot be established without being Popish. For all establishments settle forms upon posterity and settle money upon forms,—in fact connect interest with opinion, affix a premium on immobility, and a penalty on free thought.

This is either useless,—trying to perpetuate what cannot be perpetuated, or tyrannical, attempting to perpetuate by some form of force or favour, that which opinion would otherwise condemn.

"No true Protestant (says Toulmin Smith, 'Local self-Government,' pp. 333–4), can suffer any disability for any civil office to attach to any one by reason of his religious faith. The laying down such disability is an act and mark of Popishness. The true Protestant must *resist* all means by which the free development of the faculties of man is sought to be hindered."

Religious liberty therefore demands the abrogation of all laws and usages which inflict disability, or confer privilege, on ecclesiastical grounds, upon any subject of the realm.

The disabilities inflicted on Dissenters are fewer than in past days, but still remain much as follows. "As a general rule, Dissenters cannot act as masters or trustees of the ancient Grammar Schools, which are national property; while Dissenting scholars must use the formularies of the

Church of England, or be excluded. A Dissenter cannot take a higher degree than that of B.A. at Oxford University, and M.A. at Cambridge; while at both universities he is excluded from the fellowships, and from every post involving authority and emolument. The Dissenter cannot avail himself of the services of his own minister, in the burial of the dead, in the English churchyards; and, in the case of Dissenters dying unbaptized, the parochial clergyman may legally refuse to perform any funeral service. No Town Councillor, Alderman, or other municipal functionary, can take office without making a declaration acknowledging the legal supremacy of the Established Church. The canons of the Established Church denounce both Dissent and Dissenters in the severest terms. On the other hand, the Bishops of the Church of England sit in Parliament, and legislate for Dissenters as well as Episcopalians. Its ministers monopolise nearly all the masterships of public schools, and hold many public offices; preside by law over parish vestries, and, in virtue of their legal position, claim precedence of all other ministers of religion, and frequently treat them with studied contempt. As the result of this repression on the one hand, and favoritism on the other, Dissenters are placed at a serious disadvantage in respect to their opinions, worship, and religious efforts, as well as to their social and political position. What is wanted in lieu of this state of things is *Religious Equality* —the State protecting all men in the expression and practice of their religious views, but neither patronizing nor endowing any religious body."

§

Religious Liberty also demands the application to secular uses, after an equitable satisfaction of existing interests, of all national property now held by the United Church of England and Ireland and the Presbyterian Church of Scotland; and, concurrently with it, the liberation of those Churches from all State control.

As Lord Brougham said in his Irish Church Bill speech of 1836, "when the Christian Religion was first planted in this land, it was supported by the voluntary oblations of the faithful," Equality, therefore, in this respect also, is but a return to the ancient ways.

The power of the State over all public "Church" property is settled by right, precedent, authority, and necessity.

The law recognises the personal and official right of the officiating individual, but has never safely allowed, nor could safely allow, such an imperium in imperio as a Church absolutely possessed of national public property.

The State has as much power over the property of the "Church of England" as over the revenues of the army and navy. It has changed the conditions of its tenure five times already. [See Mackintosh and Brougham hereon, and note the manner of past changes. Also "Edinburgh Review," January 1835, Lord Chancellor Hardwicke,

Fuller, Dean Milman, and Lords Campbell, Melbourne, Althorp, and Palmerston.]

It was not the Church, but King, Lords, and Commons that changed Roman Catholicism for Protestant Episcopalianism. Queen, Lords, and Commons next reversed the process. Elizabeth and her Parliament again sent Romanism to the right-about. The Commonwealth established Presbyterianism, and Charles II made the last change. Through all changes the endowments remained and the establishment was altered. The Church always held from the State and subject to the State, the Church being only a system of ecclesiastical rule.

Montesquieu (of Laws in Monarchies), thus extols the subjection of the Church to the Law :—

"The English to favor their liberty, have abolished all the intermediate powers of which their monarchy was composed. They have a great deal of reason to be jealous of this liberty: were they ever to be so unhappy as to lose it, they would be one of the most servile nations upon earth."

And this great master of political science further says :—

"Though the ecclesiastic power be so dangerous in a republic, yet it is extremely proper in a monarchy, *especially of the absolute kind.* A barrier ever useful *where there is no other*; *the very evil* that restrains a despotic Government is beneficial.

"With regard to religion, as in this State (a free State), every subject has a free will, and must consequently be either conducted by the light of his own mind or by the caprice of fancy, it necessarily follows that every one must either look upon all religion with *indifference, by which means they are led to embrace the established religion*, or they must be zealous for religion in general, by which means *the number of sects is increased.*

"*The clergy* (in such free State) not being able to protect religion, nor to be protected by it, *only seek to persuade.* (Vol. i, pp. 21, 415, 416.)

"But the political state of the Government received the greatest injury from his (Justinian's) project of *establishing a general uniformity of opinion in matters of religion*, and in circumstances that rendered his zeal as indiscreet as possible.

"The ancient Romans fortified their empire by indulging all sorts of religious worship; but their posterity *destroyed* it by rooting out the various sects, whose doctrines were not predominant.

"But when she (the Church) appears triumphant to the eyes of the world, she is generally sinking in adversity.

"A universal bigotry had stupified and emasculated the whole empire.

"Those who may happen to read the history written by Pachymerus, will be effectually convinced of *the unalterable inability of divines to accommodate their own disagreements*, and will see an emperor who spent his days in assembling people of that class, listening to their disputations, and reproaching them for the inflexibility of their opinions: they will likewise behold another engaged with a hydra of controversies, &c. The same artless pliancy to their intrigues, joined with the same deference to their aversions, *will never reconcile these implacable ecclesiastics while the world endures*.

"*An unacquaintedness with the true nature and limits of ecclesiastical and secular power*, was the most pernicious source of all *the calamities that befel the Greeks*, and involved both priests and people in perpetual errors.

"*This great distinction, which constitutes all the tranquillity of a nation, is founded, not only on religion, but on reason and nature*, which never confound things really distinct in themselves, and which can only subsist in consequence of that very distinction."—*Montesquieu*, vol. iii, pp. 154, 162-3, 171-2-3, "Grandeur and Declension of the Roman Empire."

And to this should be added the opinion of one of the very first of modern philosophers upon history.

Mr. Draper, discussing the union of Church and State, under Constantine, the questions of religious unity and individual freedom, of the hierarchical principle, of toleration, and of the true and ultimate meaning of the Reformation, thus expresses himself:—

"The unavoidable consequences were a union between

the Church and State; a diverting of the dangerous classes from civil to ecclesiastical paths, and *the decay and materialisation of Religion*. . . . The fatal gift of a Christian Emperor had been the doom of true religion."

"This decline of its (ecclesiasticism) ancient influence, should be a cause of rejoicing to all intelligent men, for *an ecclesiastical organisation allying itself to political power can never now be a source of any good.* In America we have seen the bond that held the Church and State together abruptly snapped. It is therefore well that, since the close of the Age of Faith, things have been coming back, with an accelerated pace, to the state in which they were in the early Christian times, before the founder of Constantinople *beguiled the devotional spirit to his personal and family benefit*—to the state in which they were before ambitious men sought political advancement and wealth *by organising hypocrisy*—when maxims of morality, charity, benevolence, were rules of life for individual man—when the monitions of conscience were obeyed without the suggestions of an outward, often an interested and artful prompter—when the individual lived not under *the sleepless gaze, the crushing hand of a great overwhelming hierarchical organisation*, surrounding him on all sides, doing his thinking for him, directing him in his acts, making him a mere automaton."

"The Reformation Itself, philosophically considered, really meant the casting off of authority, the installation of individual inquiry and personal opinion."

"The history of the Reformation does not close where many European authors have imagined, in a balanced and final distribution of the north and south between the Protestant and Catholic. The predestined issue of sectarian differences and dissensions, is individual liberty of thought. So long as there was one vast overshadowing, intolerant corporation, every man must bring his understanding to its measure, and think only as it instructed him to do. As soon as dissenting confessions gathered sufficient military power to maintain their right of existence—as soon as from them, in turn, incessant offshoots were put forth, *toleration became* not only possible, but *inevitable, and that is perhaps as far as the movement has at this time advanced in Europe.* But Macaulay and others who have treated of the *Reformation*, have taken too limited a view of it, supposing that this was its point of arrest. It *made another enormous stride when, at the American revolution, the State and the Church were solemnly and openly dissevered from one another.* Now might the vaticinations of the prophets of evil expect to find credit; a great people had irrevocably broken off its politics from its theology, and it might surely have been expected that the unbridled interests, and instincts, and passions of men would have dragged everything into the abyss of anarchy. Yet what do we, who are living nearly a century after that time, find the event to be? Sectarian decomposition, passing forward to its last extreme, is the process by which individual mental liberty is engendered and maintained. *A grand and imposing religious unity implies tyranny to the individual;* the increasing emergence of sects gives him increasing latitude of thought—with their utmost multiplication he gains his utmost liberty. In this respect, unity and liberty are in opposition; as the one diminishes, the other increases. The Reformation broke down unity; it gave liberty to masses of men grouped together in sufficient numbers to ensure their position; it is now invisibly but irresistibly making steps, never to be stayed until there is an absolute mental emancipation for man.

"Great revolutions are not often accomplished without much suffering and many crimes. It might have been supposed before the event,—perhaps it is supposed by many who are not privileged to live among the last results,—that this decomposition of religious faith must be to the detriment of personal and practical piety. Yet *America, in which, of all countries, the Reformation at the present moment has furthest advanced,* should offer to thoughtful men much encouragement. Its cities are filled with churches built by voluntary gifts; its clergy are voluntarily sustained, and are, in all directions, engaged in enterprises of piety, education, and mercy. What a difference between their private life, and that of old ecclesiastics before the Reformation! Not, as in old times, does the layman look upon them as the cormorants and curse of society; they are his faithful advisers, his honoured friends, under whose suggestion and supervision are instituted educational establisments, colleges, hospitals,—whatever can be of benefit to men in this life, or secure for them happiness in the life to come."—*Draper's* "Intellectual Development of Europe," v. i, pp. 269, 274; v. ii, pp. 220-1-2.

These principles are vindicated equally in the splendid advance of the latest of the Anglo-Saxon empires, as in the declension of that of the Romans.

The Hon. C. Gavan Duffy, returned from Victoria, at a dinner given to him at St. James's Hall, in May last (1865), states :—

"If Mr. Gregory wished to present to Parliament a startling contrast between the old country and the new, he would furnish him one which had the advantage of being founded in fact. He might ride over a district in Victoria larger than the county he represented without meeting a man who had not sufficient to eat and drink and wear, and without seeing a farmer who did not own the land he tilled in fee simple, or hold it on terms of independence; *without seeing a clergyman living at the cost of the country without a flock, or a church built by the State without a congregation.*"

The weight of authority against this money connection, this "protection" of the Church by the State, is as encyclopœdic as it is against any other prostitution. And as spiritual freedom is of the essence, we add the following from Milton, De Tocqueville, Hegel, Macaulay, Goldwin Smith, Mill, Guizot, Humboldt, and Adam Smith.

"M. Guizot has not overlooked, but impartially analysed, the mixed character of good and evil which belonged even in that age, and still more in the succeeding ages, to the power of the Church. One beneficial consequence which he ascribes to it is worthy of especial notice; the separation (unknown to antiquity) between temporal and spiritual authority. He in common with the best thinkers of our time, attributes to this fact the happiest influence on European civilization. 'It was the parent,' he says, 'of liberty of conscience.' The separation of temporal and spiritual is founded on the idea, that material force has no right, no hold, over the mind, over conviction, over truth."—V. ii, p. 243, "Dissertations," by *John Stuart Mill*, "Edinburgh Review," October, 1845.

"If proceeding further,—than removing obstacles, the legislator ventures to direct or diffuse a spirit of religiousness; if he shelters or encourages certain definite religious ideas; *or if, lastly, he dares to require a belief according to authority* in lieu of a true and sincere conviction, *he will most effectually thwart and deaden the soul's noblest aspirations, and throw fatal impediments in the way of true spiritual culture, and he can never produce virtue. For this is independent of all peculiar forms of religious belief, and incompatible with any that is enjoined by, and believed on, authority.*"—*Baron A. von Humboldt*, "Sphere and Duties of Government," p. 86.

"The principles of Christianity would be infinitely more powerful than the false honour of monarchies, the humane virtues of republics, or the servile fear of despotic States.

"The religion sent from heaven is not established by the same methods as the religions of the earth. Read the history of the Church, and you will see the wonders of the Christian religion. Has she resolved to enter a country?—she knows how to open its gates, and all instruments are proper for that purpose. Sometimes God makes use of a few fishermen; at others, he places an emperor on the throne, and makes him bend his neck under the yoke of the Gospel. Is Christianity concealed in caverns and subterraneous abodes? stay a moment, and you will see the Imperial Majesty speak in her behalf. She, whenever she pleases, crosses the seas, rivers, and mountains, and no obstacles here below can stop her progress. Place repugnance in the mind; she will make it fly before her: establish customs, form habits, publish edicts, make laws; she will triumph over the climate, the laws that result from it, and the legislators who made them."—*Montesquieu*, "Spirit of Laws," v. iv, p. 256.

"But if politics had never adopted the tenets of one sect more than of another, it would probably have dealt impartially with all the different sects. The concessions which the teachers of each sect would find it convenient and agreeable to make to one another, might in time probably reduce the doctrine of the greater part of them to that *pure and rational religion*, free from every mixture of absurdity, imposture, or fanaticism, such as wise men have in all ages of the world wished to see it established; but such as positive law has perhaps never yet established, and probably never will establish in any country. If this plan of no ecclesiastical Government (proposed to be established by the Independents towards the end of the civil war) had been established, it would probably by this time have been productive of the most philosophical good temper and moderation with regard to every sort of religious principle. In countries *where there is an established religion, the Sovereign can never be secure unless he has the means of influencing in a considerable degree the greater part of the teachers of that religion.* The clergy of every established Church constitute a great incorporation. Their interest is never the same with that of the Sovereign. It is to maintain their authority with the People, and this depends upon the supposed necessity of adopting every part of their doctrine with the most implicit faith, in order to avoid eternal misery."—*Smith's* "Wealth of Nations," v. iii, pp. 201-207.

"As a nation assumes a democratic condition it becomes more and more dangerous to connect religion with political institutions. American legislators succeeded to a certain extent in opposing the permanence of the religious world to the continual shifting of Politics. In Europe the living body of Religion has been bound down to the dead corpse of superannuated polity."—*De Tocqueville*, v. 2, p. 266.

"*Religion* as such is Reason in the soul and heart. *Thus Freedom in the State is* preserved and established by religion. . . . *The Church* was (in the middle ages) no longer a spiritual power, but an Ecclesiastical one. . . . The third kind of contradiction is the Church itself in its acquisition *as an outward existence*, of possessions and enormous property—*a state of things which*, since that Church despises or professes to despise riches, *is none other than a Lie*. . . . The corruption of the Church was not an accidental phenomenon. . . . The element in question, which is innate in the Ecclesiastical principle, only reveals itself as a corrupting one when the Church has no longer any opposition to contend with,—*when it has become firmly established*. It is that *externality* in the Church itself which becomes evil and corruption."—*Hegel's* "Philosophy of History."

"It is an unquestionable and most instructive fact that the years during which the political power of the Anglican hierarchy was in the zenith, were precisely the years during which national virtue was at the lowest point."—*Macaulay's England*, vol. i., p. 181.

"Shall I believe that Christianity deprived of State support must fall, when I see it without State support not only standing, but advancing with the settler into the remotest West? Will the Laity of Europe long remain under their illusion in the face of this great fact?"—*Goldwin Smith.*

"The whole freedom of man consists either in spiritual or civil liberty. As for spiritual, who can be at rest, who can enjoy anything in this world with contentment, who hath not liberty to serve God, and to save his own soul, according to the best light which God hath planted in him to that purpose, by the reading of his revealed will, and the guidance of His Holy Spirit?"—*Milton.*

All goes to this,—that material, political, and religious freedom are the complement of Democracy, or national self-Government, but that every nation that aspires to self-Government must get also the four-fold foundation of School, Press, Church, and Assembly, and cement and perpetuate that grand victory over ignorance and despotism by the bond and guarantee of equality.

DEMOCRACY AND CENTRALISATION;

OR,

THE OLD POWER AND THE MODERN ORGANISATION.

"I contend, that in order to combat the evils which equality may produce, there is only one effectual remedy—namely, polical freedom.

"Instruct, at all hazards, for the age of implicit self-sacrifice and instinctive virtues is already flying far away from us, and the time is fast approaching when freedom, public peace, and social order itself will not be able to exist without instruction."—*De Tocqueville.*

"The Lower House of Parliament, is not, in proper language, an *estate* of the realm, but rather the image, and representative of the Commons of England; who, being the third estate, with the nobility and clergy, make up and constitute the people of this kingdom and liege subjects of the crown." —*Hallam's Middle Ages*, v. iii, p. 105.

"Without a ministry, the working of a Parliamentary Government such as ours must always be unsteady and unsafe. It is essential to our liberties that the House of Commons should exercise a control over all the departments of the executive administration. The ministry is a committee of leading members of the houses, and is almost as essential a part of our polity as the Parliament itself. It consists exclusively of Statesmen whose opinions on the pressing questions of the time agree in the main with the opinions of the majority of the House of Commons."—*Macaulay*, 434-5, v. iv.

"In all communities, some one principle of action may be discovered which preponderates over the others."—*De Tocqueville.*

"The simultaneous accordant action of the executive and legislature is essential to a perfect Government."—*Walter Bagehot.*

"With the rise of new functions and the increase of complexity, unity obtains its completest form and fullest expression. This is a great law of universal progress. By virtue of it, a nation is a living organism."

"Entails are founded upon the most absurd of all suppositions, that every successive generation have not an equal right to the earth and all that it possesses."—*Adam Smith.*

"Laws frequently continue in force long after the circumstances which first gave occasion to them, and which could alone render them reasonable, are no more. The right of primogeniture, however, as it is the fittest to support family distinctions, is still likely to endure. In every other respect, nothing can be more contrary to the real interest of a numerous family."—*Adam Smith*, "Wealth of Nations," v. i, p. 84.

"An equal *division of lands* cannot be established in all Democracies. We are not always obliged to proceed to extremes. If it appears that this division, designed to preserve the People's morals, does not suit with the Democracy, recourse must be had to other methods."—*Montesquieu.*

"In Aristocratical Governments *there are two principle sources of disorder:* EXCESSIVE INEQUALITY between the governors and the governed, and between the governors.

"This inequality occurs, likewise, when the condition of the citizens differs as *to taxes:* which may happen four different ways; when the nobles assume the privilege of *paying none;* when they commit frauds to *exempt themselves;* when they *engross the public money under pretence of* rewards or *appointments* for their respective employments; in fine, when they render the common people tributary, and divide among their own body the profits arising from the several subsidies. This last case is very rare: an aristocracy so instituted would be *the most intolerable of all governments.*

"The laws ought to abolish the right of primogeniture among the nobles, to the end that by a continual division of the inheritances, their fortunes may be always upon a level.

"When the laws have compassed the equality of families, the next thing is, &c. In fine, the laws must not favor the *distinctions raised by vanity among families,* under pretence that they are more noble or ancient than others. Pretences of this nature ought to be ranked among private weaknesses.

"Aristocracy is corrupted if the power of the nobles becomes arbitrary. *The extremity of corruption is when the power of the nobles becomes hereditary,* for then they can hardly have any moderation."—*Montesquieu,* v. i, pp. 65-68-147.

"Such powers as are established by *commerce,* may subsist for a long series of years in their humble condition, but their grandeur is of short duration."—*Ibid,* pp. 24, v. iii.

Chapter VI.

DEMOCRACY AND CENTRALISATION;

OR,

THE OLD POWER AND THE MODERN ORGANISATION.

"After providing in the most liberal manner for education, free countries have but one thing more to do for the accomplishment of the rest,—to secure *intellectual freedom*."—*Draper*, "Intellectual Development of Europe."

"*As in a country of liberty* every man who is supposed a free agent ought to be his own governor, *the legislative power should reside in the whole body of the People.* But since this is impossible in large States, it is fit the People should transact by their representatives what they cannot transact by themselves."—*Montesquieu.*

"It no longer appears to me to be the end and purpose of the present world to produce that state of universal peace among men, and of unlimited dominion over the mechanism of nature, merely for its own sake,—*but that it should be produced by man himself;* and since it is expected from all, *that it should be produced by all*, as one great, free, moral community."—*Fichte.*

"If any of the provinces of the British Empire cannot be made to contribute towards the support of the whole empire, it is surely time that Great Britain should free herself from the expense of defending those provinces in time of war, and of supporting any part of their civil or military establishments in time of peace, and endeavour to accommodate her future views and designs to the real mediocrity of her circumstances." —*Adam Smith*, v. iii, p. 465.

"The land of France belongs to fifteen or twenty millions of peasants, who cultivate it: the land of England belongs to an aristocracy of thirty-two thousand persons, who have it cultivated. This is one of the spiritual characters of our revolution. Man outweighed the land. In England, the land has outweighed man."—*Michelet.*

When the national intellect becomes sufficiently developed and organised, not only will it have superseded the reign of force and of chattel property, it will also undertake that opinions shall not be judged by interests, but rather interests by opinion.

Force could not then organise, for elements of organisation would remain above it and beyond it. Property could not organise, for it would be but the medium of preparation and enfranchisement of its master—manhood. That only can completely organise which develops by governing, and governs by developing.—In which the units are not sacrificed to unity, nor unity to the units, but in which the State and the Individual are equally and completely considered.

The harmony of organisation with power is the test of conservative adjustment. The adjustment of power with preparation and right is the crucial question with Democracies.

Centralisation and Democracy both, are of the body, mind, and character,—by force, opinion, or conscience.

That only can be and remain universal, which is complete as to numbers and character,—as to quantity and quality. That alone which is thorough as to the whole man, can be catholic as to a whole People.

Democracy is founded, as we have seen, on material, political, and religious freedom. There can be no complete centralisation until this Democracy is universal in a nation, and " the whole of the all " is (approximately) organised.

Thus an intenser individuality than of old, can

alone meet and mate, as the universal soul of the world, the vast material combinations of the present, and the vaster ones of the future.

Organisation depends on discipline; discipline upon intelligence; unity upon the quality of the units. Although in a Democracy there is no will but the People's, there is in the whole world no other concentration of will so intense, all pervading, and terrible.

Scientifically, the cohesion of the whole depends much upon the minuteness of the parts.

Politically, homogeneousness means unity, and universality of suffrage and of will is the only agency that can compete with and excel autocracy in intensity and concentration.

In tracing, therefore, the process of the destruction of local self-Government by the necessity of more comprehensive and intimate unities, and by various corporate excrescences and abuses of privilege, priestcraft, and prerogative, and the growth of factitious and gangrenous sub-unities, the true stand point is at a sufficient distance to grasp the unity of the problem. At a sufficient elevation to take in the beauty and the glory of the promised land, we see the gradual gathering of the elements of power,—a gradual perfectioning of the instrument which the People are preparing to wield. We see, in fact, how through the centuries, Democracy and centralisation, freedom and order are made meet for one another.

It may be said that we in England have no

means analogous to the "State-right" power of America, wherewith to enforce the interests of locality against generality and centralisation, and to a certain extent the allegation is at present true. When county magnates were a reality, they had their State-rights and policy, but now the machine is on too colossal a scale, and even with universality of suffrage, centralisation can never become sufficiently intense and imminent to constitute ours a true empire. At home the anti-national interest of endowed sects and families will for ages obstruct the progress of the People and the unity of the nation. Abroad, in the colonies, the "State-rights" of Canada, Australia, New Zealand, South Africa, and India, will be ever more and more powerfully advocated, and the materials for making of them one empire do not exist, and cannot be created.

The longest lived empire of the past,—Rome, was not seated upon widely different latitudes. The influences of climate were similar. This, one of the most notable facts respecting the homogeneousness of that empire, is altogether reversed in the case of our own.

While, therefore, distance, climate, and race-differences, will prevent the permanence of the English *Empire*, the oligarchic constitution of English society and politics, withstand the advance of our Democracy, and the completion of our *nationality*.

The two hostile forces are here, as always and everywhere, Democracy and Oligarchy,—that which seeks power in the sections, and that which seeks it in the whole.

The power that will constitute our material basis of Democracy is to be found in a gradual union of the forces and interests of labor and capital, which will modify, counteract, or outweigh the union of capital with aristocracy.

SAFEGUARDS.

From time to time the immemorial safeguards of local and individual rights have been, or will be, as far as possible restored, and the British constitution revindicated.

Of these safeguards there are two classes; the first are of a *primary* nature, relating to the institutions themselves which are the source of all authority, and whose special business is the assertion of the rights and responsibilities of freemen.

"I. Frequent, fixed, regular, and accessible folk-motes, to which *all freemen* shall come, and discuss *all matters*, both of local and general interest. As to the latter this ancient custom is now partly resumed, in the shape of annual meetings of members with their constituents.

"II. Open elections of all local officers, and of the representatives to the local and general assemblies, in full folk-mote, and without any delayed poll.

"III. The frequent elections of all officers and representatives."

The other class of safeguards may be called *secondary*, not by reason of their little importance, but inasmuch as they have special reference to the existence of a body having a derived authority only. It must be remembered their main object is,

—not like the primary ones, to *assert* rights and responsibilities, but,—*to prevent encroachments* by those holding a deputed authority, and *to maintain statute law in harmony with common law.*

"I. Frequent and regular meetings of (and elections to) Parliament. Attention has been already called to the frequent assertions of the necessity of this; and to the statutes, among others of 4 Edward III, c. 14, and 36 Edward III, c. 10, requiring Parliaments to meet each year once, and oftener if need be. It has also been called to the 7 Henry IV, c. 15, by which it was, as "declaratory of the ancient laws and customs of Parliament," declared that the elections should be made, notwithstanding any prayer or commandment to the contrary, and also without any commandment of the King, by writ or otherwise. Of this Act the statute 16 Charles I, c. 1, was but a re-declaration. The latter was repealed by Charles II, c. 1. But the principle thus violated has been still more *daringly, unconstitutionally, and mischievously departed from, for the first time in English history, by the "Septennial Act"* of 1 George I, statute ii, c. 38, passed so late as 1716.

"II. The constant and regular attendance in their places of all the members. The contrary is quite recent in England, and was not permitted of old. No member could depart without special licence from the House, and under heavy penalties.

"III. The holding *conference by the representatives with those whom they represent on every matter on which doubt exists.* In the 13th Edward III, the Commons answered the King that "they dare not assent (to a money vote) until they have conferred and advised with the Commons in the country. Wherefore they pray that a Parliament be summoned again at an early day;—and in the mean time every member will go down into his own part, and use all his endeavours to get the King's request agreed to."

"Taxes were over and over again asked, and very properly refused. *Members dared not vote the money without their constituents' assent.* Every man thus knew *what taxes* were asked, *and what for.*

"IV. *The reporting back* by the representatives to those whom they represent, what has been done on each matter.

* * * * * *

"VIII. *The answering of every petition* during the same sitting of Parliament.

"There is not one safeguard more important than this,

or which is alone more calculated to keep Parliament and the Crown within the proper limits of their respective functions. 'Parliament,' says the ancient document called the Modus Tenendi Parliamentum, 'ought not to separate so long as any petition remains undiscussed; or, at least, to which the answer is not determined on; and if the King permit the contrary, *he is perjured*."—*Toulmin Smith*, pp. 129, 133, 134, 140.

These are the arrangements which can alone protect local and individual rights against centralisation, and adjust them thereto.

§

Feudality itself, therefore, left to the People more complete franchises and immunities than oligarchy now permits us, tempered as it is with the influences of labor, capital, and monarchy.

Earl Russell now informs us that owing to the Chandos clause in the Reform Bill of 1832, and "the admission of £50 tenants-at-will on the same basis as independent freeholders, the county representation was, as Lord Althorpe predicted, weighed down by the influence of the great landowners."

The *conflicting principles* of the voting qualification now are :—

1st. Has the country the right to judge of a man's *capacity* to understand his own political interests,

2nd. Or ought it only to enquire if a man has already *some material stake and interest* in the public welfare?

The first principle involves some sort of educational or other arbitrary and theoretical test.

The second simply asks, "Is the man rated?" or, has he, say, a "residential" stake in the commonweal? "*Can he give hostages to the nation?*"

Let us at least agree with Earl Russell, "to trust to no nice tricks of Statesmanship, no subtle invention of ingenious theorists," &c.

As to the true principles of the British Constitution, we may further refer to the treatise of Penn thereon, a treatise of immense and exhaustive research, wherein he lays down the rights of absolute *property;* (which includes the right of fair taxation) of *voting;* and the *judicatory* right, or right to be judged by a fair jury, as the primary and immemorial rights of Englishmen. And he adds thereto, that "religion being settled by the State, was no part of the old English Constitution."

An ancient writer remarks that "the Acts of an Anglo-Saxon Parliament are a series of treaties of peace between all the associations that make up the State; a continual revision and renewal of the alliances offensive and defensive of all free men." And another writer adds that "national representative assemblies cannot without a departure from their true functions, be allowed to become oligarchies *having independent authority.*" (All their authority being *derived* not *original.*)

And Sir Edward Coke declares that what is done by Parliament "must have two special properties; the one in creation, namely, that it be given by the *common consent of the whole realm* in

Parliament; the other in the execution, namely that it be given and employed for the *common benefit* of the whole nation, and not for private and other respects."

The duty of reformers is plain. It should be to restore the observance of the principles of the British Constitution and of popular self-Government, and to adjust them in practice, as Disraeli recommends, "to the moral and material development of the nation." To restore in fact the harmony of "organisation" with "power."

And not the least evils of the present state of things is that that has now to be done *by agitation* which used to be done, and of right ought to be done or prevented, *by the direct action and participation of the People* in Government.

"Propose," said Bentham, "anything good; the answer is at hand—wild, visionary, theoretical, utopian, unpracticable, dangerous, destructive, ruinous, anarchical, subversive of all Governments—there you have it.—Well, but in America there it *is*: and no such evil consequences. Aha!—and so the United States Government is your Government, is it? You are a Republican then, are you? What you want is—to subvert this Constitution of ours: the envy of nations—matchless in rotten boroughs and sinecures.

"Propose anything that would put power into the hands of those of whose obedience all power is composed—you propose Democracy.

"What, according to these men, is the use of the Constitution? To make the *People* happy? What then? Only to make the *one* man happy, with the small number of others.

"Now by this bugbear *Democracy* are the People of this country to be frightened out of their senses?

"Here we have one partial separate sinister interest—the interest of the ruling One with which the *universal*, the democratic interest has to antagonise. And here we have another partial, separate, and sinister interest—the aristocratical interest—with which the democratical interest has also to antagonise."

Nevertheless "the privilege of starting new subjects of deliberation, and in short of *propounding* in the business of legislation, which, in England, is allotted to the representatives of the People, forms another capital difference between the English Constitution and the Government of other free States, whether limited monarchies or commonwealths, and prevents that which, in those States, proves a most effectual mean of subverting the laws favourable to public liberty, —namely, *the undermining of the these laws by the precedents and artful practices of those who are invested with the executive* power in the Government."—*De Lolme* "on the Constitution," pp. 478-479.

Evidently, to make this house, which thus propounds and initiates, the actual house of the People, is a great part of the problem of "Democracy and Centralisation."

As regards our Foreign affairs, the less said respecting the virtues of Oligarchic Government the better. The whole virtue and energy of the country barely, even now, suffices to make its national action negative. A Government by the nation's manhood would permit no abject diplomatic wars; and, by a clear, decisive policy, would make most wars impossible.

Since Cromwell, until lately, our international interventions and non-interventions have combined the evils of a policy of permissive wrong with those of a policy of active wrong. We have first murdered our brother in the name of principle, and then declared in the names of policy and of peace that we are not our brother's keeper.

COLONIAL POLICY.

Let us, as a sample, contrast the results of Government by the few with those of Government by the all, as admitted by Mr. Russell, and as just drawn by the Hon. Joseph Howe, of Canada, who anticipates in Canada the rival, or probably the future enemy of England :—

"Our columns of gold and our pyramids of timber may rise in your Crystal Palaces, but our Statesmen in the great Council of the empire, never.

"When the independence of the United States was established in 1783, they were left with one-half of the continent, and you with the other. You had much accumulated wealth, and an overflowing population. They were three millions of people, poor, in debt, with their country ravaged and their commerce disorganised. *By the slightest effort of statesmanship* you could have planted your surplus population in your own provinces, and in five years the stream of emigration would have been flowing the right way. In twenty years, the British and Republican forces would have been equalised. But you did nothing, or often worse than nothing. From 1784 to 1841, we were ruled by little paternal despotisms established in this country. We could not change an officer, reduce a salary, or impose a duty, without the permission of Downing Street. For all that dreary period of sixty years, *the Republicans governed themselves, and you governed us.* They had uniform duties and free trade with each other. We always had separate tariffs, and have them to this day. They controlled their foreign relations,—you controlled ours. They had their ministers and consuls all over the world, to open new markets, and secure commercial advantages. Your ministers and consuls knew little of British America, and rarely consulted its interests. Till the advent of *Huskisson*, our commerce was cramped by all the vices of the old colonial system. The Republicans could open mines in any part of their country. Our mines were locked up, until seven years ago, by a close monopoly held in this country by the creditors of the Duke of York. How few of the hundreds of thousands of

Englishmen who gazed at Nova Scotia's marvellous column of coal in the Exhibition, this summer, but would have blushed had they known that for half a century the Nova Scotians *could not dig a ton of their own coal* without asking permission of half a dozen English capitalists in the city of London. How few Englishmen now reflect, when riding over the rich and populous States of Illinois, Michigan, Missouri, and Arkansas, that *had they not locked up their great West*, and turned it into a hunting ground, which it is now, *we might have had* behind Canada *three or four magnificent provinces*, enlivened by the industry of millions of British subjects, toasting the Queen's health on their holidays, and making the vexed question of the *defence of our frontiers* one of very easy solution."—*Russell's Canada*, pp. 195, 196.

When Downing Street and republican rule are thus compared by Canadians, the gravitation of Canada to the Republic appears a less unlikely thing. Russell (p. 241) also speaks of British Northern America, as—"a country which suffers from the early neglect of the home Government, the studied aspersions and misrepresentations of powerful agencies."

These results of our Colonial policy represent, amongst other things, the absence of the sympathies and full national manhood from the national councils.

They represent, also, middle-class superciliousness at *popular* self-Government amongst the Anglo-Saxons, witness the Hon. C. Gavan Duffy, at St. James' Hall, May, 1865, on Australia. We quote his picture, as the companion to the Hon. Joseph Howe's. Both empires are flouted, misrepresented, and scorned alike :—

"Long residence in a country where *material prosperity was universal*; where, *in nine years, he had seen only three beggars*; where those who held the plough, as a rule, cultivated their own land, and were at no man's mercy; where there was *absolute religious equality* in all respects; where the population was constantly increasing; where the *Government of the country and the laws of the country spring directly from the will of the People*, and where the soil was guarded by *citizen soldiers*,—would not fit him, he feared, to look with much patience on the spectacle which Ireland presented at present. He rather turned to a country of which he might speak freely, as having recent knowledge of it, and in respect of which he had only to guard against the temptation to exaggerate its advantages which springs from a sense of gratitude. No man, indeed, had more reason to be grateful. He had found in that country all the essential conditions of happiness—work to do which he was pleased to be engaged in, and which had sufficient success to be easy and agreeable—a liberal, and even a bountiful reward for labour—friends, health, and contentment. Coming back with such recollections and impressions, he felt surprised and wounded at the tone which prevailed in respect of the Australian colonies in the press and in the Parliament of this country. He thought there was a great mistake of policy, and a strange lack of good feeling, in the eagerness with which every fact that appeared to damage or lower the reputation of the Australian communities was received in England. A century ago, the same prejudices existed towards the colonies of North America; and the evil consequences had not died out yet, and perhaps would never die out. There was a generous and cordial feeling towards their native country among the mixed population of Australia; but they had the sensitiveness to unjust criticism which distinguishes every new People; and they might be made as hostile as America had been by the same causes. He was puzzled to account for this sentiment towards Australia. What had Victoria, for example, done to provoke hostility? She had never cost the Imperial treasury a guinea, except for strictly Imperial purposes. She had managed her own affairs without pestering the Imperial Parliament, and managed them with notable success; she had poured a tide of gold—averaging nearly a quarter of a million sterling every week—for the last dozen years into the commercial capital of England, and from which wealth every class, and almost every individual, in this community were more prosperous than they would otherwise have been.

"If the colonial Parliaments sympathised intensely with the colonial communities, he would cite against the conclusions of a political philosopher like Mr. Lowe the doctrine of a greater political philosopher, Edmund Burke,—that it was a more natural and tolerable evil, that Parliament should be infected even with popular epidemics, as this would indicate some consanguinity with the nation, than that they should be wholly untouched (as a certain moribund House of Commons seemed to be) by the opinions and feelings out of doors."

INTERVENTION AND NON-INTERVENTION.

It is wonderful to see how fine phrases about "the Principle of Non-Intervention," lead men to suppose that non-intervention *as a principle* is either moral, logical, or possible. And yet the interventions and non-interventions of a nation are the best test of its essential spiritual life.

For ages, interventions have been on the wrong side. It is true that France intervened for Democracy and nationality in Italy. We are told she had her ideas and her interests, and we hear always the same weary wisdom against the right. But the great lesson sought now to be impressed on Statesmen and People, was derived from the great wars for the balance of power, from the wars against Bourbons and for them, from the war against the American nation, and the French Republic, the war against Napoleon and with Napoleon, and the war in the Crimea.

Weak and wicked interventions have prejudiced the English mind against intervention. Our Statesmen are not trusted to make a good and holy war under any circumstances, and the argument from the abuse is made to tell not for, but against the use.

Were it not that human nature is wiser than those who aspire to manage her, this "reaction" against intervention would take an age or two of infamous neutrality to teach John Bull that neutrality may mean dishonour, but cannot always mean inaction, and that neutrality itself, is often, in this vicinage of European States, one of the intensest forms of complicity and of intervention.

Non-intervention may be, upon occasion, often Statesmanlike, moral, and possible. But it is rarely in this world of action and interaction, "a principle."

The "Principle of Non-Intervention" amounts simply and solely to this. The Creator has subdivided the race, and planted the various families of man in diverse regions, climates, and conditions, to work out separate problems, and to complete amongst themselves the various national individualities, which the providential education of the world requires.

For an alien *material force,* to interfere with this separate and preparatory isolation, tends obviously to obstruction or anarchy.

But *ideas* must and will enter everywhere, and carry on an inevitable propagandism.

Well, the training progresses. Ideas are generated within, or enter from without. Of two things one, authority adjusts itself to the advancing enlightenment and civilisation of the People, or it opposes these processes.

In the latter case, soon or late, authority is deposed, or it calls in physical force from authority elsewhere. Without this, local progress is inevitable, for the local force would always finally be overmatched by the inevitable moral propagandism of the outer world, and by the local resistance and organisation. This is the common sense of non-intervention.

But the rule, hitherto, has been that Government helps Government,—that Priests join with King, and Despot with Despot, and that so, fraud and physical force oppose and extinguish in detail the progress and ideas of mankind.

This has been the practice and "principle" of *Intervention*.

Thus, if we content ourselves with asserting the *principle* of Non-Intervention against the *practice* of Intervention, we simply meet as children, as traitors, as atheists, as murderers, or as idiots, the most tremendous political problem which events ever set before the doers and thinkers of the world.

Let Non-Intervention *mean* Non-Intervention, and we are content.

But if it do mean Non-Intervention,—if principle be not another term for license, then Non-Intervention must include Intervention, as the ultima ratio of law, of civilisation, and of justice, against barbarism and brute force.

The battle of the world is to be won by opinion or by arms. Opinion against opinion, the right will hold its own. Arms against arms, the wrong cannot conquer. But if the wrong is to ally itself with wrong, and if right is to isolate itself from right,—if wrong is to be allowed to concentrate, and extirpate one by one the thoughts and aspirations of the People striving for resurrection or for life, then, once for all, we say, human nature is not bad enough for this,—cannot—in *this* world—be *made* bad enough for it, and that they who would lead it to such a consummation, either betray freedom and religion peacemeal, or are preparing for some final and tremendous arbitrament.

We assume, therefore, when men extol the great principle of Non-Intervention, that they do not understand their own meaning, that they are too simple for the ways of this wicked world, or that they are consciously betraying the right. There are but three meanings to the phrase. The first expresses the theory of the separate providential training of nations. The second asserts that that separate training process and national individuality shall be respected. The third says that it shall *not* be respected. That a wrong may be helped, but that the right shall not be helped, and they who knowingly teach this doctrine, will never hold power in England. Theirs is the teaching, and upon their brows will be the brand of Cain. Soon would they be sent upon their wanderings, and though they should seek to build great cities in the West, the West would cast them out. For it is not the great Republic of the People that will divide People from People in the right, or unite tyrant against tyrant for the wrong.

The criminal nature of our foreign and colonial policy is owing chiefly to the want of political education and power amongst the masses.

How we come to be wanting in this respect, after the glorious advance in our national education and character two hundred years since, is for the dominant parties and sects since that period to answer. Then was begun again an English nation from the beginning. America left in England all the advantages and evils of its existing organisations, and yet of the three great wars of the West two were for Independence, and the third is the holiest that ever was waged.

Responsibility educates, and we here have always feared the People, because we have always used them up body and soul for unjust wars, and withheld from them free *secular* and *religious* teaching.

Is it strange, then, that the Pope and the Devil should have gone on tick to the descendants of the Puritans? That our debt should be owed for putting down republics, and setting up legitimists?

First we intervened, next we make the consequences of intervention indelible by proclaiming the great principle of non-intervention.

First we settled, or allowed to be settled, the future of the world at Vienna; we accept, or allow to be accepted, the theory of the balance of power, and then allow exceptions and unsettlements,— on the wrong side.

Look at the diplomacy of Cromwell:—"I will sail a fleet over the Alps to stop that." "The guns of England shall be heard at St. Angelo." "I tell you England has much to do with this Hungarian business." How he encouraged the trade of the

Puritan colonies of America. What a legacy of glory to the Puritans. What majestic traditions for the nation. What minute insight. What Titanic grasp. Look at these things, and then mark how England, not being strong enough for Democracy then, has indeed "done many great and glorious works in the name of Christ," by individuals or societies, but *as a nation among nations,*—murder and treason against policy and right continually.

We have got at last, after two hundred years, to the era of compromise! Indeed! and are glad,—we that came from Cromwell, to thank God for *that.* We are got to the era of non-intervention for right,—we that intervened for wrong for three ages,—we whose non-intervention to repeal our former interventions, is itself intervention perpetuated. We are got to "neutrality,"—we who shook the den of every despot, and startled the legitimists of Europe like vermin to their holes!

If we have come from intervention for the wrong to non-intervention for the right,—if we are preparing to go from non-intervention and neutrality to activity for the right,—*it is because the masses are marching on power*, and because the great fight of the People in the West warns the holders of power to make terms with Democracy while they may.

If any now turn to the People and demand, "Where have been the Ironsides of England?" We say, for the West, they were with the legions of Lincoln; and for old England, history does not in this sense repeat itself,—but our Democracy, which could not last in 1660, has stepped back to organise itself upon a broader base and a more enduring platform.

The words of the great diplomatist are sometimes truer than those of the more sincere philanthropists. Talleyrand well said of *non*-intervention,—"*C'est un mot métaphysique et politique, qui signifie à peu près la même chose qu'intervention.*"

PARALLELS AND PROGRESS.

In England the great principles of Material, Political, and Religious Equality are yet undeveloped, but are advancing. Our Democracy and our Centralisation are therefore alike incomplete.

A nation can only advance by a principle or by a man, and as our own "Statesmen," not of our "compromise era" (for that only begun lately with non-intervention for the treaties of Vienna), but of the era of the betrayal, without compromise, for eighty years, of the whole ruling power of England to despotism, superstition, and feudality, pass away from the scene (like "Statesmen" of a similar era in America), it becomes possible that this great trading, fighting, praying, and deceived nation may get its will for freedom and nationality thoroughly done by its Government for itself and on the world.

There can be no guarantee for permanently good Government without the People. They will never have power till they deserve it. When they deserve it, they will conquer it by the help of the real aristocracy, and of the politically well informed and truly liberal portion of the middle class. The Commons, truly, are absorbed by the Lords, and the Lords represent themselves, and if we compare the present with the last great crisis of American Democracy, we shall find that the centralisation and the safety, *the progress, and the honour, are in proportion as the Government is popularised and open.*

Then a great historical figure contended with the aristocracy on behalf of the People. Then Chatham denounced the farce of virtual representation of America and of the English. Then, as now, the English Constitution was unbalanced. Chatham denounced it then,—Gladstone and Bright now. In some points the contrast is striking. In others the similarity is more striking still. Then Pompadour and Yarmouth were powers in England and France till, as to England, George III took prerogative for his mistress, and worshipped her with desperate and live-long chastity. Then the English Government was in the market for French or Indian scalps. The slave trade was forced upon America,—upon South Carolina, and Virginia even, by repeated and categorical instructions from England. Then Austria was to be detached from Spain by the offer by England of territory in Italy or in Silesia. Then the Empress of Russia was in the market for fifty thousand dollars; the English King got seven hundred thousand pounds as his share of the spoils of French merchant ships seized in full peace. Protestantism and Frederick were to be extinguished in Europe, that France might be provided against, there, and in Canada. Pitt, just married, poor, and in office, left it rather than support prerogative and privilege against the People, and Pitt and Frederick seemed about the two honest and capable men of the age and hemisphere. Then did America unite herself against Prerogative, and Prerogative and Privilege, Peers, Bishops, and Kings' Mistresses, conspired with prerogative against England.

It was because the English People were unrepresented, that these things could be. It was to Pitt, as the Minister of the People, that all things for a time seemed possible. It was Chatham and the People of England and America, who kept the empire for a time together, but ultimately drove king and aristocracy into alliance against them, till at last Chatham was hustled from power and life, *and the first step in the dismemberment of the British empire was accomplished.* But man proposes and God disposes. The spirit that waked first in Cromwell and puritan England, stirred the mighty Frederick, the, perhaps, mightier Chatham, and it animated the American nation and returned in revolution upon Europe.

"Pitt prepared with one hand to smite the whole family of Bourbons, and to wield in the other the Democracy of England." England has ended by acknowledging Napoleon and *watching* Austria out of Italy.

Had England not persecuted, Emigrants had been, not middle-class Puritans, but traders, speculators, cadets, or felons!

Had England not oppressed, the States might have remained separate Governments to this day, and the true principle of Federation had had no exemplar.

Had England not forced the slave trade on America, there had been no Lancashire cotton famine, no Southern cotton monopoly. There probably had been a regular trade with India, but slavery being in the South and remaining, the South could hardly do either better or worse, or less or more than it has done.

Had England not warred against the French Democracy, France had not got panic-stricken by coalitions, and then drunk with glory, nor had Napoleon arisen to do *the greatest secular work since the disruption of the Roman Empire,*—the breaking in pieces of the feudal system, and all the four-fold despotism and ruin, of standing armies, autocrats, oligarchies, and priestcraft.

The Americans and the English are one People. America drew its blood and its creed from the heart of England.

It won its Independence by the sword, but at a time when Prerogative against Privilege, and Privilege against Prerogative, or both against Popular rights, were the only combinations that troubled much either the King, the Lords, or the Commons.

We know the Pedigree of that great People, both after the flesh and after the spirit, and we will swear that it is worth its breeding.

It left Europe for Freedom. Its utterance breathed the very spirit of the pure Democracies and of Gospel antiquity. Its battle now is set for Principle, as well as Democracy. Throughout its history, it has based its rights on those of the common human nature, and on the inalienable gift of the Creator.

There are no muniments in the universe like the Title Deeds of the American nation, and the pedigree of its rights.

Its Declarations appealed to the rights of representation. The representative principle was the main feature in the British Constitution. The British Constitution adopted them as the natural and inalienable rights of man. And they were conferred upon man by the will of God!

The "Book of its Generation," as well as the story of its progress, is unlike that of any other People or Government, and fifty years but confirm the thought of Washington in his inaugural address:—"Every step by which they have advanced to the character of an independent nation, seems to have been distinguished by some token of a providential agency."

THE SITUATION.

The only danger in England now is this,—that the "power" and the "organisation" may not harmonise soon enough or fully enough to guarantee progress from violence or haste.

The spirit is at variance with the forms.

England has advanced from local self-Government to centralisation. She must remain where she is, or return to local self-Government, or accept the centralisation, and balance it by INDIVIDUAL SELF-GOVERNMENT,—by making the suffrage and the political competency universal.

"The English Aristocracy," says De Tocqueville, "is perhaps the most liberal which ever existed. It cannot, however, escape observation that in the legislation of England the good of the poor has been sacrificed to the advantage of the rich, and *the rights of the majority to the privileges of the few*. The consequence is, that England, at the present day, combines the extremes of fortune in the bosom of her society, and her perils and calamities are almost equal to her power and renown."

And Montesquieu points out similar dangers, as also the remedy, and the reason why they have not been more injurious.

In language already quoted, he denounces the two kinds of inequality which are in aristocratical Governments the principal sources of disorder: he speaks of unequal burthens, exemptions, monopolies, primogeniture, and hereditary power. He then proceeds:—

"*The mischief is when excessive wealth destroys the spirit of commerce.*

"Such powers as are established by *commerce*, may subsist for a long series of years in their humble condition, but their grandeur is of short duration; they rise by little and little, and in an imperceptible manner, for they do not perform any particular exploit which may make a noise, and signalize their power; but when they have once raised themselves to so exalted a pitch, that it is impossible but all must see them, every one endeavours to deprive this nation of an advantage which it had snatched as it were, from the rest of the world."

"The British Government is one of the wisest in Europe, because *there is a body which examines it perpetually*, and is perpetually examining itself; and its errors are of such a nature, as never to be lasting, and are frequently useful by rousing the attention of the nation."—*Ibid.*, pp. 24-60, v. iii.

The principles of Democracy are as clear as the dangers of oligarchy.

Manhood-development,—the foundation of freedom and of nationality, must be gradually relieved of its shackles, and oligarchy, the rule of privilege and force, exchanged for aristocracy, the free rule of the People, and the best of every class.

All obstructions whatsoever to this master principle of "Development and Association," must be abolished or destroyed. All monopolies whether in office, land, religion, commerce, or the franchise, must be extinguished. *Education should be the freest and most universal of all things.*

In fine, the course of the last thirty years must be persevered in, till *our* nation and Democracy are also made, and the power and the will of the all shall rule.

That particular situation "when the chiefs and the People deliberated and the People decided," and when "the kings were neither fathers, elders, imperators, nor despotic lords, but the creation of a social wisdom far more excellent in conception, and beneficent in practice," must of necessity belong to a primitive or to a very advanced epoch,—when the objects of society were extremely simple, or its organisation nearly complete.

A dilemma soon presented itself to our Teutonic ancestors. Unless the all voted directly on public questions there could be no freedom : if the all voted there could be no Government. To avoid despotism on the one hand, and confusion on the other, the representative system was invented, —a system of governing by proxy.

But another dilemma. If the all do not vote for representatives, there is a mixture of despotism and representation : if the uneducated all vote, there is anarchy and misgovernment. Practically, despotism and oligarchy are providential provisional governments for the minority or dotage of States, when, of necessity, masters represent a large proportion of the population (as Sharon Turner tells us was the "constitutional practice" in the national council of the Anglo-Saxons), "like the rest of their property."

Without virtue, Democracies miscarry as entirely as without freedom, and virtue, which, as Hume well says, "is nothing but a more enlarged and cultivated reason, never flourishes to any degree, nor is founded on steady principles of honour, except where good education becomes general."

In fine, unity can exist only in an extremely simple and rudimentary state of society,—a state which cannot and ought not to be perpetuated, or in that complete state where the units are prepared by education, and by an infinite complexity of interests, for a high civilisation, and an entire national self-Government,—where the whole of the all is developed and organised, and the single final preponderating power, is the universal one of the People.

INDIVIDUAL SELF GOVERNMENT.

God and the Soul, are the alpha and omega; the beginning and the end of politics. To perpetuate the exclusive rights of the few, you must perpetuate the universal wrongs of the many. To destroy the *rights* of the People, you must deny and destroy their God. A policy of concession, a policy of suicide, or a policy of despair, therefore, awaits the Governments of the old world, and except as a question of time, Democracy is no experiment to any who comprehend the meaning, the nature or the history of man.

Man is generically one, and this secures, within a State, association of persons or parties, and without it, of States and nations. The solidarité of Peoples is only the ultimate expression of the unity of the species.

Creation is Democracy, and there is no lasting aristocracy, save that which is identical with a true Democracy, and is set to destroy all other aristocracies whatsoever, which addresses all and is revolutionary, and which teaches the unity, equality, and freedom of man.

What then is the issue *now* of this philosophy?

It is for America the making of that nation as the sign and flag of the Peoples everywhere.

It is for England (which was not ripe for Democracy two hundred years ago, and is not ripe now), a constitutional balance, popular rights, and a national strength and progress, unchecked and unmeasured. In fact, an honest enacting of such Constitution as we have. We shall have our army under constitutional control. Our diplomacy not a screen for partisans or a mask for conspirators, but open, national and true. We shall no longer have a monopoly of power by one estate, tempered only by an unrepresented public opinion,—a practical revolt of opinion against forms and force. We shall have done with a mere mechanical balance of power, which is socialism applied to politics. We shall replace the present solidarité of families (a communism of whigs within, and legitimists without) by a solidarité of Peoples.

Where, as in England, self-restraint is of the national genius and character, and where opinion rules, ASSOCIATION is the power that will effect this change. Where opinion does not prevail, *revolution* is the last resort of necessity and of nature.

Meanwhile non-intervention must be the safeguard of the Peoples, to prevent all propagandism save that of ideas ; but if civilisation is to be maintained, intervention must wait upon non-intervention, as penalty waits upon law.

A propagandism of ideas and religion cannot fail to regenerate the world, if only brute force be kept at bay. Non-intervention does not mean that the right is to be destroyed piecemeal, *that* were to sacrifice the spirit to the letter, and to cause non-intervention itself to intervene,—*that* were to yield the rights of the world to its wrongs, to unite the one and isolate the other.

From the mere commercial point of view, we

want everywhere higher civilisation, completer education, that we may have more employment for labour, and greater economy and better direction of the social resources of power. For there are no new continents to be discovered, and "over production" of men, and "over production" of commodities, must neutralise each other.

With or without, or against its rulers, England must advance, else, if she fall not back amongst the ruck and refuse of nations, she will at least cease to lead them.

As to Democracy, to overthrow *that*, there must be found a power more universal than the People's, and more deeply rooted than the human soul, more certain than the constant reach and progress of man after knowledge, self-interest and power.

§

Whithersoever America may tend, it is her own hand that grasps the helm,—her own voice that directs her servants, her own soul that (as far as human agency may) presides over her destiny.

The policy that in any country does not enact the will of the intellect and character of the country, is anarchical and doomed. The policy that does not rest on the intellect and character of *at least* the majority, is weak, uncertain, and precarious.

There are but two perfect *theories* of Government, Democracy and Theocracy. The one, where

God conducts the People by outward voice and sign; the other where the whole People is represented, and is by education and morality fitted for representation. From the one to the other,—from the God-Government of the garden and the wilderness, to the continent and nation, and Government of the People, the world has advanced. Every state of Government between has been a compromise and an interregnum. God or man must govern. If man govern, then the usual course must be from power to justice; from prerogative to privilege; from virtual to actual representation, and the march of progress is strewn with the wrecks of systems that man has left behind. The warrant for the existence of any oligarchy is, not right, but necessity, the necessity for order. The warrant of the doom of every oligarchy that has failed, has been that it has not used order for progress,—that it has failed to hand down the Government to an oligarchy less exclusive, or to a representation more numerous and complete.

Thus order is the warrant of oligarchies. Progress is the term of order. Democracy is the ultimate goal of progress, and rests on the nature of the soul and the law of God.

It is "the Son of man, which was the Son of God."

CONCLUSION.

As the result of this enquiry into the spirit of the English nation and the forms of the British Constitution, and the relations between Freedom (or Equality) and Order, self-Government and Centralisation, we can only say that the principles of Locality and Generality, of Individuality and of Empire, have, in every age and by every People, to be accommodated as best they may to its living spirit and to the actual facts.

On a small scale they were admirably united in England by "Local and Representative self-Government."

On a large scale, they are admirably carried out in America, by "State" and National Governments, and by *Popular Sovereignty.* These never really clashed, except under the influences of an Oligarchy, called there "Slavery."

The *negative* assertion of inviolable and absolute Local or State right is found in Germany, and results in a dead lock, in a neutralisation of the German *nation,* and in a "constituted anarchy."

The *positive* assertion of absolute State rights was found in "the South." State right there meant the right of the parts not only to arrest the development of the nation by a gigantic economic blunder, but to destroy the life of the nation by forcing a sectional sin upon its soul.

The assertion of the Southern theory was active,—and the South is destroyed. The assertion of German provincialism is partial, and the nation neither progresses nor dies, but remains.

In England and America the People have power to overcome and to use an obstructive or vicious organisation, by and for their own Sovereignty.

For England, the *positive* lesson seems to be the fatuity of withholding, or of not urging on, that universal Manhood-Development and consequent variety and fullness of character, and that political equality, which can alone complete our nationality, and enable it to hold its own amongst Democracies in the coming era.

For Her, also, the *negative* lesson seems to be that it is especially unstatesmanlike to yoke to the sovereign power another power—the Church,—which is in its essence sovereign, and which in conflict with any other sovereignty must destroy or be destroyed. And that, moreover, that or any other corporate power of a certain immobility and closeness of nature, tends to anarchy, is an imperium in imperio, is another "Southern" exaggeration of the rights of the parts, and against the interests and progress of the whole,—in fact, directly contravenes unity, magnifies forms against spirit, and minor organisations against the national organisation.

That the triumph of oligarchy and privilege over local self-Government resulted in centralisation, but Democracy balances centralisation with Equality, and combines the two for the best national uses, and the maximum national power.

The battles of the future, whether of peace or war, will be fought and won, not so much by nations that are wielded by the strongest Governments, as by nations that are the more individually complete, by those that best deserve the name of "national individualities."

For England and the world the great lesson seems to be that, on a large scale, *Federation* is the only mode by which the rights and the progress of the whole and of the parts can be accommodated.

That for building on so vast a scale, *the Atoms* must be bound together by the adamantine cement of freedom. That nations can only obtain or qualify for freedom by securing its four-fold assertion in School, Press, Church, and Assembly;—the first and second to educate universally, the third to guard religion against secular taint, or complicity of State *craft*; the last as the forum and Parliament of the actual People. That thus educated, man *must* associate for political action. That thus associating, he *must* win political equality. *That a nation of such men is the only true national unity, and is alone fit to enter with other such nations into those grander combinations of economy, of harmony, and of the progresses and ambitions of Peace, for which the world prepares.*

Whilst, therefore, towards Federation is the tendency of Governments, universal manhood suffrage and equality is not only the right of educated Peoples, but *the only Factor of Unity,* and the Necessity, and the Conservatism, and the Balance of States. Democracy begins with the Individual. It ends only with the world.

PRINTED BY HARRISON AND SONS, ST. MARTIN'S LANE.

www.ingramcontent.com/pod-product-compliance
Lightning Source LLC
LaVergne TN
LVHW021134110826
845150LV00005B/1027